Penguin Specia...
Political Murder in Northern Ireland

Martin Dillon was born in Belfast in 1949. He was educated at colleges in Romsey (Hampshire) and Belfast. He spent two years in England and Southern France before joining a Belfast Newspaper in 1968. He reported on the violence in the province and later joined the *Belfast Telegraph* in June 1972. He has spent much of his spare time since boyhood writing and reading poetry.

Denis Charles Lehane was born in London in 1949. He was educated at Brockley Grammar School in London and Pembroke College, Oxford where he graduated in Modern History in 1971. He worked on *Cherwell*, the university newspaper, and went into journalism on leaving Oxford, working for specialist newspapers and magazines before joining the Thomson Organisation in 1972. He joined the *Belfast Telegraph* in January 1973.

Political Murder in Northern Ireland

Martin Dillon and Denis Lehane

Penguin Books

Penguin Books Ltd, Harmondsworth,
Middlesex, England
Penguin Books Inc., 7110 Ambassador Road,
Baltimore, Maryland 21207, U.S.A.
Penguin Books Australia Ltd, Ringwood,
Victoria, Australia

First published 1973

Copyright © Martin Dillon and Denis Lehane, 1973

Made and printed in Great Britain
Set in Monotype Times

Contents

Outline plan of Belfast 7

Foreword 9

Part One – The Background

1 The point of no return 19
2 The 1966 killings and the U V F 27
3 The Troubles begin again: 1968–71 36

Part Two – The Killings: 1972

4 Ulster has its back to the wall: January–June
   1972 49
5 The I R A call a truce – the Protestant extremists
   declare war: 26 June – 9 July 75
6 The truce is over but the assassinations continue:
   10 July–31 August 91
7 Two Catholics killed for every Protestant:
   September and October 118
8 A brief pause, but the killings continue:
   November and December 140

Part Three – The Killings: January–June 1973

9 The U D A call off the assassins: January 1973 159
10 The assassins unleashed: 29 January–28
   February 177
11 Plebiscite and new constitution – but the
   assassinations go on: March and April 199

12 'We are responsible' – the emergence of the U F F:
   May and June   213

Part Four – The Killers

13 The killers (I) – the I R A   245
14 The killers (II) – the Protestants   264
15 The killers (III) – the British Army   292

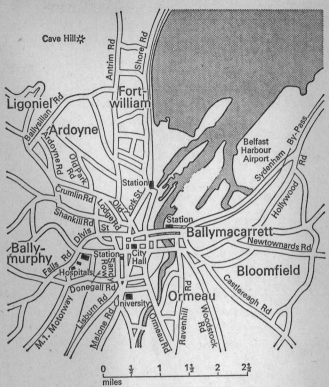

Outline plan of Belfast showing some of the places mentioned in the text.

Foreword

This book began in the first few months of 1973 as a series of articles we produced in our own time for the *Belfast Telegraph*, for which we both work. Early in March four articles were presented to the *Telegraph*, but were turned down. By that time we both felt that the information that we had amassed in our researches was of such public interest that it ought to be published in some form.

When we began, we were thinking only in terms of a series of newspaper articles, but even before the *Telegraph* turned down the pieces we produced, we had started thinking in terms of a book. In the first few months of 1973 we handled about 130 killings, but as time passed the killings increased until at the time of writing the figure has passed the 200 mark. We realized that it would be impossible to produce more than a general picture of the assassinations in newspaper articles, and that a larger vehicle would be necessary to put before the public what we had discovered. But we think it is a pity that the original articles never saw the light of day, for although they contained far less detail than is contained in this book, at the time they were written the general points they made were quite startling. The main conclusion they draw, and which is continued here, was that Protestant groups were responsible for the majority of the assassinations. In March 1973 such a claim would have been rejected by a wide section of the Ulster population. It was only in June that the Ulster Freedom Fighters became the first Protestant group to accept responsibility for any killings. In the articles we sought to show that the killings were neither random nor motiveless as was currently believe at the time. We gave a breakdown of the 'squad' system, and illustrated the degree of discipline and organization involved in the assassinations by reference to chosen examples. At the time the articles were written not a single conviction had been obtained in court for any of the killings. When we came to write the book, our task was made immeasurably easier by the fact that in the spring and early summer of 1973 a number of cases did come to trial. In every instance the version of events that came out at the trials supported the claims we had made earlier in our articles. There were two changes in the situation, however. First, before such trials we could never back up our arguments with hard factual evidence. Second, once such cases came to trial and gained publicity, it was no longer possible for people in Ulster to dismiss our arguments out of hand, as they had done in March.

Our basic conclusions from the research we have now undertaken over a period of six months are what they were in March: namely that the bulk of the assassinations were carried out by Protestant groups, and that these started as an organized and concerted campaign of sectarian killings that began in the spring of 1972. In March this year these conclusions were so unpopular that we were denied the opportunity of presenting them and the findings on which they were based, before the Ulster people. They are probably just as unpopular today, but they are no longer so incredible.

What follows is an account of these assassinations in which we have tried to put them in the context of the Troubles as a whole. We are aware that the book will be unpopular and that it will be criticized from various sources. This is only to be expected. Much of the criticism will be justified. Much of it will not be. It must be stressed that our sole aim in writing this book has been to present the truth. To say that we approached the task without any preconceived ideas would be untrue. But it would be true to say that virtually every preconceived idea that we held before we examined the killings was swept aside by what we found. We have not had an axe to grind in writing this book. We did not set off with the intention of 'blaming' Protestants for the killings. But having made our investigations into almost 200 of the assassinations we could not avoid the conclusion that

Protestant groups were responsible for most of them. But we do not attach 'blame'. We have tried earnestly not to judge anything or anyone in this book. This has meant that we have had to make conscious efforts to eliminate our personal feelings from what we have written. We do not claim that each of us does not have a personal position on the killings and on the Troubles as a whole, but we do believe that as far as has been humanly possible this has been left out of the book. In a very real sense the fact that two of us have been working on the book has assisted us here. We have differing views on such things, and probably could not present a composite judgement anyway. But we have not sought to sit in judgement on anyone or any organization involved in the assassinations. This position too, of course, may be attacked. There will be those who will say that we had a moral obligation to criticize what they may regard as immoral acts. It may be claimed that we do not accord the fullest respect to the victims by presenting their deaths in a cold, emotionless manner. Such criticisms will be valid from the point of view they are made, but we have approached our task from a different angle. We have sought to put before the public in as accurate and detailed a form as possible the truth about the sectarian assassinations. It may be that the truth sometimes hurts, but that is something we have accepted.

The truth has many facets, and it is often difficult to distinguish it from falsehood. What we have perceived to be the truth will be rejected by many. As well as setting forth the facts of individual assassinations, we have tried to explain and relate them to the context of the security situation at the time. We have thought it significant that the main onslaught did not begin until the late spring of 1972, almost three years after the Troubles started. From this we have drawn certain conclusions that have validity only if the first basic truth is accepted. If one were to claim that it makes no difference whether most of the killings started in 1972 or 1969, then our conclusions and most of the interpretive side of the book would be invalidated. Truth, therefore, is a volatile substance, and we cannot, and do not, claim a monopoly of it. All that we do claim is that we have tried to the best of our ability to seek the truth without prejudice, and to present what we have found without bias, and without fear of the consequences.

We have founded everything that we have written on fact, and it is necessary, to assist the reader, to explain precisely what we mean by this. Our facts fall into three basic categories. The first is what we term 'hard facts'. These are facts about which there is no possible doubt or question from any side. Into this category fall forensic evidence and the proceedings of court hearings, whether trials or inquests. These facts are documented and cannot, for all practical purposes, be challenged. The second category of facts are those of equal solidity but which are not documented and, for various reasons, not unchallengeable. For example, various aspects of killings that are known to be true cannot and do not appear either in the courts or in forensic reports. The police in Ulster are aware that a number of killers are now in gaol serving sentences for lesser offences. These people cannot be brought to court because there is not sufficient evidence to secure a conviction. But the fact of their involvement in killings, once it is known to be true, is as valid for our purposes as if they had been convicted. The third category is what we would term 'soft facts', although this tends to suggest that the evidence of this category is less valid than the other two. This would not be correct. Into this category comes the question of 'balance of probability'. This evidence is largely circumstantial, but one must remember that so too is most evidence presented before the courts. Thus, the balance of probability would suggest that it is most unlikely that IRA assassins would travel deep into Protestant East Belfast in the early hours of the morning following the 'Twelfth Night' to dump a body. They could have dumped it in their own area, in the certainty that no one would talk to the RUC about it. Yet this is what was claimed had happened to UDR man Henry Russell in 1972, when his body was found in Larkfield Drive, Sydenham. On its own, evidence in this category probably is sufficient in most cases for one to make a definitive statement on a killing. But we have chosen not to rely on it, and only to use it to support evidence of the other two types.

Thus, in the Russell case, the balance of probability, based on the place where the body was found and the time it was dumped, would suggest Protestant assassins; but it was only after other evidence of a more direct and personal nature linked Russell's death with Protestant assassins in the area of Larkfield Drive that we felt justified in ascribing his killing to the Protestants.

As the reader will appreciate, in most cases the evidence has been a mixture of all three categories, and we have been able to weigh each against the other. In many respects we have been in a better position to investigate the killings than the detectives assigned to the task. We have not been bound by normal court rules of evidence and have been able to pursue rumours and the most unlikely lines of evidence. Not all of it has been terribly fruitful, but much of it has.

The terms of reference that we set ourselves included only the civilian assassinations. Occasionally we have included UDR men, but only when we felt, as in the case of Henry Russell, that membership of the UDR had no influence on the killing. Because of this, it can be argued that the book does not present a balanced picture, that we depict a situation in which Protestants are responsible for the majority of killings, while overall it is the Catholic IRA that has caused most of the Troubles. More soldiers have been killed by the IRA than civilians by Protestants. More bombings have come from the IRA, and it has claimed in its campaign of indiscriminate bombings of civilian targets many more victims than the Protestant groups have in their assassinations. This criticism is valid and one of which we have been very aware. We have not engaged in a macabre value-judgement of human lives that ignores the deaths of security forces and highlights those of civilians. This is a book intended solely to cover one aspect of the Troubles in Ulster, and as such it must almost inevitably appear unbalanced. The alternative would have been to have written an enormous work on the Troubles as a whole to include the over 800 fatal casualties of the past four years. This would not have been practicable. Instead we have striven constantly to remind the reader throughout the book of the context in which the assassinations have taken place. We have referred as often as possible to acts of IRA violence that ran parallel to, and were frequently the cause of, Protestant killings. And we must make clear that while it is our contention that most of the assassinations were committed by Protestants, the IRA were responsible for a sizeable minority of them. We do not want to engage in moral arguments or judgements, but the reader may chose to reflect whether there is any moral distinction between killing one person and one hundred.

On this issue as on every other, it is ultimately for the reader to make up his own mind. We have tried to put before him the truth of the killings as we have seen them. We recognize there are limitations to the book. It was produced very quickly, and had we time we think we could have made it much better. We have striven at all times to be fair and impartial. It is up to the reader to decide whether we have succeeded.

We have divided the book into four parts for convenience. The first part is an introduction, setting out the background to the assassinations prior to 1972. Parts Two and Three are devoted to the assassinations in 1972 and the first half of 1973 respectively. Part Four is an analysis of the three groups involved in the killings: the IRA, the Protestants and the British Army. We felt obliged to include the last chapter on Army involvement, not so much because the evidence of Army killings was great – there have been only two known Army victims – but because many people genuinely believe that there is a concerted assassination campaign by plain-clothes troops. We have not dealt with cases where civilians have been killed by uniformed troops, because after some consideration we have not classified such killings as assassinations.

In conclusion, let us reaffirm that we have not written this book in support of any of the protagonists in the Ulster conflict, whether Catholic IRA, Protestant paramilitary groups, or the British Army. In our opinion we don't think any group comes out of the book with particular credit, but others may think differently, and that is their privilege. We have not been concerned with creating heroes and villains in Ulster. This has been done too often and we do not have any heart for such an enterprise. For if there is one conviction that we have gained through our researches, it is that there are no heroes or villains in Ulster's Troubles – only victims. This book is about the victims.

We wish to acknowledge our debt to Faber & Faber for permission to quote extensively from Brigadier Frank Kitson's book, *Low Intensity Operations – Subversion, Insurgency and Peacekeeping*, in Chapter 15 of this work.

MARTIN DILLON
DENIS LEHANE

Belfast, August 1973

Part One
The Background

1. The point of no return

When the New Year 1972 came to Northern Ireland there was a feeling of hope in the air. For over three years the province had been in crisis, and the year just past had seen violence and destruction grow at an unprecedented rate. In 1971 a section of the Roman Catholic population had turned against the British troops – troops initially sent in 1969 to protect the Catholics from a possible massacre by some of their Protestant neighbours. In March three young off-duty Scots soldiers – two of them brothers – had been shot in cold blood by IRA men who had spent the evening drinking with them. The deaths brought a reaction of shock and horror in Britain as well as Ulster. But in Northern Ireland it was to be but the first of many acts of horror that were to strain to the limit the people's capacity to be shocked.

The dawn of 1972 brought Ulster's people, weary after more than three years of marches, riots, and finally shootings and bombings, the precious hope that the corner had been turned, and that peace, so elusive for so long, was at hand. It was a false hope, and 1972 was to prove easily the worst year in Northern Ireland's history for violence and destruction. Instead of a gradual return to normality, the year saw Ulster slither even more swiftly into chaos and anarchy. The rule of law all but ceased to run in the province, and a new and more terrifying phase of the war emerged in full force: the sectarian assassinations.

But on Saturday 1 January, it did not look quite like that at all. 'THE IRA IS BEGINNING TO LOSE THE WAR', read one of the front-page headlines in the evening *Belfast Telegraph* – Ireland's largest-selling newspaper with a sale of 210,000 copies daily, and an estimated readership in the province of 600,000. The main story of the day was a public message the then Home

19

Secretary, Reginald Maudling, had sent to the Ulster Prime Minister, Brian Faulkner. Under the headline 'MY WISH IS PEACE' Maudling was reported to have told Faulkner that he hoped for three things in 1972 for Northern Ireland: an end to violence; an end to internment; and an agreement on an active and permanent role in public life and the affairs of the province for both communities.

But only in the first hope did Faulkner have any enthusiasm. He had repeatedly urged a hard line towards the IRA during the premierships of Terence O'Neill and James Chichester Clark. When in turn he became Prime Minister, he introduced internment without trial under the Special Powers Act on 9 August 1971 – a policy which he still believed would ultimately defeat the IRA. He found the idea of sharing power with anyone who did not accept the permanent status of Ulster in the United Kingdom anathema. So only in an end to the violence did Faulkner concur with Maudling's New Year message. And in this hard line there is little doubt that he was supported overwhelmingly by Protestant Ulster. Faulkner's weak flank lay to his right, not to his left. He was safe as Unionist leader and Prime Minister as long as he was not seen to compromise with the Roman Catholics.

However, this was precisely the policy Mr Heath's government at Westminster – aware now after three years that Ulster would not go away of its own accord – had decided upon. If Maudling was out of touch with Belfast, so too was Faulkner ignorant of the true feelings in Whitehall. Gently but firmly Maudling was telling him that the old Ulster was gone, and that to survive, Faulkner and the Unionists would have to make a fresh start, and include the Roman Catholic population within the system. In his message Maudling wrote: 'It will be a year that calls for statesmanship from all the leading people in Northern Ireland.' The times were difficult but the crisis could be overcome:

There can, to my mind, be no doubt that given a concerted effort by all involved throughout the province, 1972 can produce a lasting solution. There is equally no doubt that in the absence of such an agreed solution, further and renewed tragedy lies ahead for the people of Northern Ireland in the year that is now opening.

Put quite simply, Maudling was saying that 1972 was a make-or-break year for Northern Ireland: Ulster had reached the point of no return. The *Belfast Telegraph* Leader for 1 January echoed his sentiments:

If it is true that the darkest hour precedes the dawn, then Northern Ireland may hope for streaks of light in the sky in 1972. At times the year just past could hardly have seemed worse. The turning-point must come soon ... This is the year of decision, when Ulster must decide if it is to be peace or war, a hope of progress or the prospect of a steep descent into the morass.

These were sensible and common-sense words on the part of both the British Home Secretary and Northern Ireland's only non-aligned daily newspaper. But both contained within them the germs of the subsequent failure of 1972 to be the turning-point in the search for peace. Maudling talked about an 'agreed solution' and the *Telegraph* said 'Ulster must decide if it is to be peace or war.' But how could there ever be an agreed solution between two groups who were implacably opposed on the fundamental question of the very existence of Northern Ireland? There had never been an 'Ulster' in the terms the *Telegraph* talked of that could make the sort of positive decision required. The solution that had worked since 1921 had been imposed by one community on the other: the minority had never agreed, merely submitted. If it ever chose to, this minority, or even a small but determined section of it, could totally disrupt the fabric of society within the province and make normal life impossible. The *Belfast Telegraph*'s Ulster did not and could not exist. Instead, there existed two groups, bitterly antagonistic, each believing itself to be in the right and to be wronged by the other, and each fearing a sell-out from the British government that would imperil its very existence. This was the reality of Northern Ireland when the New Year 1972 arrived.

In the early days of the New Year, if Faulkner and the Unionists were lukewarm to most of Maudling's hopes for 1972, the representatives of the minority, legitimate and illegitimate, were alike implacably opposed to them. At an anti-internment rally of Roman Catholics held at Falls Park on Sunday 2 January,

Austin Currie, one of the six SDLP members of Stormont who had walked out of the parliament as a protest against internment, proclaimed to huge applause: 'I have no doubt that within the next six or seven months Brian Faulkner and his rotten Unionist system will have been smashed,' and he added in reply to Mr Maudling's appeal to minority representatives once again to take part in the political process: 'But I say to Maudling: Why the hell should we talk to you? We are winning and you are not.'

The SDLP would not talk to Maudling until Faulkner, the leader of the democratically elected majority party in the province, had been removed, and the system he and the majority stood for was abolished. 'Why the hell should we talk to you? We are winning and you are not.' This was an evaluation of the previous three and a half years that was shared as much by Protestants as by Roman Catholics in the province. The silent majority in Ulster was Protestant. It had seen its society and way of life attacked by people who professed allegiance to an alien culture and national state. It had seen its major cities bombed, its commerce and industry attacked, its soldiers and police killed. And after each outrage, the offending minority had been granted concessions by a distant government who had no real knowledge, feeling, or interest in Ulster. Yes, the Catholics had won for three years, but only because the majority had remained quiescent and had trusted the government in Westminster to take care of its legitimate interests. But that trust had been misplaced. Loyal Ulster had been forced to accept unpalatable measures to placate an unruly minority, and each succeeding concession had only sharpened the minority's appetite for more. It seemed that the Catholics would not stop until the British government sold the six counties down the river and into a Catholic-dominated, reactionary, united Ireland.

In the way of this stood one implacable obstacle: Stormont. As long as the Protestant majority retained its own parliament and democratic Constitution Ulster would be safe. And at the helm in these troubled times was Brian Faulkner, a man of impeccable credentials as far as most Unionists were concerned. Though Faulkner appealed neither to the far-out extremists nor to the aristocrats who had ruled since 1921, he was a man who had his finger on the pulse of the people who mattered: the vast mass of Ulster's Protestants who were neither aristocrats nor far-out extremists, the people who simply wanted an end to the violence and a return to the tranquillity and normality that had existed when Lord Brookeborough had been Prime Minister. In a speech to the quarterly meeting of the East Down Unionist Association on Saturday 24 January, Faulkner caught the mood of these people and their feelings towards the Roman Catholic community, whom they believed supported the IRA virtually to a man:

We are speaking of hard-faced men. And I do not use that expression as an epithet, but as an accurate description of certain bitter and vicious countenances we have seen on public display – who shoot men in their own houses and before their own children; who place a deadly charge of high explosives next to an innocent victim in a pram; who drive a petrol-tanker with a booby-trap into a busy residential area; who shower a downtown shopping street with fragments of glass to tear the faces of women and young girls; who leave office-workers involved in a vital public service scarred and shattered; who break the knees of confederates whom they suspect of some offence against their code; who shave and tar young girls whose heinous offence is to love someone of whom they disapprove. That is real violence.

He then went on to discuss the alleged social grievances of the Roman Catholic community. Protestants in Ulster, he said, were also poorly housed, unemployed and suffering under the same adverse economic and social conditions as the Roman Catholics: 'But no one has yet suggested that there would be moral justification for them to make a protest in the form of killing or maiming, totally at random, some unfortunate number of their fellow citizens.' Not yet, perhaps, but Protestant Ulster had sat back for over three years and watched its most cherished beliefs demolished. The so-called 'Protestant backlash' had been derided with scorn by Catholic politicians, not taken seriously by the British government, and despaired of by many Protestants who were neither extremist nor bigoted. But by the start of 1972, Ulster's Protestants had learned one major lesson from their

Roman Catholic neighbours: namely, that under certain circumstances, when non-violence failed, violence could succeed. It was a lesson that was to be applied with deadly effect later in the year when, with the suspension of Stormont in March, the Protestants felt they had their backs to the wall and the sell-out to the South, long feared, was imminent.

The story of the sectarian assassinations in Ulster is the story of the Protestant backlash. There can be no questioning the simple truth that the greater part of the near-200 such assassinations were committed by Protestants organized in groups, often for this specific purpose. The Provisional IRA, for whom the authors have no sympathy, have committed atrocities that shame not only the name of Ireland, for whom they profess to be acting, but the whole human race. The bulk of the assassinations of civilians, however, are not to be laid at their door. The story of this phase of the Troubles is that of a small group of Protestants, concentrated mainly in Belfast, who were driven to despair of the legitimate constitutional procedures they had been brought up to revere by an indiscriminate campaign of killing and destruction that seemed all too likely to succeed in its every aim. That the backlash took over three years to emerge was due chiefly to the fact that the people involved were deeply interested in preserving the *status quo*. Only when that *status quo* seemed to be crumbling before them, and no other course seemed open, did they act.

Three years of concession and compromise to the Roman Catholic community, against the background of a rapidly increasing escalation in violence and destruction, had made the Protestant community very angry. In all communities at all times there are men and women who are not content to sit back and let themselves be dictated to by events. So too in Ulster's Protestant communities, men and women, often living in the same appalling social conditions that had led their Roman Catholic neighbours to commit or support acts of violence against the State, felt the need to do something to preserve those things they believed in. But the Catholic activists, the IRA – whos, main grievance, it had been revealed over three painful years was not adverse social conditions or the lack of full civil rights, but the very existence of the government and society that used these to keep them down – these people had a ready-made target for their frustrations in the visible forms of that government, in its soldiers and policemen and in its industry and commerce. It made no sense for Protestants to shoot soldiers or policemen, to bomb shops and factories, because these were the things they sought to preserve. To them as to the IRA this was Ulster: the Protestants wanted to save it, and a section of the Roman Catholic community wanted to destroy it.

Thus the only avenue left open to Protestant activists was to attack the Catholics – the 'enemy'. It was only too easy for them to see in the Roman Catholic community a fifth column within Ulster's midst, dedicated to its destruction. They saw a ruthless campaign of violence and destruction by the Catholic-based IRA which aimed at having the province absorbed into a backward sectarian state whose culture, society, and standard of living was completely opposed to the traditional values of Protestant Ulster. They acted accordingly.

If, before the Troubles began, most Protestants could make a distinction between the IRA and the Roman Catholic community, by 1972 there were few who did so. The reaction of the Catholic population in August 1971 when internment had been introduced was massive. Faulkner had moved only against the Catholic extremists. The UVF Protestant extremists who had feared that Faulkner would intern them, too, in order to demonstrate his impartiality, were not touched. The Catholic community, led by its elected politicians, protested vehemently at what it saw as a blatantly sectarian act. Catholics staged strikes – strikes that were bitterly resented by their Protestant work-mates who did not down tools. Led by the SDLP, Catholic politicians and appointed officials in all walks of public life boycotted all organs of the Northern Ireland State, and announced that the boycott would last until internment was ended. At the same time, the IRA unleashed a new and more deadly onslaught against the security forces and property in Ulster. It was hard, if not impossible, for the average Protestant to distinguish in his mind between the violent and non-violent reactions of the Catholic community to internment.

After August 1971 in the Protestant community there were no illusions about the Catholics: those who were not actually in the IRA were supporters. The polite term for the effects of internment was that it 'polarized the communities'. In simple terms readily understood in Sandy Row, the Shankill, or East Belfast, every Catholic was a Fenian. And as every good Protestant knew, it was the intention of the Fenians to bomb and murder loyal Ulster into an alien 32-county Catholic republic.

In this climate of opinion, which had the tacit support of some Unionist politicians, it was not difficult to translate words into actions. If all Catholics were the enemy, and the enemy was ruthless and merciless – men, as Faulkner said 'who place a deadly charge of high explosives next to an innocent victim in a pram' – then all Catholics were legitimate targets in a campaign of counter-aggression aimed at doing what the security forces had lamentably failed to do: namely wiping out the IRA and returning Ulster to peace and prosperity.

The sectarian assassinations were a counter-attack by a group of Ulster Protestants who agreed with Austin Currie and the IRA that the Catholics were winning and the the Unionist system was about to be destroyed. They were the product of frustration by a group of people who felt their only crime had been loyalty. The year 1972, we shall see, was not the first occasion when Protestants had gone out and killed Catholics in order to hit back at the IRA. Nor were Protestants responsible for the first civilian assassinations in these Troubles. But when the killings increased dramatically in the first half of 1972, and continued unabated thereafter, it was as a result of a deliberate and concerted campaign of sectarian assassination by Protestants. The anger, the bitterness of a people who felt their only crime had been loyalty, was translated into the most ruthless and dedicated campaign of civilian killings that had been seen in Western Europe since the Second World War. The Protestant backlash had been a long time coming, but when it finally came it made its presence felt with a vengeance that only the righteous can inflict.

2. The 1966 killings and the UVF

When Brian Faulkner said in January 1972 that no one had suggested that Protestants might 'make a protest in the form of killing or maiming, totally at random, some unfortunate number of their fellow citizens', he was not technically correct, as he probably knew. For in June 1966 he was a member of a Northern Ireland cabinet under Terence O'Neill that made the Protestant Ulster Volunteer Force an illegal organization under the Special Powers Act.

In March 1966, before the present Troubles began, a number of Catholic-owned premises in Ulster were petrol-bombed. The province had been at peace since the end of the last IRA campaign in 1962, but it was a tense time. Easter 1966 would mark the fiftieth anniversary of the rebellion in Dublin that eventually had led to independence for most of Ireland and the partition of the North to leave it within the United Kingdom. Republican celebrations of the Easter Rising were planned and there was some fear in Protestant areas that these might be the prelude to a new IRA campaign.

This fear was fanned by a rising political force, a fire-eating orator and Free Presbyterian minister, the Reverend Ian K. Paisley. In April and the first week of May, after the celebrations had passed off without serious incident, there were five more fire-bombing incidents. Of these the most serious occurred on 7 May when a bomb was thrown from a passing car at a Catholic-owned bar in Upper Charleville Street in the Shankill area of Belfast. The bomb missed the bar and instead went through the window of an elderly Protestant widow, Mrs Matilda Gould. Mrs Gould, 77, later died from the burns she received in the attack. The killing was subsequently attributed to a group called the

'Shankill UVF' and in a later court hearing this was confirmed by Mr Justice Gibson, who said: 'The bombing was the work of the Ulster Volunteer Force, a seditious combination or unlawful association whose activities were directed to asserting and maintaining the Protestant ascendency, in areas of the city where there was a predominantly Protestant majority of the local population, by overt acts of terrorism.' At the time of the attack on Mrs Gould, however, the UVF was not illegal, and the Ulster Prime Minister of the day, Terence O'Neill, shortly after refused to make it so.

The Ulster Volunteer Force, like the IRA, can trace its origins back to the troubled years in Ulster before the First World War. But unlike the IRA, it had no continuous history until 1966, when an organization of that name suddenly emerged on the Northern Ireland stage. A fortnight after the attack on Mrs Gould, on 21 May, Belfast newspapers were given a statement by a man describing himself as 'Captain William Johnston, Adjutant, First Battalion, Belfast UVF'. He said:

From this day we declare war against the IRA and its splinter-groups. Known IRA men will be executed mercilessly and without hesitation. Less extreme measures will be taken against anyone sheltering or helping them, but if they persist in giving them aid, then more extreme measures will be adopted. Property will not be exempted in any action taken. We will not tolerate any interference from any source and we solemnly warn the authorities to make no more speeches of appeasement. We are heavily armed Protestants dedicated to this cause.

Within a week events were to prove that these words were no idle boast. On 26 May a meeting of the new UVF took place in a back room of the Standard Bar in the Shankill Road. It was the first of a number of regular weekly meetings that were to be held in the bar. On this night it was decided to assassinate Leo Martin, a prominent Belfast IRA man. Four men were assigned to carry out the order the following night. On the 27th these men cruised around the Roman Catholic Clonard where Martin lived, but could not find their man. They did, however, pass a man returning home from a bar. Unfortunately for him, he was singing Republican songs, and this was sufficient information for the four UVF men to brand him an IRA man and shoot him. The victim was John Patrick Scullion, 28, a Catholic engineering worker of Oranmore Street. He died in the Royal Victoria Hospital three weeks later, and an anonymous caller to the *Belfast Telegraph* claimed the UVF were responsible for the killing.

The upsurge of Protestant militancy – reflected in the petrol-bombings and the deaths of Scullion and Mrs Gould – aroused anxiety in many quarters in Ulster. Not, however, in the highest. On 23 June, the Prime Minister, Terence O'Neill, announced in Stormont that he had no intention of invoking the Special Powers Act and outlawing any Protestant organization. Within a week he was to change his mind.

The incident that was to make him do so occurred in the early hours of Sunday 26 June, one month after the Scullion shooting. At two in the morning the people living in Malvern Street, off the Shankill Road, heard gunfire. The shots they heard were those that cut down four Roman Catholic barmen: Andrew Kelly, 27, Liam Doyle, 24, Peter Ward, 18, and Richard Leppington, 20. Two young girls who had been listening to music on the radio ran out to see a gang of men shooting the Catholics. The victims had earlier gone into the Malvern Arms public house. This was a time when there was little or no sectarian strife in Belfast, and Catholics and Protestants drank in each other's bars without fearing for their lives. The four were barmen at the International Hotel and had easily recognizable Southern accents. Unhappily for them, members of the UVF were in the pub planning to execute an IRA man, and the UVF men recognized the four as Catholics, and decided upon them as victims. Ward was shot through the heart and died almost immediately in the ambush that followed.

Three Protestant men were subsequently charged with Ward's murder: Augustus A. Spence, 33, a stager of Hertford Street, Belfast; Hugh Arnold McClean, 46, of Larne Road, Carickfergus, a bricklayer; and Robert James Williamson, 33, of Dagmar Street, Belfast. After the capture, McClean seems to have lost his nerve somewhat, and in an effort to minimize his own part in the killing, told all, implicating Spence heavily. In a statement to police shortly after his arrest McClean said that the UVF had met regularly in a back room of the Standard Bar where they plotted to assassinate members of the IRA. On the night in question he had attended a regular UVF meeting in the Standard Bar at which Augustus 'Gusty' Spence had taken the chair. Also there according to McClean were: Leslie Porter; Williamson; a cousin of Spence named Henry Hayes; and James 'Rocky' Burns. Burns, a 46-year-old labourer, was of particular importance to the group because he had served a prison sentence during the war, and had come to know a number of IRA men who were interned at that time. McClean said Burns was able to supply the UVF with the names and addresses of IRA men for assassination.

That night Spence did most of the talking, and the target was fixed, as in the previous month, as Leo Martin, who Burns said lived in Baden-Powell Street, although he did not know the number. Porter was sent to find out, and on his return, Burns and McClean were sent out with him. 'Burns and I were told to shoot Martin,' McClean said in his statement, and added that Spence made sure that he had a gun with him. The three drove to Baden-Powell Street, where, McClean said: 'Burns and I arranged that we would knock on Martin's door and if he answered the door we would shoot him.' Fortunately for Martin, he was out when his unexpected visitors arrived.

Rather than have a wasted journey, however, they then broke into Martin's house and set fire to it before reporting back to Spence in the Standard Bar. There they had some drinks before adjourning to the house of Spence's sister, Mrs Cassie Curry, in Belgrave Street. There, McClean said, the conversation was of arms 'for the volunteers'. At about 10·00 p.m., still having failed to assassinate any IRA men, the group moved to the Malvern Arms, a bar noted for its late hours. McClean testified:

When we were in the bar for about an hour, four lads came in and went for a drink at the counter. The conversation came up about the religion of these fellows. Spence asked the company if they would be

Catholics ... Spence then went up to the bar beside the four lads to buy a drink. When he returned to our table he said: 'I have been listening to their conversation and they are four IRA men.' We had some more drinks ... Spence said: 'These are IRA men and they will have to go.'

Shortly after midnight, Spence, McClean, Williamson and an unnamed fourth man left the bar. When the four Catholics left at 1·45 a.m. the four UVF men had taken up firing positions and were waiting for them. Ward was killed immediately. Kelly and Doyle were seriously wounded, and Leppington managed to run off, receiving a bullet-wound in the foot. The four gunmen returned to Mrs Curry's house in Belgrave Street. Once there, 'Spence produced a sack,' McClean said, 'and we all put our guns into it ... Somebody produced a bottle of porter and I drank it. Spence said: "That's the job done," or words to that effect.'

In his statement, McClean described Spence as his 'immediate boss' but said he thought Spence was taking orders from somebody else. In police questioning on how he came to join the UVF he was alleged to have said: 'I was asked, did I agree with Paisley, and was I prepared to follow him. I said that I was.' And after being charged he allegedly said: 'I am terribly sorry I ever heard tell of that man Paisley or decided to follow him. I am definitely ashamed of myself to be in such a position.'

It was the UVF men's misfortune that night that among the other customers in the Malvern Arms were a group of off-duty RUC men, and the three accused were rounded up soon after, and appeared in Belfast Magistrate's Court on 28 June. Spence is alleged to have said on his arrest: 'So this is what you get for being a Protestant!' Spence was also accused of the Scullion murder, and the three accused were closely questioned about the petrol-bomb attack on Mrs Gould's house.

Against the Rev. Ian Paisley, whom McClean had tried to implicate in the UVF, there was not the slightest shred of evidence to indicate complicity. Indeed, he was one of the first churchmen to condemn the shooting when he said in a statement to the Belfast *News Letter*: 'Like everyone else I deplore and condemn this killing, as all right-thinking people must do.

Incitement, direct, or indirect, must be treated with the full rigour of the law.'

Another version of the events of that evening was in the form of a statement Williamson, one of the accused, was alleged to have given the police shortly after his arrest. The statement was read at a special hearing of the case in August prior to the trial, and was widely quoted in the press at the time, although Williamson's counsel strongly protested at its publication. The statement was taken at 2·35 a.m. on 29 June by Detective Constable Leo McBrien at Tennent Street police station and read:

I went to McDowell's bar [Standard] at the corner of Agnes Street, Shankill Road about 8·00 p.m. last Saturday night [25 June]. I went with Gusty Spence, and we attended a meeting of the Ulster Volunteer Force. The following men were at the meeting: Rocky Burns, Leslie Porter, Hugh McClean, Des Reid, Gusty Spence and myself. McClean, Burns and Porter were sent up to Baden-Powell Street to see if a man called Martin was in and, if he wasn't, that was it. They came back and said he wasn't in. The whole lot of us left McDowell's at closing time and went to Curry's house in Belgrave Street.

Rocky Burns's coat was lying open and I saw a revolver sticking in his trousers. We had some more drink there and, in fact, I had quite a lot of drink that night in McDowell's. Some time after 11·00 p.m. I went to Watson's bar [Malvern Arms] in Malvern Street with Gusty Spence, Frank Curry, Porter, Reid, and McClean. Rocky Burns did not come. We had a few drinks in there and then me and Porter and Reid went out in the direction of Glengormley. Reid left the car and came back with a parcel which he put in the boot. I never saw what was in the parcel but Reid told me it was gelignite. We drove to Craven Street and I left them at the car and went to Curry's house. I was standing outside Curry's house with Henry Johnston. I don't know where the jelly went to. I went round to Watson's bar. I had a Luger gun in a shoulder-holster with me. It was loaded with six rounds of small-calibre ammunition. I joined two comrades who I don't wish to name. I was told there was four IRA men in the bar.

There was instructions given by one of my comrades to scare them. I took up my position at the corner of Malvern Street and Ariel Street. My comrades took up their own positions. The four IRA men came out of Watson's pub. I moved towards the centre of the road. I drew my gun and fired towards the men, but low. Everybody was told to fire low. I mean my comrades. My gun jammed twice, and I had to cock it and a round was ejected each time. That's how I know that I fired four rounds. We all ran down Langford Street and made our way to a certain place, where we all put our guns in a sack. I went home after that. This was not a deliberate attack. It happened on the spur of the moment. I think that the one who got away had a gun on him. I did not know that these I R A men were going to be in Watson's that night.

Perhaps the most frightening description of that night came from one of the victims. At the trial, Liam Doyle, who had been seriously wounded in the ambush, broke down and cried when asked by the Crown Prosecutor, Mr Frank Reid Q.C., to look at the pathologist's photographs of his dead colleague, Peter Ward. When he recovered, however, he described what happened when he and the three other young barmen left the Malvern Arms shortly before 2·00 that morning. As they entered the street, he said he heard a number of bangs and saw some flashes coming from four men standing at the corner: 'I did not know where it was and just stood there. I saw Andy falling and felt a pain in my leg. I ran across the street.' He saw the men move in on them, and on running across the street he fell to the ground near a lamp-post with his head to the wall and his feet facing the roadway.

I saw this man running after me. I saw flashes coming from him and he started to shoot into me. He fired five or six shots into me. I was hit six times. I asked him what he was shooting at us for as we were doing nothing. I pleaded with him not to shoot at me and shouted 'please don't' or something like that, but the man made no reply and did not stop shooting.

Doyle identified the man who had shot him as Gusty Spence. All three accused were found guilty of murder in October and sentenced to life imprisonment by the Lord Chief Justice, Lord McDermott, who recommended they serve a minimum period of twenty years in gaol. They were found not guilty of a charge of conspiracy to murder, which at that date was a capital offence. Later that week at the trial of Burns, Porter, and two other men on arms and explosives offences arising out of the events of that night, Porter volunteered the information: 'Spence is the Colonel of the Shankill Division [of the UVF] so far as I know and his official name is Colonel William Johnston.'

The immediate effect of the Malvern Street shootings came a few days after they took place. The Prime Minister, Terence O'Neill, had been in France at the time, ironically, as it turned out, attending a ceremony commemorating the men of the old UVF who had joined the British Expeditionary Force in 1914. He returned to Belfast on Monday 27 June, and in the early hours of the next morning held a crisis cabinet meeting. Later in the day, Tuesday 28 June, he addressed Stormont with the following statement:

Information which has come to hand in the last few days makes it clear that the safety of law-abiding citizens is threatened by a very dangerous conspiracy prepared at any time to use murder as a weapon ... The Minister of Home Affairs has this morning made regulations under the Civil Authorities (Special Powers) Act (NI) 1932 to declare an organization which has misappropriated the title 'UVF' an unlawful organization ... This organization now takes its proper place alongside the IRA in the schedule of illegal bodies.

Thus O'Neill took the action he had been pressed to take, and declined, one week earlier, and banned the UVF. Interestingly, the Minister of Home Affairs responsible for implementing the ban was a William Craig, MP for Larne, about whom we shall hear more. Also of interest is that, despite the ban being passed in June 1966, not one person was charged with being a member of the UVF until January 1973 – six and a half years later.

The significance of these events in 1966 – the deaths of Mrs Gould, John Patrick Scullion, and Peter Ward – lies in the similarity in both motive and execution with later killings in the 1970s. At the time the killings were abhorred by ordinary people in both communities. Apart from one or two exceptions, Spence and his colleagues were regarded as criminals in the Protestant community, not as patriots.

At no time does the UVF appear to have constituted more than a handful of men who met once a week in the Standard Bar.

There was at that time no threat from the IRA. In 1969 when serious rioting broke out in Belfast it was discovered that the Marxist Chief-of-Staff of what consisted of the IRA, Cathal Goulding, had sold all their arms and ammunition in the belief that the future role of the movement lay in political rather than military action. The inability of the IRA to defend the Roman Catholic areas in Northern Ireland during these riots led to the birth of the militant Provisionals with their philosophy of total war.

But in 1966, for all practical purposes, there was no IRA in Ulster, and consequently no threat from it. The province was enjoying a period of peace, and economic expansion seemed to promise a better future for both Protestants and Catholics. There was as yet no support for militant sectarianism on either side, but events were to change all that, and to turn Spence from a villain into a hero.

3. The Troubles begin again: 1968–71

At the time there were few to mourn the incarceration of Spence and his colleagues. They were not considered martyrs to the cause in 1966, but events over the next few years were to make them so. By 1970 Ulster was in a very different situation. Rioting and sectarian warfare had led to a complete breakdown in law and order, only stemmed by the sudden injection of the Army into the streets. One Northern Ireland Prime Minister had fallen, another was tottering, and the IRA threat, unreal in 1966, was seen by every Protestant in the province in far worse a form than had ever been dreamed of only a few short years before. By then Gusty Spence was a folk-hero to the Protestant working class. His imprisonment was now seen to be unfair – another example of the injustices the Roman Catholics had perpetrated on the Protestants.

When elements in the Protestant working class organized to meet the threat they saw before them – organized as Spence had urged them in 1966 – it was the UVF leader who was the inspiration. He occupied a place reserved for very few in political life: that of the man who had held an unpopular conviction but who had been proved right. In his gaol cell in the 1970s, it is highly unlikely that Spence played a decisive role in the political events in the Shankill and East Belfast; but he was nonetheless the guiding light, and it was his tactics that were adopted when Protestants hit back at the Roman Catholics.

The identification of the Catholic community with the IRA, the compilation of lists of known Catholics who could be assassinated, the squad tactics of three or four men sent to carry out an assassination, the tactic of shooting men at their own homes or as they leave public houses: all of these features of the assassinations in the 1970s were present in the UVF killings in 1966. Then the activities of the UVF drew equal hostility from both the Protestant community in Belfast and the Catholic. But by the 1970s, a section of the Protestants, concentrated in the working-class districts of the Shankill, Sandy Row, and East Belfast, had come to regard the killing of Catholics as legitimate military action. These killings were seen as a last resort, a last line of defence for a people with their backs to the wall, against an alien and enemy community that sought to destroy them.

By 1972, it had become clear to many of these people – not criminals or psychopaths, but good, decent people who had only asked to be left in peace to go about their everyday lives – that Gusty Spence had been right in 1966. There had, after all, been an IRA threat to Ulster, and the only way to stop a republican takeover now was to hit back hard at the IRA: to meet fire with fire. The events of recent years had proved beyond doubt to a great many Protestants – people who were not bigoted – that there was no distinguishing the Roman Catholic community as a whole from the IRA. They were both one and the same thing: those Catholics who were not active members of the IRA, sheltered and harboured the terrorists.

It was a tragic belief, but it was sincerely held by many thousands of decent working-class Protestants, and there was not a small amount of justification in it from the Protestant point of view. Austin Currie's 'Why should we talk, we are winning?' sentiments were not isolated. Catholic leaders and politicians had poured scorn and contempt on Protestants and their institutions all through the Troubles. The Protestants had taken it all, but they had remembered. For every concession, the Catholics had produced new demands, and become more confident that they would get everything they asked for. But the Protestants had not been impotent, merely inactive. Spence had shown the way in 1966. By 1972 the time was ripe for his strategy to be put into practice.

The militant Protestants were ready to hit back. They had, as they saw it, been extremely patient under the most extreme provocation, but the suspension of Stormont in March 1972, followed by the truce negotiated by the British government with the IRA in June, were the last straws: the backlash emerged. The campaign of sectarian assassinations that burst on Ulster in June and July 1972 can be understood only in the context of what had happened in Northern Ireland in the six years since the UVF killings in 1966.

The Troubles began in the autumn of 1968 with the organization of civil rights marches and demonstrations. In all of the many phases of the Troubles till 1972 the Roman Catholic community in Ulster held the initiative. From marching in 1968 the situation developed to rioting, with, in the summer of 1969, serious riots in Belfast that required the infusion of troops to separate the two communities. Rioting continued in 1970 when the IRA gunmen and bombers first appeared. By 1971 sniping at soldiers and bombings in the centres of Belfast and Londonderry had become frequent occurrences.

O'Neill was replaced as Prime Minister by James Chichester Clark in April 1969. He in turn was replaced by Brian Faulkner in March 1971. One of the contributary factors in Chichester Clark's downfall had been the brutal slaying in March by three IRA Provisionals, led by Martin Meehan, the Ardoyne commander, of three young Scots soldiers. These killings were seen as particularly shocking because the IRA men had spent the evening drinking with the soldiers, who were off duty, and had taken them to a lonely spot outside the city, ostensibly for more drinking. Two of the soldiers were brothers, and one was only 17. The three were taken to a deserted spot where the killers shot each of them in the head in turn.

By the time of Faulkner's arrival as Prime Minister, the B-Special Constabulary had been disbanded, and the RUC disarmed by the British government after the recommendations of the Hunt Committee. In August 1971, Faulkner set up internment without trial to try to crush the IRA campaign. It had the opposite effect. Only Roman Catholics were interned, and the Catholic community erupted in violence. It was a gamble which failed, and the failure was recognized by the Westminster government the following March when the Northern Ireland government was suspended and Direct Rule from Britain was imposed.

It is within this fabric that the advent of the sectarian assassinations of civilians is to be placed. The first of these took place on the night of 23 December 1970. Andrew Jardin, a 65-year-old Protestant company director, was shot dead by masked gunmen who entered his luxury home at Hannahstown, a suburb of Belfast. At the time, police were quick to issue a statement that the killing was not connected with the Troubles. Instead, robbery was suggested as a motive.

With hindsight, however, the circumstances of the Jardin killing would tend to suggest otherwise. Three armed men called at his house at 9·00 p.m. The door was answered by Jardin's daughter, Mrs Sylvia Murphy. The men asked for Jardin by name and forced their way into the house. They were met by Jardin himself who was armed with a revolver, and it is unclear who fired first. What is clear is that Jardin was shot dead by the gunmen, who then fled without taking any valuables. Police later found traces of blood outside the Jardin home that led them to believe that one of the gunmen had been wounded or even killed.

A number of factors tend to suggest that the Jardin killing had a political motivation. First, Jardin was no ordinary businessman. He was a prominent member of the Orange and Masonic Orders. He also belonged to the *élite* of the Orange Order, the Royal Black Preceptaries, the 'Blackmen'. As well as this, as part of his business activities he was the owner and managing director of the Black Mountain Quarry. Through his quarry he had access to large amounts of explosives. After his death, rumour in Roman Catholic areas said that he had died at the hands of the IRA because explosives from the Black Mountain Quarry had been used by the Protestant UVF in the bombing of Catholic bars.

But of the greatest interest is a curious link between the killing of Jardin and that of a 28-year-old Roman Catholic, John

Joseph Kavanagh, just over a month later. Kavanagh, a roof tiler of Kashmir Road in the Lower Falls, was found shot in the head on the banks of the Blackstaff river at Roden Street, in the same area, on 27 January 1971. This was the first killing in the Troubles to be considered by the police as an assassination for political motives.

Kavanagh had been executed by the IRA as an informer. His death was to set a pattern for executions to come. The pathologist's report on Kavanagh said that he had been shot where he was found. He had been shot in the head at close range, and had probably been kneeling when the death-blow had been administered. He died instantly. The killing sparked off a full-scale murder hunt with detectives being flown over from Scotland Yard. It was early days, and police could afford the luxury of a 'real' murder investigation with no stone unturned. Not that it availed them much, for the Yard men returned home in the autumn with no solution, grumbling about lack of co-operation from the population.

What was interesting, however, was that a few days after Kavanagh's body was found, the front page of the Belfast *News Letter* ran a big story linking Kavanagh with Jardin. A John Joseph Kavanagh from the same area of Belfast as the dead man had been employed by the late Andrew Jardin at the Black Mountain Quarry. Could this be a coincidence, the *News Letter* asked? Jardin's daughter confirmed that such a man had existed. 'We have been deeply interested and concerned about this latest case,' she said. But a foreman working at the quarry stated that a photograph of the dead men was not of the John Joseph Kavanagh who had worked for Jardin. Significantly, perhaps, the photograph he was shown was four or five years old. The police were far from convinced that there was no connection between the two deaths. Kavanagh's sister told them that he had been working outside Lisburn until shortly before Christmas. The Black Mountain Quarry was situated just outside Lisburn. The police issued an appeal for the John Joseph Kavanagh who had worked for Andrew Jardin at the quarry and who lived in the Lower Falls to come forward. Nobody did.

There are two possible conclusions to be drawn from this. One is that there were two John Joseph Kavanaghs living in the Lower Falls. Each worked outside Lisburn, some ten miles from Belfast. One worked for Andrew Jardin at the Black Mountain Quarry; the other did not, and it was he who was killed in Roden Street on 27 January 1971. The surviving John Joseph Kavanagh, who managed to live in a small tightly knit community like the Lower Falls with no friends or relatives, disappeared shortly after the deaths of his former employer and his namesake. Nobody he left behind in Belfast had ever heard of him. The other conclusion is that there was only one Kavanagh, and that he both worked for Jardin and was killed in January. This Kavanagh was deeply involved in the IRA. The Provisionals later accepted responsibility for his death on the grounds that he was an informer. He had been in prison and was known to the police, for whom he may have been a source of information. Through his job at the quarry he would have been able to give the IRA the information that explosives were being passed to the UVF. After Jardin's killing and the subsequent police investigation, Kavanagh's knowledge, and perhaps his willingness to part with it to the authorities, may have signed his death warrant.

There were four more assassinations in 1971. Each was the work of the IRA and, interestingly enough, like Kavanagh, three of the other victims had been in gaol quite recently. These were Albert Edward Bell, 26, a Protestant of Olympia Street, who was killed on 7 February; Robert George McFarland, 32, a Protestant of Spencer Street, Holywood, killed on 26 October; and Thomas Henry Malcolm Kells, 19, a Protestant of Alliance Avenue, killed on 31 October. The final victim was a Unionist politician, Senator John Barnhill, 65, who was shot by the official IRA at his home in Strabane near the border in December. His death will be discussed more fully in Chapter 13.

Albert Edward Bell was a Protestant member of the IRA. He was found at Nutt's Corner, off the Crumlin Road, a deserted spot high above the city on the road to Aldergrove Airport, not far from the place where the three Scots soldiers were to be killed the following month. He was the victim of a clinically executed IRA killing. The pathologist's report showed that he had been shot twice at close range by a .38 revolver. The first bullet had entered the brain from the back of the head and had travelled upwards. The second bullet had been administered after the body had fallen, and had entered the brain behind the right ear and exited on the other side of the head. Death was instantaneous. This pattern of execution was to become, with slight variations, the standard IRA killing. Kavanagh's had been the first death to be considered by the State Pathologist's department as an assassination. He had been shot through the left nostril at very close range, and this, together with the other circumstances of the death, led to the conclusion that the killing had been an assassination. Jardin's death, to this day, despite the subsequent killings of men in identical fashion, is still officially regarded as attempted robbery without any political motive.

This early phase of assassinations, in which six men were killed between December 1970 and December 1971, was dominated by the IRA gunmen. Five of the victims were Protestant and one, Kavanagh, was a Catholic. It was not until 1972 that the Protestant gunmen emerged.

The next man to die in 1971 was Robert George McFarland, a 32-year-old Protestant who lived in the almost exclusively Protestant town of Holywood on the fringe of East Belfast. His body was found in an alley at Altcar Street, off the Mountpottinger Road in East Belfast at 8·00 a.m. on the morning of 26 October. East Belfast is separated from the West by the river Lagan. On the west side are found the hot spots of the Falls, Shankill, Sandy Row, New Lodge, Ardoyne, Ballymurphy, Andersonstown, and most of the other names that have become familiar throughout the world because of the Troubles. In the East, however, the overwhelmingly Protestant population has meant that most of the area has remained relatively quiet. An exception to this has been the Short Strand area, just across the Albert Bridge. This area contains a Catholic population and it was a strong IRA enclave in the East. This was where McFarland was found.

He had been gagged and hooded and shot through the head.

The killing bore the hallmarks of an I R A execution, and although the police at the time said they were keeping an open mind on the matter, there is no doubt that the IRA were responsible. For a considerable period of time as the assassinations mounted, police pursued the theory that killers were shooting their victims in their own areas and then dumping the bodies in 'enemy' territory. In the context of the sectarian geography of Belfast this theory is untenable, and no evidence has ever been produced to back it up. No Protestant, in the McFarland case, would have dared to dump a body in the early hours of the morning in an IRA stronghold like the Short Strand. R UC and Army patrols kept out, and IRA patrols were heavy on the ground. Such a policy would have entailed a heavy, and unnecessary, risk to those dumping the body. The climate of fear in both communities engendered by the Troubles and the growth of private armies to fill the vacuum left by the normal forces of law and order was such to ensure a wall of silence that protected the assassins from the consequences of their actions – at least through the courts of law. Witnesses rarely, if ever, were prepared to risk their own lives by giving information to the police or Army that would lead to the arrest and conviction of those responsible for such killings. The assassin was secure in the knowledge that he could dump his victim's body in his own area – sometimes only a short distance from where he himself lived – because no one would tell the story afterwards. In the McFarland case, it was later confirmed that he had been shot where he was found, and this was a pattern that was repeated with frequency as the killings multiplied.

Unlike his Protestant co-religionist, Bell, or the Catholic Kavanagh, McFarland was not a member of the I R A. But he was a frequent drinker in bars in the Short Strand frequented by IRA men, and he was well known to them. Also known to them was that the cause of McFarland's gaol term of nine months in 1970 was that he had been found carrying a can of petrol in the grounds of St Colmcille's Roman Catholic Church, Holywood. He had been released from prison early in the year at about the same time as Bell, and the reason for both deaths was the same.

McFarland had gone into the Bridge Bar in the Short Strand and tried to get a cheque cashed by the barman. The bar was frequently used by local IRA men, and McFarland got into conversation with a group of them. He asked them if he could join the IRA. They in turn asked him if he wanted to join the Officials or the Provisionals. He replied that he did not care, and the men said they would see to it for him. Later that evening, McFarland was picked up by the IRA in the Short Strand and interrogated. He was executed because they believed he was an informer giving information, gathered on his drinking visits, to the UVF on IRA activity in the area. His attempt to join the IRA of whichever wing was seen as a crude attempt to infiltrate the organization to spy on its operations.

The fourth assassination victim in 1971 was Thomas Henry Malcolm Kells, a 19-year-old Protestant labourer of Alliance Avenue, Belfast. His body was found on the Flowbog Road, Dundrod, south of Belfast, on the afternoon of 31 October. Kells's arms had been tied behind his back, and he had been blindfolded and gagged. He had been shot four times in the left back in the region of the heart. A fifth bullet had then been fired through the left temple. Like the other deaths, a .38 revolver had been used.

Coming so swiftly after the McFarland killing, that of Kells was bound to attract comment. 'RUTHLESS ASSASSINATION BY "MURDER SQUAD"' was the page-one headline in next morning's Belfast *News Letter*. In that evening's *Belfast Telegraph* there was a story headlined: 'GAGGED MAN'S DEATH: JAIL LINK INQUIRY', in which the coincidence of Kells, McFarland and Bell having all left prison within a few weeks of each other at the beginning of the year was spotlighted. The RUC were said to be keeping a 'very open mind' as to who might be responsible for Kells's death and whether it was linked with the other two. But, the story concluded: 'Clearly the police are puzzled. They are trying to discover if, in fact, the common denominator in the three assassinations could date back to their terms in prison.'

For some reason, Kavanagh was not included in this list, although he too had undergone a recent prison term shortly before he died. With hindsight, it becomes somewhat clearer why these four men should have met the fate they did. All were ex-convicts, people involved in petty crime and not, with the exception of McFarland, in gaol for political offences. Kavanagh's family, it is true, did claim that he had been gaoled for his part in the defence of a Catholic area during a riot, but this puts rather a favourable gloss on his offence, and the family's story appears to have been aimed more at the IRA who killed him than anyone else: they were attempting to counteract the rumours that he had been an informer, and present him as a patriot.

The picture that emerges in all four cases is of men with little grasp of the political realities who got involved in very deep water, just at a time when the political situation in the province was deteriorating and becoming something approaching civil war. The story of McFarland walking into an IRA pub in the Short Strand and asking if he could join the IRA typifies the men. McFarland said he did not mind which wing he joined. The Provisionals and Officials were bitter ideological foes who had quarrelled violently on more than one occasion, involving fatal casualties. McFarland lost whatever credibility he may have had and signed his own death warrant by his ham-fisted approach in a very dangerous situation.

All four men were killed by the IRA, who believed they were informers or spies. Kells, the last to die, lived in Alliance Avenue, a mixed street at that time, on the fringe of the IRA stronghold, the Ardoyne. He was believed to be giving information on IRA activity in the Ardoyne to the security forces. Prison was a denominator in all four cases. There they became known to the security forces, and they would have been under observation once they left. The opportunities for such men to collaborate with the forces of law and order were extensive. The glamour of giving information and the (admittedly small) sums of money they would have received for their knowledge could have overcome what little sense they may have possessed. In all societies the police rely for much of their information on crime from people such as these. The 'copper's nark' is to a very real extent an invaluable weapon in the armoury of police all over the world.

Certain types of people, often petty criminals, derive a disproportionate amount of satisfaction from talking to the authorities, whether they have useful information or not. Police forces are not the only bodies patronized in this way. Newspapers also receive their full share of people who insist they have valuable information to give. In a normal situation such people are harmless and often do provide quantities of useful intelligence. But Northern Ireland during the Troubles was not a normal situation. It will never be known how many people met their deaths because they talked too much to the wrong people, or gave the impression they knew something when they knew nothing. Those who dabbled in the murky world of the terrorist campaign and counter-campaigns were putting their heads on the chopping-block. They were in a deadly business, and they were the suckers.

By the end of 1971, six men had been assassinated in the current phase of the campaign. No Protestant organization was involved in any of these killings. Like the bombings and the killings of members of the security forces, the IRA, based in the Roman Catholic community and supported solely by Catholics, was completely responsible. There were not to be any Protestant-initiated assassinations until the New Year 1972 when the very existence of Northern Ireland seemed to be in jeopardy. Then, when the last defence of the Protestant Constitution was swept aside by the British government, who then proceeded to treat on equal terms with the IRA, the floodgates were opened.

Part Two
The Killings: 1972

4. Ulster has its back to the wall: January–June 1972

As we have seen, the New Year 1972 brought a glimmer of hope in Northern Ireland that the worst of the Troubles was over. It was soon dispelled. Violence and destruction of property continued unabated, and originated entirely from members of the Roman Catholic community. As so often happens, hope of an improvement in a bad situation, once held, no matter how briefly, and then dispelled, leads to an even greater disillusionment and gloom than before. This was the feeling in the Protestant community in the early months of 1972. Added to this, there was unease as the continuing rumours that the British government might abolish the Northern Ireland Parliament and integrate the province into the rest of the United Kingdom.

The average Protestant did not want to see the Stormont government abolished, and even if the prospect of full integration had some support on its own merits, increasing animosity towards the Roman Catholics made Protestants cling the more tenaciously to the old system. The Rev. Ian Paisley's Democratic Unionist Party stood on a platform of full integration, but so too did the IRA, though, of course, for different reasons. Paisley and the DUP believed full integration would strengthen the union; the IRA that it would weaken it. But full integration was not on as far as most Protestants were concerned: to many it would seem like another unjustifiable concession made to the Catholics, and another step on the inexorable road to a 32-county Irish republic. No, Stormont always had been the first and the last line of defence of Protestant Ulster, and so it must remain.

The first few months of the New Year saw the hardening of much Protestant opinion on this issue in particular, and against the Roman Catholic community *en masse* as supporters and providers for the IRA, in general. Everything Ulster's Protestants had believed in for fifty years appeared to be crumbling away. They felt betrayed by the attitude of successive British governments, both Conservative and Labour, none of whom had made a real effort to arrest the process. The governments in Westminster seemed too often, to the ordinary Protestant in Belfast, to be more concerned with maintaining good relations with the government of the Irish Republic in Dublin. And yet it was this very government, led by John Mary Lynch, that was turning a blind eye to the activities of the IRA and allowing its territory to become a safe haven for wanted terrorists from the North.

Ulster's Protestants, it seemed, had no friends anywhere. The world's press was virtually unanimous in its hostility to their cause. They had seen a law-breaker such as Bernadette Devlin turned into a latter-day Joan of Arc by the media. Foreign politicians, such as Edward Kennedy, had made political capital out of the Northern Ireland tragedy at the expense of the majority Protestant community who only wanted to be left in peace inside the United Kingdom. The former head of Belfast's Provisionals, Joe Cahill, had been built up as a modern revolutionary hero by the British and Foreign press after he had the audacity to hold a press conference in the heart of Belfast under the noses of the military. In September 1971 Ulster's Protestants could read that Cahill had said in an interview: 'I want to see peace, prosperity, and happiness in my country, and I think the way we are going about achieving it is the best way.' This could hardly be expected to go down well in a community that ran a daily gauntlet of bombs and bullets from Cahill's colleagues in the IRA.

By 1972 Cahill was safely sheltering in the Republic of Ireland. Hundreds of thousands of Protestants in Northern Ireland were enraged at the government in the South – a government that allowed the terrorists a safe refuge from which to mount their attacks on Ulster. A letter to the *Loyalist News*, a militant Protestant news-sheet, summed up all the anger and frustration felt by many Protestants, and called for a strong reaction from the Protestant community:

I want to remind Protestants that these animals are crawling into Ulster, hitting vital points like R UC stations etc. The ugly thing is that the bastards are getting away with it. Then the question arises, what the hell is the U VF doing about it? You've got to fight fire with fire, and personally I don't think they've enough fire to make the animals sweat! I'm not against the U VF but I would like to see a new U VF fighting for the cause and willing to give their lives to hold on to what others gave their lives for.

Just as in 1969, when they had felt under attack, members of the Roman Catholic community had asked, 'What the hell is the I RA doing?', so in 1971 history was repeated on the Protestant side. And the parallel went further than that, for, just as in 1969 the I RA was completely caught by surprise at the political turn of events, so too in 1971 what was left of Spence's U VF was woefully inadequate to meet the needs of the situation as the militant Protestants saw it. Thus with chilling irony, just as the Provisional I RA grew out of the frustrations of activist Catholics, so in 1971 the militant Protestants created another outlet for their grievances: the UDA. In August 1971, less than one month after the above letter appeared in the *Loyalist News*, leaflets were distributed in the Shankhill, Sandy Row, and East Belfast by a group of men, at least one of whom was to become prominent in the Ulster Defence Association. The leaflets read:

Being convinced that the enemies of the Faith and Freedom are determined to destroy the State of Northern Ireland and thereby enslave the people of God, we call on all members of our loyalist institutions, and other responsible citizens, to organize themselves *immediately* into platoons of twenty under the command of someone capable of acting as sergeant. Every effort must be made to arm these platoons, with whatever weapons are available. The first duty of each platoon will be to formulate a plan for the defence of its own street or road in cooperation with platoons in adjoining areas. A structure of command is already in existence and the various platoons will eventually be linked in a coordinated effort.

Here we have the birth-certificate of the Ulster Defence Association. The timing of the leaflet is significant. It was distributed on 12 August, three days after Brian Faulkner interned hundreds of Roman Catholics under the Special Powers Act. The leaflets came at a time when the Province was still un-nerved in the wake of the worst violence in its history that had followed internment. There was a strong fear among Protestants that the violence might spread into their areas and that the IRA might take reprisals against them. Hence the emphasis on defence on a street-by-street, area-by-area basis. This was the reality of a troubled city divided on sectarian lines. The UDA was formed to defend Protestant areas, not to attack Catholics. It grew spontaneously out of a genuine fear among members of the Protestant working class that their very existence was in peril. As such it immediately had overwhelming local support. At last people could see that something was being done within Protestant communities to defend the Ulster way of life and the values that had been revered for fifty years. From defence, it was then only a short but logical step for some to offence. After all, the best defence is attack.

One year later this step had been taken, and in September 1972 in a loyalist news-sheet called *Ulster Militants* a group of men who had joined the UDA explained in a letter why they had come to take offensive action against the Catholics:

Most of us, with the exception of two groups, were at one time members of all the other organizations, but we got sick and tired of training with only a general idea of what we were supposed to be training for. We wanted action and we were not allowed to have any. It was always 'tomorrow'. Gradually, through a contact man, we were convinced that a number of small groups, basically unknown to each other for security reasons, but cooperating in attacks on known enemies, would be a more effective weapon against the IRA Provos and their 'passive' sympathizers. The idea was tried out and proved very successful. But the success was undoubtedly dependent upon anonymity. While the contact men – there are now three – know each other, they are unable to contact their own group leaders. The leaders do the contacting ... People who can carry out an attack on a target and remain silent are few and far between, yet any other type, until the Loyalists openly go on the streets, are dangerous to us ... Our motto is simple but very apt: '*volens et valens*' which means 'willing and able'.

The authors of the letter claimed that they were first contacted in the summer of 1972 at about the time of the IRA truce. This same period saw a dramatic rise in the number of assassinations and saw the worst phase in the whole assassination campaign with almost forty killings inside five weeks from 26 June to 31 July.

This statement tells of men of action champing at the bit at a policy of static defence. They were contacted by others who felt the same and who had been 'cooperating in attacks on known enemies'. The 'enemy' is interpreted very liberally. The letter speaks of the attacks as a 'more effective weapon against the IRA Provos *and their passive sympathizers*' (our italics). 'Attacks' is almost certainly a euphemism for assassinations, and the category of 'passive sympathizers' would seem to have included virtually every Roman Catholic in the province and every Protestant suspected of associating with Catholics. And the letter tells us that these 'attacks' proved 'very successful'.

The story of the first six months of 1972 is one in which the Protestant population in Ulster became increasingly frustrated by, and alienated from, the policies of the British government in Westminster. By the time of the June truce with the IRA, some of these people, like those who wrote to *Ulster Militants*, were ready to take the initiative from the British and the IRA. The campaign of assassinations was the result. But there had been a steady trickle of such killings during the previous six months that could have been seen as a warning of what was to come, if only someone had been looking.

The first civilian assassination victim in 1972 was Peter Gerard Woods, 28, a Roman Catholic publican who was shot dead at his home at Lowwood Park, Shore Road, North Belfast, on the night of 8 January. Woods was counting the takings from his Gibraltar Bar after closing, and his killers escaped with £500. Robbery was a possible motive here, but one does not have to shoot a man to rob him. Whoever the killers were – and it was probably the IRA – they were obviously quite ruthless. Life does not seem to have had a very high value for them.

The second killing in January was equally ruthless. Sidney

53

Agnew, 46, was a Protestant who lived in the Protestant Mount-pottinger district of East Belfast adjacent to the Catholic Short Strand enclave. A bus-driver, Agnew was due to give evidence at the trial of three local IRA men charged with hijacking a bus. The night of 18 January, the day before he was due to give evidence, a meeting of the Ballymacarret IRA (Short Strand) discussed the matter. It was decided that Agnew should be killed to stop him from talking. The belief held at the meeting was that if Agnew were removed in this way, the case against the three IRA men would collapse and they would be freed. Accordingly, a young man and a young girl were sent to Agnew's house, where they shot him down at his door in front of his wife and children. It was an assassination carried out in a way similar to that of Jardin in December 1970.

This killing horrified a province that had thought its capacity for horror had long been exceeded. It showed quite clearly the lengths to which the IRA were prepared to go on the grounds of expediency. No man or woman was now safe, even in their homes, from the long arm of the IRA assassins. The most tragic aspect of Agnew's death is that it was pointless. The IRA men knew very little about the law. In earlier deposition hearings Agnew had given his full evidence. At the trial his depositions were ruled admissible, and his posthumous evidence was sufficient to convict the accused men on all charges.

Agnew and Woods were the only killings in January, but developments on the political side were to have a direct bearing on the later killings. The very day that Agnew died, the Stormont Cabinet had decided to extend for a further twelve months the ban on parades in the province. Retrospectively, when so much has happened in Ulster, it seems a little odd that this should have caused so much fuss at the time. But it did. It was seen in Loyalist circles as another indication that Ulster was being sold down the river, and that the effective decisions were being made, not by the Unionist government at Stormont, but in Whitehall. The extension of the ban had a significant part in the establishment of a new political group in the province that was to play an increasingly important role in the coming year: Vanguard.

It was led by former Home Affairs Minister, William Craig, and supported by a pugnacious shipyard worker and former Northern Ireland Labour Party man, Billy Hull, and the Grand Master of the Orange Order, the Rev. Martin Smyth. Vanguard was to provide the political focus for the growing Protestant discontent.

The heart of this discontent lay among the Protestant working class, and here Billy Hull had his own separate power base in the Loyalist Association of Workers. LAW was based mainly, though not entirely, on Belfast's Harland & Wolf's shipyard which employed over 10,000 workers, almost all of them Protestant. Craig addressed a meeting of 500 LAW members on Thursday 27 January in the Apprentice Boys' Memorial Hall in the Catholic city of Londonderry. In fighting terms he threw down the gauntlet of resistance to the British government if Westminster were to try to tamper with Northern Ireland's Consititution:

We in Ulster are intent on seeing that we have a constitutional organization that can effectively preserve and maintain in Ulster the British heritage. It is not the Constitution that matters to us. It is the British way of life. The Constitution is only the vehicle. Any tampering with our Constitution would merely be the beginning of the inevitable sell-out and would expose us more and more to the caprices of British politicians who, for the sake of expediency, are all too likely to betray their friends.

But the Londonderry LAW rally at which Craig formally announced the setting up of Vanguard was overshadowed within three days by events in that same city that became known to the world as 'Bloody Sunday'. During the course of an illegal civil rights march through the city on Sunday 30 January, soldiers of the First Battalion, the Parachute Regiment shot dead thirteen civilians, none of whom was a known terrorist and none of whom was found with a weapon. The events of that afternoon shook the very foundations of the Unionist system. The Roman Catholic community throughout the province reacted with strikes, and in Dublin an angry mob burned down the British Embassy. Brian Faulkner was a worried man when he gave the Stormont parliament an account of the incidents two days later:

'This is a very grave moment indeed in the history of Northern Ireland,' he said. Bloody Sunday sounded the death-knell for the old Unionist system that had existed since 1921. The British government was given exactly the right excuse it needed to dismiss the Stormont government and treat with the IRA terrorists. This point was not missed in certain quarters in Ulster.

Protestant Ulster was in the midst of a grim battle for survival against ruthless and successful foes. It was a crisis, and crisis measures were called for. At the inaugural meeting of Vanguard at Lisburn on 12 February, Craig arrived in a car flanked on either side by an impressive uniformed motorcycle escort. He was announced to the assembled crowd simply as 'The Leader', and read out to them a 'Declaration of Intent and Covenant to Act' modelled on the 1912 Covenant of Carson's UVF from an earlier crisis in Ulster's history. It was a scene reminiscent of Nuremburg, and after the Declaration was received with acclamation, Craig announced that he was ready to accept drastic measures:

'We are determined, Ladies and Gentlemen,' he said, 'to preserve our British traditions and way of life. And God help those who get in our way.'

Craig did not spell out precisely what he meant by that last remark. However, it is not too difficult to guess how his deliberate ambiguity was interpreted by many in the emotional atmosphere of the rally. What we can know is what one individual Protestant felt at that same time. In the February edition of another newssheet, the *UDA Bulletin*, there was published a letter, claimed to have come from a woman, in which it was stated:

I have reached the stage where I no longer have any compassion for any nationalist, man, woman, or child. After years of destruction, murder, intimidation, I have been driven against my better feelings to the decision – it's them or us. What I want to know is this, where the hell are the MEN in our community? Have they any pride? Have they any guts? Why are they not organized in, not defence, but commando groups? Why have they not started to hit back in the only way these nationalist bastards understand? That is ruthless, indiscriminate killing . . . If I had a flame-thrower, I would roast the slimy excreta that

Slimy excreta...

pass for human beings. Also I'm sick and tired of you yellow-backed Prods who are not even prepared to fight for your own street, yet alone your own loyalist people. When civil war breaks out and, God forgive me, but I hope it's soon I, at least, will shoot you along with the Fenian scum.

Whether this letter did in fact originate spontaneously from a woman reader is to a large extent irrelevant. What is important is that someone in the Protestant areas was trying to whip up support for the idea of 'commando groups' to give the Catholics a touch of their own medicine, namely to 'hit back in the only way these nationalist bastards understand. *That is, ruthless, indiscriminate killing.*' (Our italics.) And these sentiments were given support by the publishers of the *U D A Bulletin*, an official organ of the association, both in the fact that the letter was printed and in a leader that accompanied it.

'Without question most Protestants would agree with your sentiments,' the leader began. 'We do. The greatest contribution you can make to the destruction of the murderous Provos, I R A, and nationalists, is to direct your energies into the UDA.' Protestants were being prepared for a counter-attack against the I R A and their sympathizers. The form this would take was clearly apparent in the early months of the year, but no action of any kind was taken by the security forces to prevent it.

There was only one assassination in February, that of Bernard Rice, 49, a Roman Catholic who lived at Mountainview Parade, off the Crumlin Road. The circumstances of Rice's death are puzzling. The Crumlin Road is one of the most dangerous thoroughfares in Belfast. It divides the Roman Catholic Ardoyne stronghold from the Protestant Shankill and Woodvale bastions. Lower down it is bordered by the Oldpark and Bone areas.

Rice was shot dead by two men in a car on the evening of 3 February as he was on his way to a meeting of the Catholic Ex-Servicemen's Association (CESA) in the Ardoyne. As Rice left his house in Mountainview Parade, his killers were lying in wait for him outside the Crumlin Road Fire Station. They apparently knew their victim and probably knew that he was heading for the CESA meeting in the Ardoyne. But Rice was not expected at this meeting. The invitation to the meeting may have been part of a set-up, which would almost certainly exclude any Protestants from responsibility. There is some evidence that this actually happened at his place of work in Mullusk, and this is given some credence by the killing six weeks later of one of Rice's workmates, Sean McConville. One flaw in this theory, however, is that the car Rice's assassins used made its getaway in the direction of the Protestant Woodvale. This is the only direct evidence, such as it is, however, to link the killing to Protestants, apart from the simple fact that Rice was a Roman Catholic worker in the largely Protestant Mullusk factory.

McConville, 17, a Roman Catholic who lived in the Crumlin Road itself, not far from Rice, was shot dead in similar circumstances on the evening of 15 April. He was walking along the Crumlin Road when he was called to a stationary car. As he went to the car he was shot five times in the head and chest and died soon after. The killers drove along the same escape route used in the Rice killing, along Twaddell Avenue towards Woodvale.

The similarities between the two deaths suggest a connection. Both men were Roman Catholics working in the mainly Protestant factory at Mullusk. Both lived in the Crumlin Road area, and many of their Protestant workmates would have lived not far away in the Shankill and Woodvale. Both men were killed from stationary cars that appeared to have waited for them and to have known their victims. Both cars were seen to escape into Woodvale. The balance of evidence would suggest that the killers were Protestants working from Woodvale who possibly knew the men through the Mullusk factory. Rice could have been overheard by a Protestant workmate the day of his death discussing the CESA meeting in the Ardoyne, and a similar remark by McConville could have disclosed his intentions on the evening of his death. Or, more simply, the killers may have waited for a period of time for their victims near their homes in the belief that sooner or later they would emerge. Rice would therefore seem to be the first victim of Protestant assassins.

Though Rice's death was the only assassination in February,

this month, like January, was not without importance on the political scene. In a month of crisis following Bloody Sunday, on Tuesday 22 February the I R A hit back at the Parachute Regiment in a bomb attack at the Regiment's H Q at Aldershot in England. However, instead of the intended military victims, the blast killed six cleaning-women and a Roman Catholic padre. Three days later, on Friday 25 February, the Official I R A managed to shoot the Minister of State for Home Affairs, John Taylor, six times without killing him. The following evening, Craig addressed a Vanguard rally at Enniskillen, County Fermanagh:

We in Vanguard feel the time for talk is over. We want the Ulster loyalists to commit themselves to the course of action. We are finished with all this wishy-washy approach to the menace which threatens our province, and by the time we all come together in an all-Ulster rally in Belfast on 18 March every part of the world will know where the Ulster loyalists stand and will know that the Ulster loyalist is capable of doing more than talk. Late as the hour is, and it is jolly late, I can say with confidence we are going to win this struggle ... We are going to beat this conspiracy into the ground and we make no accommodation with the enemies of this country, the enemies of democracy.

Tough words indeed from the man who had outlawed the U V F almost six years earlier. Underlining the new toughness among some Protestants, the following night two Roman Catholics were shot down from passing cars.

Lawrence McMurtagh, 44, was shot outside his father's public house, the Star Bar, at the junction of Mayo Street and the Springfield Road in the Lower Falls. A white Cortina approached and stopped outside and a man jumped out and fired four shots at McMurtagh, who survived although hit by two of the bullets. The car disappeared down Mayo Street.

In the second incident, Felix O'Neill, 43, a Roman Catholic from Artoe, County Tyrone, was shot when masked men entered his lodgings at Highland Parade off the West Circular Road. O'Neill was lodging with a Protestant family in a strong Protestant area. This evening the raiders burst into the house, and while two stood guard outside, three went in. One gunman entered the sitting-room and shot O'Neill five times. The intended victim survived, however. None of the Protestants in the house was harmed in the attack.

The O'Neill shooting was unquestionably the work of Protestant extremists. McMurtagh almost certainly was as well, but at the time it was claimed that plain-clothes troops were responsible. No proof has ever been produced that Murtagh's would-be killers were British troops but to what extent such a 'Third Force' operated in the killings, will be discussed at greater length in the last chapter of the book. For the meantime we will pass on.

March saw one of the worst atrocities in the whole of the Troubles. On Saturday 4 March, a bomb exploded without warning in the crowded Abercorn Restaurant in the heart of Belfast's shopping centre, an area crowded with Saturday afternoon shoppers. Three people were killed, but these casualties do not tell the full horror of the scores of others wounded, some hideously mutilated for life. In the British House of Commons a few days later, Maudling said: 'These crimes are the work of psychopaths. I would not think there was any concerted plan, but there is a new pattern of uncoordinated bombing by psychopathic killers.'

Maudling hit the right chord. The bombing appalled people on both sides of the sectarian divide in Ulster. But to Protestants the Home Secretary had articulated what they had felt for so long: the IRA bombers and killers were aggressive psychopaths. They were people who could not be regarded as normal human beings at all. In an interview on Radio Telefis Eireann (RTE), the Eire broadcasting service, a few days later Craig discussed what action the Loyalists might feel compelled to take against Ulster's enemies in the present situation. 'Would this mean the killing of all Catholics in Belfast?' he was asked. 'It might not go as far as that,' he replied. 'But it could go as far as killing.'

The man who had banned the UVF had turned full circle. It might not be necessary to kill all Roman Catholics. But some might have to be killed. There were more than 100,000 Roman Catholics in Belfast at the time. On Friday 28 April, in a speech to the Conservative Party's Monday Club in London, Craig went further when he said he was prepared to 'shoot and kill' to keep Ulster British.

'When we say force,' he said, 'we mean force. *We will only assassinate our enemies as a last desperate resort when we are denied our democratic rights*' (Our italics).

Between the two statements – one to RTE, the other to the Monday Club – Stormont had been suspended. It was later to be abolished in its pre-1972 form. To an audience at Carickfergus, County Antrim, on Wednesday 8 March, Craig had spelled out what he meant by Ulster being denied her democratic rights: 'We have been guaranteed our Constitution by the British Government,' he said. 'If we let them alter that original Constitution they will let us down. Once they let you down one way, they will let you down another.'

Ten days later, on Saturday 18 March, Vanguard held a monster rally at Ormeau Park, East Belfast. The suspension of the Stormont Government was less than a week away, and the rally was held in an atmosphere of crisis and high excitement that is best captured in the scene described by the *Belfast Telegraph* report that evening:

Thousands of people from every corner of Ulster poured into Ormeau Park, Belfast, this afternoon, for the mammoth Vanguard rally. With scores of people still arriving on foot and in cars and buses, the official Army–RUC estimate of the crowd was a staggering 75,000. And long before the rally was due to get under way thousands of men and youths – some of them in combat-style jackets – lined up for inspection by the Larne MP and Ulster Vanguard chief, Mr William Craig. One group of youths lined up carrying a banner which read 'Shankill Battalion' and another 'Shankill Tartan'.

To this vast mass of Protestants Craig brought an uncompromisingly tough message. It was music to the ears of a people who believed their way of life and very existence was about to be destroyed. Let the British government try to abolish Stormont, Craig said. Nothing that government did would matter, because Ulster's Protestants would not surrender their heritage without a fight:

We will be preparing to implement contingency plans which will make any political initiatives that are unacceptable to the majority unworkable. We will be launching a fighting fund setting up an organization that could intensify a trade war with the Irish Republic and identify the real enemies within Ulster. And we will establish a more sophisticated intelligence service than is available at the moment ... *If the politicians fail it will be our job to liquidate the enemy.**

Two days later Craig underlined this message when he told Unionists at Newtownbreda that Direct Rule was coming soon – it was, in fact, only four days away:

The great majority want no political juggling. The course of action is pretty clear – liquidate the IRA. That is, put down the IRA. Any truce or agreement with the IRA will only last as long as is convenient for them and, as sure as day follows night, a build-up of armed strength will be immediately embarked upon for a further campaign of violence ... The days of the union may be drawing to a close but our British heritage and way of life will be saved. We may be moving into a situation close to war.

Craig in these crucial days prior to Direct Rule was able to articulate the gut mood of many thousands of working-class Protestants. They had seen the gradual diminution of the traditional role of the Ulster parliament in the province while more and more authority seemed to be concentrated in hostile hands in London. The Constitution carefully created in 1921 to look after their interests and guard against absorption into the Irish Republic was crumbling away before their eyes as a direct consequence of the IRA terror campaign.

Craig clarified their attitude when he stated that if (a) the Stormont government were to go and Direct Rule imposed, and then (b) the British government were to enter into an agreed truce with the IRA, Ulster's Protestants would be left to their own devices to preserve their accustomed way of life.

Direct Rule was imposed on 24 March, and on 26 June the IRA and the British government began a truce. These two events unleashed the full fury of the Protestant backlash upon the Roman Catholic population. Craig was not bluffing in March.

* Italics ours – M. D. and D. L.

At Newtownbreda he told his audience: 'Let there be no doubt that Ulster loyalists will fight if they have to fight. It is important that we get on with speed in compiling dossiers on known IRA supporters.'

The reaction had already begun. On the evening of Monday 13 March, a young Roman Catholic, Patrick McCrory, 19, from Ravenhill Avenue in the predominantly Protestant East Belfast, was shot dead as he answered his front door. His father later claimed that the local Tartan gang had previously beaten his son up and given him a warning that they would get him. Patrick McCrory lived in a Protestant area, and he was killed by young men of his own age-group because he was a Roman Catholic. His girlfriend later identified to police two of the youths whom she said were involved in the earlier beating and threats, but no action was taken against them. As will become apparent as the story unfolds, the amount of evidence required to convict a murder suspect in Northern Ireland in these troubled times was so great as to place most assassins beyond the reach of the law. Evidence that would secure conviction in the rest of the United Kingdom frequently would not ensure suspects reaching trial in a society overwhelmed by the consequences of virtual civil war. And even when cases did get to trial, juries and witnesses were so open to intimidation, both direct an indirect, that men whom the police were certain were guilty were let off. The killers of Patrick McCrory went free to commit more assassinations. In the period covered by this book, this was to prove the rule rather than the exception.

There was one other killing in March, and it was one that provides an insight into the mood in the working-class Protestant areas at the time. Ingram 'Jock' Beckitt, 37, a Protestant docker of Crimea Street, off the Shankill Road, was a big man by any standards. A Scot, he was in the words of a man who knew him well, 'an old-fashioned Prod. The sort of man who would take on six peelers in a bar. But he was straight. He never stole anything. He was no criminal, but the hard man of the Shankill.'

Beckitt and his brother 'Pinky' were strong men, widely respected as leaders in their area before the Troubles began.

They cooperated with the local police for the good of the Shankill community, often using their weight and influence to defuse potentially explosive situations as the Troubles developed. Ingram Beckitt was an early member of the UDA. His sister, Mrs Jean Moore, was later to head the women's section of the Association. But there were certain elements in the emerging UDA that Beckitt was opposed to. He was not sympathetic to those who joined the organization with backgrounds in crime, and who saw their new status as defenders of the community as a means to furthering their criminal careers.

On Friday 24 March the British Prime Minister, Edward Heath, announced that he had suspended the Stormont government and imposed Direct Rule on Northern Ireland from London for one year. The reaction in Protestant areas was instant. The long-feared sell-out seemed to be upon Ulster.

On Sunday evening, 26 March, a number of meetings of Protestant militants were held in the Shankill to discuss what to do in the light of the new political situation. At one of these meetings Beckitt is reported to have attacked a particular group of men who had been involved in illegal activities and described them as 'not men at all, only a bunch of thugs and gangsters'. He is said to have threatened to reveal all he knew about their activities to the police.

Later that same evening, Beckitt's brother Pinky, who had loyally supported his brother's views at the earlier meeting, was badly beaten in one of the clubs in the Shankill Road. When he heard of what had happened to his brother, Beckitt is said to have been outraged, and to have rushed down to the club to deal with those responsible. However, the men concerned were waiting for him. He was shot a number of times by two men, William Spence and John Thomas Boyd. Both men were later to be the victims of Protestant assassins. Beckitt's body was taken to near-by Conlig Street, where it was dumped. However, contrary to the belief of the assassins, Beckitt was not dead, and when they got to Conlig Street he regained consciousness and attacked his assailants. He was shot once more in the head, and this time he was killed.

Beckitt's death appalled the Protestant working-class community. The morning of his funeral, Wednesday 29 March, a huge advertisement appeared in the *News Letter* signed by virtually every branch of the UDA condemning the killing as the work of 'gangsters and hoodlums'. At no stage was it ever suggested that the IRA was responsible. The dead man's sister openly accused a 'UDA faction' of killing her brother. As we shall see, in due course the 'gangsters and hoodlums' responsible were later to receive their reward for the killing.

But though Beckitt's death was sincerely regretted in the UDA, there was a certain logic to it. He was a man who would not countenance confrontations between Protestants and the security forces. But with the imposition of Direct Rule the growth of Protestant militancy was bound to lead to clashes with the RUC and the Army, as the security forces became the direct instruments of the government in London. And Protestant militancy was on the increase. In the months after Direct Rule the UDA snowballed in size and influence within Protestant area. When it first appeared on the streets in May it boasted an active membership in excess of 50,000 and few commentators were prepared to doubt the claim. The emergence on the streets of Northern Ireland of this body, apparently well organized along paramilitary lines and with its members uniformed and hooded, was a profound psychological shock to both the Roman Catholic community and the British government. One day the Protestant backlash was the subject of discussion and speculation. The next it was there for all to see, marching through the streets of Ulster. The backlash had arrived, and it was not confined to marches.

In April three men were assassinated. Sean McConville was killed on the 15th. On 20 April the killing of a Roman Catholic taxi-driver, Gerald Patrick Donnelly, by two Protestant gunmen, was to set a pattern that would be repeated with variations in a number of subsequent assassinations.

Donnelly, 22, of Cliftonville Road, worked for Arkle Taxis in Clifton Street at the lower end of the Crumlin Road. At 11·30 p.m. this Monday night two men went into the Arkle Taxis office and asked for a taxi to take them to the Ardoyne. By this date the sectarianism in Belfast had become so grave that only Catholic taxi-drivers would as a rule take fares for Catholic areas and Protestants only to Protestant areas. In asking for a taxi to the Roman Catholic Ardoyne the two men could be certain that they would be given a Catholic driver. Donnelly was the unlucky victim.

To get to the Ardoyne he had to skirt predominantly Protestant areas on either side of the Crumlin Road. Before he got anywhere near the Ardoyne, however, his passengers produced guns and made him drive into Harrybrook Street, a Protestant street off the Crumlin Road. At Donnelly's inquest in January 1973, a woman living in the street told how at about midnight she heard a car pull up outside her door. She heard what she took to be the sound of a number of men beating up another, followed by what sounded like a car back-firing. She went out to find the body of Donnelly lying in the road by the side of his taxi, bleeding to death from five bullet-wounds in the chest. Another woman testified that she had seen two men running off in the direction of the Shankill down Sydney Street West. There was no apparent motive in the Donnelly killing. There was never any evidence to suggest a connection with the IRA. He was shot at random simply because he was a Catholic. His was the first of many such deaths.

The other man killed in this month was also a Catholic. But Martin Paul Owens, 22, of Tullymore Drive, Andersonstown, was not a victim of Protestant assassins. Owens, an ex-internee, was executed after a trial at a kangaroo court by the Provisional IRA. His brother had been lifted by the Provisionals earlier in the day on 15 April in mistake for Owens. The brother was released, and Owens was picked up by a squad at 11·45 p.m. from his home in Andersonstown. He was later dumped from a white car at Horn Drive in the same area. He had received the standard IRA execution, being shot in the head at close range.

The following month of May saw ten assassinations – the most so far in one month. There had been two in January, one in February, two in March, and three in April. In 1971 there had only been five altogether, and only the Jardin killing in 1970. It was no coincidence that the jump in sectarian assassinations in May should coincide with the visible manifestation of the new Protestant militancy: the UDA. In succeeding months, the regular tally of such killings was only to drop below ten in one month, November, which had eight.

The first May victim was an IRA man – one of the few to fall into the assassins' net during the whole campaign. But Victor Andrews, a Roman Catholic of Pacific Avenue, was a seaman and returned home only two or three times a year. He was killed by a Tartan gang, and his death was particularly vicious. Unlike most of the victims, Andrews was not shot but stabbed a number of times. At least fifteen deep stab wounds were found on his body, which was dumped in an entry off Baltic Avenue on Thursday 4 May. Death notices in the Belfast *Irish News* for Andrews were placed by the IRA, the Civil Rights Association, and the Joe McCann Republican Clubs. The killing is of interest because Andrews was one of the few IRA men to have been killed by the Protestant assassins. But, even so, his contribution to the IRA terror campaign could not have been considerable as he had spent the greater part of the Troubles away from Ulster at sea. In addition, his allegience lay with the less militant Official wing of the IRA. Also of significance is the use of the knife and the fact that the killing involved a ritual in which more than one person used the knife on the victim.

Just over a week later, on Friday 12 May, another Roman Catholic, Patrick Joseph McVeigh, 44, was killed in mysterious circumstances. McVeigh, of Ladybrook Park, Andersonstown, was a member of CESA, and was one of five CESA members on unarmed vigilante patrol in Finaghy Road North when they were hit by a burst of automatic fire from a group of men in a car. McVeigh was killed and his four companions were wounded. The attackers disappeared up Riverdale Park South towards the Lisburn Road. The interest in this shooting lies in the fact that the men inside the car were not Protestant extremists but plainclothes soldiers. Immediately after the incident the Army Press Office in Lisburn issued a statement in which it claimed that a uniformed Army patrol had come under fire from snipers. Fire had been returned and five gunmen had been hit. But this statement was retracted, and a later statement put out which claimed that the five men had been shot by 'persons unknown'. Later still, the Army admitted that McVeigh and his companions had been shot by a plain-clothes Army patrol in error. The full ramifications of this and other incidents will be dealt with in Chapter 15.

The next killing followed on Sunday 14 May when a 25-year-old Catholic, Gerard McCusker, of Marchioness Street in the Lower Falls was found shot through the head at Ireton Street off the Shankill Road. His mother claimed he was killed by Protestant extremists. He was last seen a number of days earlier walking in the direction of the Protestant Millfield area. He appeared to have been tortured before being killed. His body had lacerations and bruises consistent with a heavy beating, hair had been pulled out, and both wrists were broken. He was the first victim to bear the marks of torture. This was a characteristic that arose only with the advent of the Protestant assassin.

The McCusker killing was followed on Wednesday 17 May by that of Bernard Moane, 46, a Catholic drink representative of Ailesbury Drive, Ormeau Road, Belfast. Moane's job took him into many hard-line Protestant areas visiting bars with his samples. On the afternoon of his death he was escorted out of a bar on the Shankill Road and taken in his own car to the Knockagh Monument, Greenisland. Situated just outside Belfast to the north, the site was a well-known beauty spot towering high above the city and an ideal place for a picnic giving a magnificent view of South Antrim and the Irish Sea. At the monument, Moane's kidnappers drank his samples of drink and then shot him dead, making their escape in his car.

Four Protestants were later charged with the Moane killing. One of these, Alexander 'Joker' Andrews, 19, an unemployed labourer of Argyle Street, said in the pre-trial hearing that his father had been killed at the Four Step Inn explosion. The Four Step Inn was a bar in the Shankill that had been bombed without warning on 29 September 1971.

The charges against Andrews in the Moane case were dropped but he still figured in the story. While he was in Crumlin Road gaol he gave orders to the other loyalist prisoners that were scrupulously obeyed. He stopped them behaving in a disorderly fashion and shouting abuse at the police and prison officers. He made them drill and behave in a military manner with rank respected. On his release, however, the discipline he instilled seems to have crumbled and the prisoners lapsed into their earlier non-military habits.

The trial of the three other men took place in June 1973. Before the jury were Samuel James Welshman, 25, an unemployed driver of Ainsworth Street, Joseph McAllister, 19, a labourer of Argyle Street, and Samuel Swain, 38, unemployed of Montrose Street. The main evidence against the men was given by some people who had been at the monument when the killing took place that afternoon. Strict secrecy was enforced. The witnesses were identified only by letters of the alphabet and they gave their evidence wearing hoods and dark glasses.

The first witness, Witness A, told the court that on the afternoon of 17 May he was at Knockagh War Memorial when he was approached by a man whom he identified as Welshman who asked him if he was a 'Mick or a Prod'. He replied that he was a Presbyterian, and was then told: 'You have walked into something here. We are going to fill a chap in.' Witness A then claimed Welshman told him that the victim was an IRA man who had been responsible for the death of a UDR man and pointed out Moane as the man in question. Witness A was then made to let down the tyres of a car belonging to another witness, Witness C. He heard Moane say: 'Ah, no, boys,' followed by three shots. He was then taken from the scene by the men and dropped off at a road-junction where he telephoned the police. Moane's car was later found abandoned at Ainsworth Avenue, and fingerprints on the car matched those of Swain, Welshman, and McAllister.

Witness B told a similar story. He said that he and his wife and child had gone to the beauty spot to have a picnic. They were sitting near the edge of the cliff when a man, whom he identified as Welshman, tapped him on the shoulder and asked if he could speak to him.

'I just got up to see what he wanted,' the witness said. 'He saw me clasping a lemonade bottle and he said: "Don't do anything stupid, I am only trying to do you a favour."' Welshman then showed him the butt of a gun which was tucked into his belt: 'He said that he was going to knock off an IRA man who was connected with the killing of UDR man Elliot. He just said he did not want the child to see anything unpleasant. That there were enough unpleasant things happening.' He was told to go over the hill and not to come back for at least an hour. The witness went straight over the hill with his family where he met Witness C. Together the two telephoned the police at Greenisland at 3·30 p.m., but by this time Moane was dead.

The UDR man that Welshman referred to was James Elliot, 33, a Protestant lorry-driver of Aughnavalley, Rathfriland. He was found in a crater near the border at Newtownhamilton on 19 April. He had been held by the Provisionals for almost two days before being shot in the back of the head as he knelt on the ground. After the execution, the IRA men had strapped explosives to the body with wires leading to the other side of the border. One of the first people on the scene was a *Belfast Telegraph* reporter who arrived before the Army after a woman living near by had telephoned the newspaper that there was a body on the border. The reporter looked closely at the body and stepped over it, but fortunately for him he did not touch it. A few hundred yards away on the other side of the border, IRA Provisionals viewed the reporter through binoculars waiting for the expected Army patrol to appear so that they could detonate the corpse. When troops did arrive on the scene they already suspected the trap and were able to defuse the macabre bomb. The *Telegraph* reporter spent that evening in the company of a bottle of whisky.

The Elliot killing was regarded as particularly horrific, and rumour spread that the body had been terribly mutilated. This was untrue, but the story spread quickly in the Protestant community and was even reported by Unionist MPs to their colleagues at Westminster. Both Welshman and McAllister believed that Moane was involved in this killing, though, as we shall learn, McAllister began to have some doubts once Moane had been killed.

Witness C told a story similar to that of Witnesses A and B, but he caused a sensation when asked to pick out the man he had seen with Moane at Knockagh that afternoon. For he picked out Alexander 'Joker' Andrews, the man who had had charges of murdering Moane dropped earlier against him.

Further sensation followed the next day. In the absense of the jury a statement McAllister was alleged to have made to the police was read in court. The statement was ruled inadmissible as evidence by the judge, but it was very revealing. In it McAllister disclosed that he had been a close friend of Thomas Henry Malcolm Kells, the 19-year-old Protestant labourer of Alliance Avenue who had been shot by the Provisional IRA in October 1971. He said that at Knockagh Swain was the man in charge and he had ordered McAllister to kill Moane.

McAllister said he told Moane to lie face downward on the ground and it was at this point that Moane said: 'Ah, no, boys.' When Moane refused, McAllister shot him through the forehead and then, on Swain's orders, shot him twice when he fell to the ground. Swain then told McAllister to empty the rest of the rounds into Moane's body. But McAllister turned to Swain and said: 'If I have to fire this revolver again it will be into your fat mouth.' He is also alleged to have told police that if he ever discovered the man who 'spread the lie that Moane was an IRA man', he would shoot him.

Swain, Welshman, and McAllister were each found guilty of murdering Moane in June 1973 and sentenced to life imprisonment. Passing sentence on all three men the judge, Mr Justice Gibson, said that he completely agreed with the jury's verdict. As they left the dock to return to their prison cells, Moane's killers each gave the clenched fist salute and shouted: 'No surrender!' and 'Keep up the fight!' This demonstration drew applause from friends and relatives of the convicted men sitting in the public gallery. Such scenes were common at trials of UDA and UVF men.

Of the other deaths in May, Adrian Barton, 18, the single

Protestant killed, lived in the Springfield Road. He had a Catholic girlfriend, and had been warned a number of times to stop seeing her. He was shot coming out of the Whitehorse Inn on the Springfield Road the night of Tuesday 21 May.

With two exceptions, the killings in May appear to have been the work of Protestant extremists. The exceptions are William Hughes, 56, a Roman Catholic from County Tyrone whose car was mistaken for a police car by the IRA, and Gerald Duddy, 22, a Roman Catholic of Inishmore Gardens, Andersonstown. Duddy was found on Monday 27 May at Finaghy Road North in the Andersonstown area having received the standard IRA execution.

June was a decisive month in the campaign of assassinations. As we have seen, in the minds of many Protestants there were two essential elements in any sell-out by the British government. The first of these, the removal of the Stormont government, had taken place in March. The second, a deal between the British government and the IRA, took place in June.

In June itself prior to the truce on the 26th there were seven assassinations, with two Protestant victims and five Catholic. One of the Catholics was Hugh Madden, 43, a greengrocer who was shot outside his shop in the Oldpark Road. He will be dealt with in a later chapter along with his brother, Thomas, who was a victim of assassins in August.

One of the Protestants killed in June was John Lunnen Brown, 30, of Blackmartin Parade in the Springmartin area. Brown, a Scot, was a member of the UDA. On Sunday 25 June, a few hours before the truce came into operation, his body was found dumped in the street where he lived. He had been kidnapped by a number of men in a Protestant area as he was on his way home earlier in the day. His body bore the marks of a considerable beating. His nose was broken and his eyes were badly gouged, and he appeared to have been battered with a rifle-butt before being shot. His death was first attributed to the IRA. But this is most unlikely. The area where he had been picked up and also where he had been dumped was Protestant. The beating he received before death was similar to later killings by Protestant extremists in the same area. It is possible that Brown was picked up and interrogated by a group of IRA men who returned his body to within yards of his home. But this would have required a degree of daring and expertise that has seldom been exhibited by the IRA. A more acceptable explanation is that Brown's death was an internal matter within the UDA.

Discussion of the Brown killing was not extensive, for a few hours after the body was found, at midnight on Sunday 25 June, the truce between the IRA and the British government came into operation. In typically ruthless fashion, the IRA stepped up its campaign of bombings and shootings in the days prior to the truce and maintained its operations right up to the moment of the ceasefire. With scarcely seconds to go before the truce, an Army patrol came under fire in the Short Strand, and Sergeant Banks was shot dead at one minute to midnight. It was a cold-blooded and pointless killing and confirmed the contempt and disgust most Protestants felt towards the IRA.

The truce came into force written in blood – the blood of the security forces and countless innocent civilians who had perished in the three-year IRA campaign. This campaign appeared to have succeeded in its main aims. Stormont was gone, and few thought it would ever come back. And now the British government had made peace with the gunmen and bombers. It was rumoured that part of the deal involved the release of all the men interned and a complete amnesty for all crimes committed by terrorists. These terms were later confirmed to have been substantially accurate.

The immediate results were sufficient to antagonize many Protestants. The Army and the RUC were bound not to enter the so-called 'No-go' areas in Londonderry and Belfast. The British government seemed to be conceding the territorial claims of a group of rebels, giving them *de facto* recognition over the areas where they held sway with the bomb and the gun.

If there was any further chance of a Protestant backlash being averted – and there was precious little once Stormont was removed – it vanished in June. The killings escalated, and for the first time it had to be faced as a reality that there was a new and deadly phase in the Troubles: the sectarian assassinations. The assassinations, as we have shown, had claimed their first victims much earlier, but it was only after 26 June that they became an irreversible process. The truce was to be short-lived, but the reaction it spawned was to continue long after it.

5. The IRA call a truce – the Protestant extremists declare war: 26 June–9 July

The truce came into effect at midnight on Sunday 25 June. Two victims were claimed within the next twenty-four hours, both killed by the IRA. Bernard Norney, 38, a Roman Catholic, was shot dead after he refused to stop at an IRA road-block. The other victim, William Galloway, 18, of Hogarth Street, was a Protestant.

Galloway was shot the evening after the truce came into operation. Rioting broke out between Catholics and Protestants in the mixed Duncairn Gardens area, adjacent to the Catholic New Lodge and Newington areas. Galloway, who lived in Duncairn, was cut down by a hail of bullets from an IRA sniper as he was on his way home. The IRA had drawn the first blood of the truce.

From 26 to 30 June Belfast and the rest of Northern Ireland enjoyed a peace it had not known for three years. Some people even began to go out at nights to bars and clubs once again in a semblance of normality. But the ceasefire had incensed the militants in the Protestant community, and while the IRA scrupulously observed the truce, the Army was faced with a new threat: the UDA No-go areas.

This was the atmosphere that prevailed on the night of Friday 30 June when a young English Jehovah's Witness, Paul Jobling, 19, from County Durham, arrived at Belfast's Aldergrove Airport. Jobling had come to Belfast earlier in the month to spend the summer doing social work in some of the areas hardest hit by the Troubles. He was a student and had stayed at the home of a student friend in the Roman Catholic Unity Flats complex while he set up an office-cum-shop in the Turf Lodge area of the city, also Roman Catholic.

It was Jobling's misfortune that he was carrying in his pocket the night he returned to Belfast a letter from his girlfriend in County Durham bearing the Unity Flats address. For the evening of Friday 30 June was a very tense one in the city. The UDA had set up barricades at various points and proclaimed their own No-go areas. Jobling was met at the airport by friends in a car who took him as far as the Protestant West Circular Road. At this point he said that he would walk the remaining distance to his shop in Turf Lodge. He told his friends to go no further with him lest their car should be taken by the UDA and used as a barricade. The friends reluctantly agreed, and Jobling was last seen alive walking across the West Circular in the direction of the Springfield Road.

On his journey home Jobling was intercepted at a UDA road-block at about 11·00 p.m. Despite his English accent, the fact that he was carrying a letter addressed to him at a Unity Flats address sealed his fate. He was taken to a house where he was interrogated and beaten before being shot in the head. His hooded body was found the next morning on a rubbish-tip at Westway Drive on the Protestant Glencairn Estate.

On the same evening that Jobling was killed, assassins from the same area struck in the centre of Belfast. Their victim was a 43-year-old Roman Catholic barman, Daniel Joseph Hayes, of Hillman Street, in the New Lodge area. At 11·25 p.m. a white Triumph Spitfire sports-car was stopped by three men on the corner of Twaddell Avenue and the Ballygomartin Road, near where Jobling had been picked up half an hour earlier. In the car were a man and his girlfriend who had been to a hotel for a drink. The driver told police that one of the men rapped at the passenger window and said: 'Sorry, sir, but we have to borrow your car for half an hour.'

The driver replied: 'Not again,' and the man said: 'No, I am sorry, sir, but we are in a hurry.' The three men allowed the owner to drive the car to his girlfriend's house, and to take his papers and other keys with him from the car. Before they drove off, the man warned the owner not to contact the police for one hour. He called Tennent Street police station at 12·20 a.m., but by that time it was too late. Though he was probably still breathing at this time, Daniel Hayes was already a dead man.

The three men who took the car were described as follows: the first, in his mid-30s, stocky build, 5 ft 7 ins, clean-shaven wearing a dark anorak with no hood; the second, early 20s, 5 ft 9 ins or 10 ins, medium build, clean-shaven wearing an anorak with the hood up; the third, early 30s, 5 ft. 7 ins., dark green combat jacket, with no hood, medium build.

Hayes, the victim, worked in the Albert Inn in Skipper Street in the city centre. The men knew his movements perfectly. He stopped work at the bar at 11·30 p.m. and began clearing up, usually leaving for home on foot at around midnight.

At the inquest the following May, Cyril Arthur Scrivener, a friend of Hayes, recalled meeting Hayes in the Albert Inn on the night of his death. 'Daniel did not have a drink, as he was working,' Scrivener said. 'But we had a chat about the RAF darts section. I left the bar at about 10·00 p.m. and that was the last time I saw him alive. He was his usual self and did not seem to be perturbed in any way. He usually walked home from the Albert Inn unless Dave Osborne, the manager, gave him a lift.'

Scrivener told the coroner that Hayes, who was separated from his wife, was living with a Mrs Eileen Sullivan; but Miss Catherine Magee, a barmaid at the Albert Inn, disclosed that there had been another woman in his life. She said that 1 July had been her birthday, but that Hayes had forgotten to buy her a present, for which he had apologised. He was in 'fine form' and the evening had passed off normally.

'I started work at 7·00 p.m.,' she said. 'Danny was in his usual good form and we worked till 12·00 p.m. together in the lounge. Pat Cambridge offered to give him a life home but he said it was a good night and he would walk home. We walked up Hill Street with him and he said he would drop in for a drink. I took it he meant Richard's Bar in Hill Street. I knew Danny had a girlfriend called Flo Hunter with whom he had a child.'

The decision not to accept the offered lift and to go and have a drink cost Hayes his life. He was found just over an hour later dumped in a children's playground in the Protestant Penrith

Street. He had been badly beaten and shot in the head and the chest. He was picked up by the men who had hijacked the white sports-car only minutes after Magee and Cambridge left him, and was taken to a club where he was 'rompered'.* What happened next was related by a witness whose name and sex have been kept secret and who is referred to as Witness A. In a statement made to police at Hastings Street on Tuesday 4 July Witness A said:

'On 30 June I was visiting a friend in Penrith Street. At 1·15 a.m. I heard a car drive up to the door and thought it was my friend's brother. It was a white colour with a black canvas roof.' The witness saw the car park on the corner of Cumberland Street and Penrith Street, and three men emerged, one of whom was being carried by the third. 'I thought the third man was drunk as the other two were practically carrying him along. All three went round to Cumberland Street into the children's playground.'

Two of the men returned to the car which drove a short distance and stopped. 'The car came to a screeching halt a few doors from me and I saw what I thought was two men kneeling. One said to me: "You are alright, it's the UDA." I said: "What?" and the man said: "Get in and you won't get hurt." As he said that I heard five single shots fired at the children's playground. I ran back into the house and heard the car drive off at a fast rate.'

The witness re-emerged on to the street and ran to the playground where a man and a woman were already standing. 'I saw a pool of what I thought was urine. I discovered it was blood. I heard a woman scream and then I saw the body of a man, I went over to see if I knew him, but there was too much blood and I ran to get the Army.'

The witness described the two men as wearing dark blue anoraks, but what made the evidence even more interesting was that the witness claimed to identify the man who had spoken as Albert Herman Moon, a 38-year-old lorry-driver. Moon was picked up by the police shortly after and charged with the murder of Hayes. But he produced eighteen individual witnesses to prove that he was in Scotland at the time, and on 19 July all charges

*For an explanation of this term, see p. 277.

against him were dropped. The witness identified the body in the playground as that of the man whom the two others had carried from the white sports-car.

Hayes was a man who stood a strong chance of being killed. Something of a Casanova, his affairs with women had, as well as estranging him from his wife, led to him receiving a severe beating from some men in the Old Lodge Road in 1968. He was also a member of CESA, having spent twelve years in the Territorial Army, and was known to have attended regular meetings in the New Lodge area. The beating he received in 1968 had been at the hands of Protestants, as the woman with whom he was having an affair at the time was a Protestant from the Shankill Road.

In view of his political connections and his sexual exploits it would not have been a wise decision for Hayes to walk home from the Albert Inn at night. He was an obvious target for Protestant extremists, and afforded an opportunity, for whoever wanted it, to settle old personal scores. His regular habits of movement were well known to the men who killed him, but even so he might have lived had he accepted the lift offered to him by Cambridge as he left the bar in Skipper Street.

At the inquest in May 1973 it was stated that Hayes had received a severe beating before being shot in the head, heart, and right lung from close range. Delivering an open verdict, the Coroner, Mr James Elliot, said:

It is a complete mystery to me. I am at a loss why barmen are so frequent victims. They seem to be singled out again and again. This unfortunate man appears to have been badly beaten up before being brought to the playground, and it would appear due to this rather than intoxication that he could not stand. An appalling murder again – a nightmare.

Less than twenty-four hours after Hayes body was found, two Protestants who had gone out for a drink were killed by the Provisional I R A. David Fisher, 30, of Nore Street, and Hugh Clawson, 34, of Shannon Street, left their homes early on the night of Saturday 1 July to drink in a Protestant social club on the fringe of the Oldpark area. The club Clawson and Fisher visited was an illegal 'shebeen' in Alliance Avenue run by the UDA.

Both men lived in an area of the Oldpark, known as the River Streets because they are all named after rivers. This area was borderline territory, and the source of much sectarian strife during the Troubles. When they set off from Alliance Avenue after midnight they were drunk. They were last seen alive walking down the Oldpark Road as they neared the Roman Catholic Bone area. It is reliably reported that a short time later they were picked up by vigilantes who handed them over to the Provisional IRA in the Bone.

Their bodies were discovered the following afternoon, Sunday 2 July, lying on waste ground at Cliftonville Cricket Ground, close to the Bone area, by some children at play. Both had been badly beaten, indicating some form of interrogation – probably about UDA activity – and they were both shot a number of times in the head and neck at close range – Fisher three times, Clawson five. It was not a typical IRA execution, but the Provisionals were in a mood for retaliation, and Clawson and Fisher were unlucky to have been in the wrong place at the wrong time.

On the same day that Clawson and Fisher were killed, two Roman Catholics met a similar fate. Gerald McCrea, 29, a haulage contractor from the Falls, and James Howell, 31, of Beechmount Avenue, were stopped and taken out of McCrea's Mercedes car early in the evening. The two men had left McCrea's house at 5·30 p.m. Several hours later, McCrea's body was found dumped at Forthriver Road, on the Glencairn Estate, a short distance from the spot where Jobling's body had been found a few days previously. Howell's body was found the following morning, hooded and bound in the back of McCrea's car, which was abandoned in the Old Lodge Road. Both men had been shot in the head. McCrea had also been shot in the back, and Howell had been badly beaten.

The next victim to die was John Patrick O'Hanlon, 38, a Roman Catholic of Carlisle Square. Friends who called at his flat after midnight in the early hours of Monday 3 July found all the lights on, as well as an electric fire. In the kitchen, the kettle had boiled away on the stove. All the signs were that O'Hanlon had either made a sudden unexpected departure, or that he had popped out for a few minutes. At daybreak, his body was found on waste ground at near-by Twickenham Street. He had been shot through the head. Marks on the body showed that O'Hanlon had been beaten. His arms were tied, and wounds around his ankles suggested that he had been tied to a chair, possibly by a form of barbed wire.

It is unclear who was responsible for the death. The victim was connected with the IRA, and prior to his death he had been arrested by the Special Branch and questioned about the IRA. His release could have suggested to the IRA that he had talked, and led to his execution as an informer. No death notices appeared in newspapers from the IRA after the death, and this would suggest that O'Hanlon was out of favour when he was killed.

However, this explanation is rejected by relatives who suggest an alternative. They claim that instead of being dragged from his flat by Provisional IRA men, O'Hanlon stepped out to the near-by Venice Café to buy some chips. On his way to or from the café, he was picked up by Protestant extremists, who took him to a near-by club, interrogated him, and then shot him. Such a story is plausible. The Venice Café, at Carlisle Circus, has been the scene of several assassinations and attempts on the lives of Roman Catholics. On one occasion two youths who were standing outside were bundled into a car and later found dead. At least four other Catholics have been assassinated in the immediate vicinity. Carlisle Circus was a highly dangerous spot, situated at the junction of the Crumlin and Antrim Roads, a short distance from the New Lodge on one side and the Shankill and Unity Flats on the other. If O'Hanlon did step out for chips that evening, he was very unwise, and was made to pay the price for his lack of wisdom.

The following day, Tuesday 4 July, the bodies of two young Protestant brothers were found on the outskirts of Belfast at Bells Road, a deserted spot on the way to Aldergrove Airport. Malcolm Orr, 20, and Peter Orr, 19, of Alliance Avenue, left their parents' home the previous evening to see some friends in the Oldpark area. They were never seen alive again. They were intercepted on their way. Their bodies were found, one on top of the other, in a ditch the next morning. They had had their coats pulled up over their heads, and had been shot through the head. Both bore the signs of beating, though only Malcolm appeared to have been beaten badly.

This killing led to an immediate outcry, and it was at once assumed that the Provisional IRA were responsible. Certainly, both boys were known to the IRA. Malcolm had a Roman Catholic girlfriend who lived in the Oldpark area, and he made frequent visits to see her, probably cutting across the Ardoyne to do so. His route would have taken him along much the same ground as Clawson and Fisher the night they were killed. His brother Peter, a student, had a Roman Catholic friend in the Bone area, an IRA stronghold like the Ardoyne. The mixed relationships of both boys would have brought them under the suspicion of extremists in both communities.

Like so many of the victims of the assassination campaign, the Orr brothers had a regular pattern of movement that may not have passed unnoticed. Their frequent trips to their Roman Catholic friends took them past many of the hottest trouble-spots in Belfast and made them vulnerable to the extremists on both sides of the sectarian divide. It is known that their relationships with Roman Catholics had caused some comment from Protestants. They had also fallen foul of the local UDA, with whom they had refused to cooperate when barricades were being erected in Alliance Avenue. This action had led to them being threatened by the UDA.

Perhaps of greatest significance is the fact that Clawson and Fisher, who were killed a couple of nights previously, had been picked up after they had left a UDA club in Alliance Avenue, where the Orrs lived. The knowledge that the Orrs were frequent visitors to IRA strongholds and had Catholic friends there, plus their opposition to the local UDA in Alliance, Avenue might have been sufficient to convince the militants that they had set up Clawson and Fisher. The site where the bodies were found would tend to corroborate this. If the IRA were responsible, they might just as easily have dumped the bodies near by as in the case of Clawson and Fisher. To travel to Bells Road, a distance of about three miles, IRA men would have had to travel through hostile territory – the same territory where the Jobling and Hayes killers operated. As we have seen, the practice of venturing deep into enemy territory to dump a body – attractive as it sounds in theory – had too many practical drawbacks to be feasible in a city such as Belfast in these times. The balance of probability, and no more than that, would place the responsibility for the Orr killings on the Protestant militants in Alliance Avenue who had previously threatened the brothers.

The day after the bodies of Malcolm and Peter Orr were found, Wednesday 5 July, a young Roman Catholic man was shot dead by a gunman in a passing car in the Falls Road. Lawrence McKenna, 22, of Denville Place, was walking along the Falls at Waterford Street at 5·00 a.m. in the early hours of the morning when he was hit in the chest by a burst of gunfire from a car that disappeared in the direction of the Shankill. Three days after the attack McKenna died in hospital, but before he died the Provisional IRA had already taken its revenge.

Samuel Robinson, 19, a Protestant of Donaldson Crescent off Twaddell Avenue, worked at Mackie's Factory in the Springfield Road, in the heart of the Lower Falls. He was shot dead by Provisional IRA men at Cavendish Street on the night of Friday 7 July as he made his way to work. The IRA claimed that Robinson was one of the men responsible for the death of McKenna. This was their revenge. At the time of the shooting, the spot where Robinson was killed was in one of the IRA No-go areas respected by the Army as part of the truce agreement. The men who shot him were able to patrol the area openly in uniform and displaying their weapons. When one reflects that Protestants such as Robinson had to travel into areas such as these often late at night, to get to work, the anger in Protestant areas at the truce can be appreciated. If Robinson was not involved in the McKenna killing, but was an innocent victim, the anger and the bitterness at his death would have been doubled. One version of his death put out by the Provisional I R A was that he was shot by vigilantes when he refused to stop at a road-block. If he was innocent, merely a Protestant on his way to work in a Catholic area, he would have been unlikely to stop at the road-block. In Belfast at this time armed men who stopped cars late at night were only on one business. A Protestant in a Catholic area or a Catholic in a Protestant area would have known only too well what to expect from such an encounter.

In the early hours of Sunday 9 July a milkman making his rounds in the Roman Catholic Grosvenor Road area of the Falls came across one of the most puzzling killings of the campaign. He saw a car parked at the side of the road, and inside lay two men who had obviously been shot. He called the police and soon after the wounded men were rushed to the near-by Royal Victoria Hospital. However, one died on the way and the other died shortly after.

The dead men were both Protestants: Alan Meehan, 17, of Finnis Drive, and Brian Patrick McMillan, 21, of Malton Drive. The car in which the men were found had been set fire to, but the fire had caused little damage. But what made the killing of special interest was that when the police came to examine the vehicle in detail they found another body – this time quite dead – in the boot. The third corpse was a Roman Catholic, Sgt Joseph Francis Flemming, 29, an instructor in the Territorial Army, who lived at Sunnyside street, Belfast. Flemming had been shot in the head and had been dead for over an hour at least when police found him.

Flemming and the two Protestants had been at a party at Finaghy, where they had met. At 5·00 a.m. the morning of the 9th they had left the party together. The milkman came across the car with its grisly contents at Little Distillery Street, off the Grosvenor Road, at 6·30 a.m. – an hour and a half after all three men were last seen alive.

Finaghy is to the south of Belfast, close to the Catholic Andersonstown area. It is conceivable that the men travelled down the Falls Road to the point where the car was found. But whether two Protestants would have willingly taken this route in the early hours of the morning, through an area where police and army kept out and the IRA patrolled, is a matter of some doubt. An alternative route would have been to travel down the Lisburn Road. Then they could have crossed to the Lower Falls at Tate's Avenue or, still further on, at Sandy Row. But it is unclear why the men should have ended up in the Falls at all. As we shall suggest later, it is probable that Meehan and Mc-Millan were heading towards the Shankill, and there is no reason why they should have approached so closely the IRA Falls area – unless, of course, they were trying to take a short cut.

The police, it turned out later, had not been the only people to fail to realize immediately that a third man was also in the car. Sources close to the Official IRA disclosed that an Official IRA patrol had opened fire on the car as it failed to stop at two road-blocks. The Officials did not search the car, and only learned of the macabre contents of the boot in subsequent press coverage. The crucial question that has to be answered is: why was Flemming's body in the boot? It is clear that he died before the other two men, who were still alive when found by the passing milkman.

He was a Roman Catholic and they were Protestants from an estate on the Upper Malone Road, near where the party had been. The two Protestants knew each other but they had not known Flemming before they met him at the party that night, and yet all three left together. Circumstantial evidence would suggest that here was a sectarian assassination that backfired on the killers. Meehan and McMillan lured Flemming from the party, shot him and placed his body in the boot of the car while they drove into home territory to dump him.

This still leaves a number of difficult questions unanswered. How, if this is the case, did the two men come to be in the Lower Falls? Little Distillery Street is only a short distance from where Flemming lived, and perhaps the two Protestants did not have sinister motives: may be they were indeed only giving Flemming a lift home. In which case, whoever was responsible for the killing may have decided to put Flemming into the boot to give the impression that the other two men had killed him. There are a number of reasons to discount this theory. At the time, the IRA made no attempt to promote political capital out of the killing, which might have been expected if they had 'set up' a Protestant assassination. And there would have been no need to set fire to the car if this were the case – if it was intended to destroy the car, it hardly mattered where Flemming's body was placed.

These three killings are clearly a puzzle – a puzzle perhaps that might be unravelled if one had access to the police files on the case. One of the two Protestants was alive long enough to give the police some clues, and it may be that the key to what happened in those ninety minutes, from the time the men left Finaghy to when the milkman spotted their car, is there. Certainly, if Meehan and McMillan did kill Flemming and were subsequently killed by the Official IRA, their deaths illustrate the dangers inherent in killers entering enemy territory to dump bodies. If the two Protestants were indeed making for the safety of the Shankill, their route was positively suicidal. At that hour and at that moment in the political climate, they would have been lucky to escape with their lives even without the body of a local Catholic in the boot.

Sunday 9 July was a busy day for police in Northern Ireland. At about the same time that the car was found in the Lower Falls containing Meehan, Flemming, and McMillan, detectives in North Belfast were searching for another body. A resident living in the near-by Cliftonville Road reported seeing three men carrying a body through the railings of the near-by Belfast City Waterworks. The Police were on the scene at 3 a.m., but darkness hindered their search. The Waterworks is situated on the Cliftonville Road, close to the Oldpark Road and not far from the spot where Clawson and Fisher had been found earlier. The call turned out to be no hoax when shortly after dawn police discovered the body of a Protestant from Heathfield Drive: David Andrews, 31.

Andrews was an epileptic who lived with his mother. He was a sick man. He was subject to fits and was partially paralysed. He had a steel plate in his head as a result of a serious brain injury, and he needed constant medical attention in the form of tablets. He was employed as a porter in Belfast's City Hospital in the Lisburn Road. People who worked with him there described him as 'a simple-minded human being'. This is hardly the material of which political militants are made. Andrews, it is clear, was an innocent, simple-minded man, whose path was crossed by people intent on killing.

His body was found dumped on waste ground. He had been shot through the head. At 8·00 p.m. the previous night he had left his home in Heathfield Drive, in the Oldpark area of the city, to go to visit the house of his elder sister at Ballygomartin Road. He was accompanied by another sister, and it was his intention to stay overnight there. However, he had forgotten some of his tablets, and rather than spend the night without them, he returned to fetch them. His sisters never saw him alive again.

Andrews was almost certainly the victim of IRA men operating out of the near-by Ardoyne or Bone areas. He had been shot before he was dumped, and his body showed the signs of a considerable beating. His assailants had also kicked him. He was dragged to the Waterworks by the three men first seen by the witness who called the police. His jacket was found soon after, but the body was not found till 6·00 a.m. There can have been no other motive for his death other than pure sectarianism. It occurred at a time when the Provisional IRA felt threatened by the rise in militancy of the Protestant extremists. They hit back in kind, killing Protestants simply because of their religion, as we shall see elsewhere shortly. Andrews had the misfortune to be a Protestant at the wrong place at the wrong time. At his inquest later, the Belfast City Coroner, Mr James Elliot, described the killing as 'a particularly brutal and senseless murder', and said: 'It is apparent from the autopsy report that this poor man was subject to considerable ill-treatment before his death. One would have thought that his condition would have been apparent to his attackers. It really is a disgusting case.'

Another blatantly sectarian killing by the Provisional IRA took place the same day, bringing the total number of victims in the past twenty-four hours to five. Gerald Turkington, 32, a

Protestant of Milady's Road in East Belfast, was found bound, gagged and shot in the head at Stewart Street in the Roman Catholic Markets area, in the early hours of the 9th. His body was found, in a macabre touch, close to the old Belfast Abbatoir. The IRA stronghold is situated immediately behind the city hall, and across the Albert Bridge from the Catholic Short Strand enclave in East Belfast.

A chilling account of Turkington's death is given by another Protestant who was also shot at the same time by the same men, but who miraculously survived. Known only as Witness A, the man provides stunning evidence of the attitude of IRA men at the time towards the Protestant community, and the UDA in particular. Turkington was in the UDA. Witness A was not, but this did not prevent him being questioned in depth on their activities. His statement to police was read at the inquest on Turkington in the spring of 1973. It said:

I was drinking in a club and left about midnight [Friday 8 July] to go across the Albertbridge Road [to East Belfast] to visit a relation. I was not sure where the relation lived and got lost. I had a few drinks in me and wandered into Madrid Street in the Short Strand. I saw about seven men in bush hats and thought at first they were UDA men. I told them I was from Sandy Row.

They led me through several streets and into a neat house in the Short Strand area. Two men and two young fellows were with me in the house and questioned me about the UDA. They roughed me up by punching me in the face and one of them stuck a glass in my face. One of them produced a .45 revolver while others kept coming and going from the house. They held me for about three and a half hours, and at one stage I tried to escape through a kitchen window but I failed and they roughed me up again.

They said they had another man in a house a couple of doors away. Eventually, they took me into a rear room, put me on my knees, and gagged and blindfolded me. A man came in and said: 'We are ready to go.' I was put into a car which moved about three house lengths and then stopped. Some other people got into the car and it seemed quite crowded in the back. We drove for about three minutes, and then the car stopped again and I was pushed out. I felt rough ground under my feet and realised that I was on a patch of waste ground. I tried to run away from the men because I knew I didn't want to be with them. As I ran, I was shot in the head and I saw a blue flash in my mind. I fell and heard one or two more shots but they didn't hit me. I knew later it must have been the other poor fellow being shot. I lost consciousness, and the next thing I remember was hearing voices. I said I was from the Shankill and I heard a man reply 'I am not worried if you are a Hindu. I am going to help you.'

Witness A was very lucky to survive, but even though he is still alive, he will never recover from the injuries he received. 'The other poor fellow being shot' was Turkington. He was a member of the UDA's 'G' Company in East Belfast, and had been on barricade duty in Dee Street, near his home, until 2·00 a.m. that morning. He was picked up shortly after and was found shot dead at 4·00 p.m. Witness A probably owed his survival to his decision to make a break for it. Turkington did not have the opportunity. The muzzle of the gun that killed him had been pressed against his scalp, and he died instantly. He had previously been beaten, and it is fair to assume that his interrogation was along similar lines to Witness A. His was the last death of the truce. Henceforth the IRA Provisionals had other things to occupy their energies.

For the truce was about to collapse. It had been a fortnight of high tension in which, though the IRA and the Army had ceased to attack each other, they had both watched the other warily. Meanwhile the Protestant extremists had hovered on the brink of outright insurrection. The truce had been a marriage of convenience for both parties – not a matter of principle – and the marriage was wearing a bit thin. The IRA did not trust the British government. It was short on political expertise and always felt more comfortable pursuing its aims on the battle-field than at the negotiating table, even if the battlefield was the homes and work-places of hundreds of thousands of people. In the back of its mind the IRA felt that the decision of the British government to treat with them was a sign of weakness in London, that it had been forced upon Heath and his government. The logic of this was that it only needed 'one more push' in the words of Sinn Fein President, Rory O'Brady, to get the IRA all its aims. The British government, on the other hand, had had a shock. It had completely misjudged the strength of feeling in the Protestant community towards the truce. The possible threat from the militants in this community if the truce continued was potentially far worse for the Army than a continuation of the IRA campaign. Thus, the interests of both parties to the truce had come to lie in ending it. A confrontation between the Army and the Provisionals at Lenadoon Avenue in the Belfast suburb of Suffolk, beyond Andersonstown, provided the Provisionals with the pretext they needed to break the truce. The local Army commander had given permission for some Catholic families to move into homes vacated by Protestants. The order had been rescinded when it was realized that the Catholics would be resisted by Protestants in the area and a sectarian riot would ensue. The Provisionals insisted on moving the Catholic families in: the Army on keeping them out. On Sunday 9 July, the Provisional IRA in Dublin announced that the truce was over. Lenadoon was responsible. The Provisionals were happy to resume their bombings and killings of the security forces. The British government had seen their serious attempt to treat with the IRA collapse in ruins. A political solution with the IRA was no longer possible. There would have to be a military solution. This was regrettable, but at least the Army had got the Protestant extremists off their backs.

6. The truce is over but the assassinations continue: 10 July–31 August

On Monday 10 July Northern Ireland awoke to find the fragile truce between the IRA and the Army was over. It had lasted for two short but bloody weeks. Before the truce began, in 1972 twenty-five civilians had been assassinated. If one adds the 1970 and 1971 killings, the figure rises to thirty-one. In the fourteen days of the Truce there were eighteen killings, an average of more than one each day. By the end of July, thirty-nine people had been killed in the previous thirty-six days since midnight on 25 June when the truce began – eight more than the combined figure for the previous nineteen months since the death of Jardin in December 1970.

The fury of the killings abated in August, when there were only fourteen, compared to thirty-six in the previous month. Thereafter the monthly figure stabilized in this region. The highest month later in 1972 was December with nineteen, and the lowest the month that preceded it, November, with eight. Just over two Roman Catholics were to be killed for every one Protestant, though there were not two Protestant assassins for every one Catholic. July was the one month in the campaign in which the number of Protestants killed almost matched the number of Catholics. There were nineteen Catholics and seventeen Protestants. Once the truce was ended on 9 July, however, the balance began to tip. Of the twenty-one killed in the rest of the month, thirteen were Catholics and eight Protestants. The IRA were once again occupied in other matters and could not spare so much time to kill Protestants as was possible during the truce.

A few days after the truce broke down, there occurred one of the most ghastly assassinations of all – probably the worst killing of the whole campaign. This was the death of David

McClenaghan, 15, a mentally retarded Roman Catholic youth, of Southport Street, off the Oldpark Road, in the early hours of Tuesday 12 July.

12 July – 'The Twelfth' – is a public holiday in Northern Ireland to celebrate the victory of the Protestant William of of Orange over the Catholic James II at the Battle of the Boyne in 1690. In Protestant areas the night before, huge bonfires are lit, and in normal times the holiday is a time of festivity that members of both communities participate in. But 12 July 1972 was not a normal time.

In the early hours of this 'Twelfth' morning, four Protestant men broke into the McClenaghan house. The men were Trevor Hinton, 23, of Coningsby Street, Oldpark Road; Ronald Waller, 18, of Lee Street; James McCleave, 19, of Glenbane Avenue, Rathcoole; and Terence Joseph Slavin, 22, of Cromwell Street. In the house at the time were Mrs Sarah McClenaghan, a middle-aged widow of three, her son David, and a Protestant lodger, Mr David Titterington. The McClenaghans were a Roman Catholic family living in a Protestant street, and what happened after the four men broke in was told in May, when all four intruders stood trial in Belfast for the murder of young David McClenaghan. Hinton was also charged with raping Mrs McClenaghan.

In his opening address to the jury at the trial, the Crown Prosecutor, Mr Robert Babbington, said that the killing had created a new dimension of violent crime in Northern Ireland:

The citizens of Belfast and all who practice in these courts have become used and hardened to details of violent and squalid crimes during these past four years. But I venture to suggest to you that the details which will be revealed to you in this case will create in your minds a new dimension. The restraints of civilization on evil human passions are in this case totally non-existent. It is said that violence begets violence. You might think that in this case we have reached the lowest level of human depravity. It will be difficult for you to envisage anything worse.

The ostensible motive for this crime was that the McClenaghan family were 'Fenians', that they had arms in the house, and that they had allowed people to shoot from the house. I say 'ostensible' because on examination you will realize that there could be no basis for such an allegation. Mrs McClenaghan, her three children, and Mr Titterington were the only occupants of the house. You might think that no rational person could hold that these persons were part of or guilty of any IRA crimes. The Crown suggests that this was in fact a sectarian outrage – a case of violent, strong, unruly thugs seeking to give a veneer of respectability to the gross behaviour they carried out in the house.

On the night prior to the attack, Mrs McClenaghan and three children had been out watching the 'Eleventh Night' bonfires in near-by streets. She returned home at about midnight with her eldest child, David, and Mr Titterington. Her two other children had earlier gone to stay with friends for the night. After the three had gone to bed, at about 3·00 a.m. they heard shooting and the sound of breaking glass. They arose and discovered bullet-holes in the glass of the front door and on the wall inside. Half an hour later the four men whom Mrs McClenaghan later identified as Hinton, McCleave, Slavin and Waller, forced their way into the house by reaching through the broken glass and opening the door-catch. The leader of the four was Hinton, who was unmasked. One of the others wore a balaclava-type mask and the other two pulled cushion-covers they found in the house over their heads. It was claimed by the Crown at the trial that Waller was the man with the balaclava, and that the two with the cushion-covers were Slavin and McCleave.

The three occupants of the house were downstairs when the men broke in. Hinton asked about guns in the house. The terrified Mrs McClenaghan told the truth, that there were no guns in the house, nor had their ever been. Hinton also asked about their religion. Titterington protested vehemently that he was a Protestant. He was taken upstairs by Waller and beaten about the face and a cigarette-lighter was used to burn him under the chin. He produced his Orange sash and claimed that, not only was he a Protestant, but that Mrs McClenaghan was too. He said she was his wife, but this appears to have made little impression because he was taken to the attic and made to kneel on his sash. He was within seconds of being killed when a shout from downstairs led Waller to go and investigate. Left on his own, Titterington escaped through a skylight into the street and he immediately headed for the nearest army post in Louisa Street. In the meantime a drama was being enacted downstairs.

Hinton must have had second thoughts as to the religion of the McClenaghans. He asked the boy David, who because of his backwardness may not have realized exactly what was taking place, what church he went to. The boy replied 'Oldpark'. Oldpark is a mixed area with Presbyterian, Roman Catholic and Church of Ireland churches. Mrs McClenaghan tried to convince Hinton that the boy had referred to Oldpark Presbyterian Church. Unconvinced, Hinton told the boy to go and fetch his prayer-book. This sealed everything, for the child dutifully obliged his captors. Not only did he bring from his mother's handbag her Roman Catholic Sunday Missal, but, for good measure, he brought her rosary beads too. Now completely satisfied that he had come upon a nest of 'Fenians' Hinton ordered the middle-aged and petrified Mrs McClenaghan to take off her clothes. She at first refused, and Hinton fired a warning shot. There was a struggle and Mrs McClenaghan had her clothes ripped off her. She was then raped on the sofa by Hinton in front of her son and the two other attackers. After Hinton had satisfied his lust, one of the others was alleged to have raped Mrs McClenaghan. She claimed it was McCleave, but no action was taken against him on this count at the trial.

After this violation, both Mrs McClenaghan and her son were taken upstairs to her bedroom. Both were made to lie face down on the bed. Hinton told her there was a bullet for her and one for her son. He then shot the boy. Mrs McClenaghan threw herself across the body of her son to shield him from the assassin's bullets, but she was in vain. She was also shot, and the four men then left the house, believing both Mrs McClenaghan and her son to be dead. But though the boy died, Mrs McClenaghan recovered. The finger-prints of the attackers were all over the house, and they were picked up by the police shortly after. At the trial Mr Babbington said that all four admitted being in the house at the time of the killing, but each tried to minimize the part he had played.

Mrs McClenaghan gave a moving testimony of the events that led up to the death of her son. She said that after the shots had been fired through the front door, Titterington had gone to investigate:

When he came back we sat talking for about twenty minutes and then I heard shooting at the front door. I went downstairs and saw four men in the hall. One was wearing a balaclava helmet. Two had cushion covers over their heads and the other unmasked man was carrying a gun and a bottle of wine. The man with the balaclava had 'UDA' written in ink on one of his hands . . . He told me he had got a telephone call from a neighbour in the street that I was involved with the IRA and that I had guns in the house. He said he wanted them.

Mrs McClenaghan identified the man with the balaclava, and related the exchange over religion. The prayer-book revealed that she and her children attended the Sacred Heart Church in Glenview Street. 'Hinton said to me, "You're a dirty Fenian,"' she testified. She was then raped twice, and claimed that on the second occasion she ripped off the mask of the man who was raping her, and that it was McCleave. She then told what happened when she and her son were taken upstairs:

I pleaded with them not to touch the boy, as he was retarded and looked so afraid. I told them that if they did not shoot I would leave the district. We both got down on the bed. Hinton told me not to scream but I started to scream and he began to shoot. He fired three shots at David hitting him about the neck and chest. I turned over to try to cover him but Hinton then shot me three times. I was hit in the thigh and hand. The four men then ran out.

At the trial, Hinton and Waller were both found guilty of murder and sentenced to life imprisonment. Hinton was also found guilty of rape. Slavin and McCleave were found not guilty of murder on the direction of the judge, but were convicted on lesser charges. McCleave was sentenced to eight years and Slavin to seven.

In passing sentence the judge, Mr Justice O'Donnell, said:

Even a community hardened by daily acts of violence must stand appalled at the human depravity manifested by this crime. I do not believe anyone, however extreme, could view this ruthless killing of a poor retarded boy while his violated mother tried to shield him, with anything other than revulsion.

Mr O'Donnell's sentiments drew agreement from an unlikely quarter. From the first, while the four men had not denied their involvement in killing young David McClenaghan, they each strenuously refuted the charge of rape. They knew that within the puritanical community they inhabited the killing of Catholics might be tolerated, and even applauded, by some; but rape was regarded as a crime, without justification, that could not be disguised as patriotism. Before the trial, Hinton, against whom the charge of rape was virtually incontestable, was held in solitary confinement in Crumlin Road gaol. This drastic measure was for his own good, to keep him away from the other loyalist prisoners in the gaol. After the trial, when all four prisoners were returned to the loyalist wing of the gaol, all four were badly beaten by their co-religionists. Their actions had shocked the hardest of hard-liners. They were considered to have brought the loyalist cause into disrepute by their actions. Loyalists could regard shooting, and sometimes torturing, of Catholics for political motives as legitimate. But their puritanical morals were outraged by such a bestial crime as the McClenaghan rape and murder. The rape of a middle-aged Catholic widow and the killing of her mentally retarded son could not be justified to Protestant extremists any more than to the average Catholic. Like Mr Justice O'Donnell, Protestant extremists viewed the crime with revulsion.

The day after the McClenaghan Shooting, Thursday 13 July, a Roman Catholic UDR (Ulster Defence Regiment) man was killed, in another killing that involved torture. Henry Joseph Russell, 21, of Sunnylands Avenue, Carickfergus, had been a member of the UDR for just one month. Very few Catholics joined this body – it had replaced the B-Special Constabulary after the report of the Hunt Committee – and the immediate assumption after Russell's body was found was that he had been killed by the IRA, who made a particular point of singling out Catholic members of the UDR for assassination. But his UDR membership played little or no part in Russell's death, and for this reason he has been included in our list of civilian assassination victims.

Carickfergus is a small mainly Protestant town on the south Antrim coast, about ten miles north of Belfast. The Russell family had moved there during the Troubles from Belfast because of sectarian intimidation. Russell had joined the RAF at the age of 15, and studied to be a nurse, but when the Troubles came to Ulster he bought himself out of the forces and returned home. He got a job as a nurse in Purdysburn Hospital a mental hospital in South Belfast, but East of the Lagan.

On Friday 12 July Russell left his local UDR base at Carickfergus at 8·00 p.m., changed at home, and set off at 9·30 p.m. to get the 9·40 p.m. train to go to work in Belfast. In order to get to Purdysburn, he would have had to travel across the city. He never made it. Somewhere between his home and the hospital he was kidnapped. At 2·00 a.m. the following morning his body was found in Larkfield Drive, Sydenham, East Belfast.

Russell had been severely tortured before his death. At his inquest in January 1973, the solicitor for Russell's parents, Mr Jack McCann said: 'For this one act alone this nation must one day answer its maker.' The UDR man had been stripped and was found wearing only his underpants. He had been branded with a red-hot poker and a cross had been branded on his back. He had also been stabbed a number of times, but death had been caused by a bullet in the head. Police described the killing as 'a ghastly brutal murder. No other words could possibly describe such a horrific crime.'

The police immediately began to follow the theory that Russell's death was the work of the IRA. But this theory is highly implausible in the light of what is now known of the assassination campaign. Certainly, there can be little doubt that the IRA would have been very likely to have killed Russell because of his UDR membership. But they would not have taken the body deep inside East Belfast – hard-line UDA territory. It is possible that a body could have been dumped a few hundred yards inside enemy territory, but the location of Russell's body would have required a drive of three or four miles into the Sydenham area, off the main Newtownards Road round small side-streets by the IRA men – and back again. And all the time there would have been the threat of discovery by UDA patrols in what was the heart of loyalist Ulster. This would have been a foolhardy course of action for IRA men to have undertaken at the best of times, but in the early hours of 13 July, with Protestants in the area emerging from their illegal drinking clubs after celebrating the 'Twelfth', it would have been positively suicidal. There can be little doubt that Russell was killed by Protestants in the area where he was found.

What clinches the matter is that Larkfield Drive was not a random spot, and Russell's death was not totally unexpected. For three months in an early period in the Troubles, Russell's family, Catholics, had lived in this same street in the depths of Protestant East Belfast. They had been intimidated out of their homes in the mixed New Barnsley Estate in the Roman Catholic Ballymurphy area. They had tried to escape sectarianism, but it had followed them wherever they fled.

When in the RAF Russell had received a bogus telegram telling him that a close relative had died. This was untrue, but concern for his family led him to forsake the safety of the forces and return to Northern Ireland. When he returned, he was followed about by unknown persons for months. One of his mother's foster-children later described him as a 'marked man', and this was probably accurate.

Russell's death was not another random killing of a Catholic. The men who killed him were of his own age, or a little younger, and some if not all of them knew their victim personally. The killers were the local Tartan gang in the area of Larkfield Drive. Russell became a marked man when he first came to live there because he was a Catholic. The fact that he was first in the RAF and then joined the UDR cut no ice with the killers. He was a Catholic, an enemy from Ballymurphy. That was enough.

The severity of the treatment he received before his death

merits comment. A number of young men were involved, and this is a common factor linking a number of deaths where violence has been used on a victim before death. Possibly there was an element of ritual about the killing in which every member of the gang had to participate to prove his commitment to the group. As we shall see, those responsible were to commit a number of other killings of a similar nature in the same area in the following months.

During the week following the discovery of Russell's body no one was killed, and this gave rise to a slight hope that the killings had ended with the IRA truce that had spawned them. Once again, this was a hope that was swiftly dispelled, and on Friday 21 July, the IRA displayed to the world that they were still capable of being just as ruthless as their Protestant counterparts.

As his name indicates, Joseph Rosato, 59, of Deerpark Road, in the Oldpark area, was of Italian origin. He was a Roman Catholic café-owner and some of his relatives were closely involved with the IRA. On the night of 21 July, at a meeting of the Provisional IRA in the Ardoyne, it was decided to pick up Rosato's son Tony, a member of the Official IRA, for question-ion, and possibly more. A group of young Provisionals were dispatched to Deerpark Road to pick up the young man.

It will be recalled that the Officials had announced on 10 July that they would continue to observe the 26 June truce with the Army. This action brought the long-simmering dispute between the two wings of the IRA once again out into the open. In the immediate weeks that followed there occurred a number of incidents in which some men on both sides were killed and wounded. The Rosato killing is to be seen in the context of this inter-IRA feud.

The men who called at the Rosato house that night were answered by Tony Rosato's father, Joseph. He told them to go away in no uncertain terms, and slammed the door on them. Immediately he did this, one of the youths fired a burst of gunfire through the closed door. Rosato collapsed dying in a pool of his own blood in the hallway while his attackers fled.

After the killing became public, the Rosato family announced through the press that they were certain that Protestants had not been involved in the assassination. Rosato's son, Tony, is said to have claimed he knew those responsible for his father's death, and stated that he would deal with them personally. In some Catholic circles, this killing was seen as particularly shocking, representing, as it did, fratricidal strife between the two sections of the IRA when many Catholics felt their community was under its greatest threat from Protestant extremists.

In a vain attempt to minimize their guilt, the Provisionals put round a story that, but for the serious nature of its content, would be ludicrous. They said that the youths sent from the Ardoyne meeting that night had been sent only to frighten Tony Rosato. They had shot low into the front door to frighten the father. Unfortunately, on slamming the street door on the Provisionals, Rosato senior tripped and fell over the door-mat. He was, therefore, lying on the floor when the bullets were fired through the door. Instead of a few slight wounds in the legs, he took the full force of the blast of gunfire in his chest.

One can only speculate on the inventiveness of the mind that thought up this explanation of Rosato's death. It is clear that whoever it was has a very slight knowledge of medicine. Even if the story were correct, a volley of bullets in the legs could have proved fatal within five minutes without proper medical attention through loss of blood.* But the story put out after the Rosato killing was untrue anyway. The pathologist's report proved conclusively that the bullets could not possibly have entered Rosato's body in this way, and the bullet-holes in the door do not back up the story either. It was merely a rather pathetic attempt by the Provisional IRA to wipe away some of the shame and guilt it felt over the killing.

By this time, feelings in the Catholic community, despite the

---

*An Official IRA man, Desmond Mackin, 38, of the Lower Falls, died at about this time in these circumstances. A Provisional IRA man fired a burst of gunfire into his thighs in the Cracked Cup drinking club in Leeson Street, and Mackin died within a few minutes through loss of blood caused by a major artery being severed.

brief pause in the killings, had reached something approaching hysteria. Although almost as many Protestants as Catholics were at this time being killed, it was the Catholic population that felt itself under attack. With hindsight and a touch of cynicism, one might suggest that this was the result of the profound psychological shock felt at the change in a position where Catholics had been led to believe they were 'winning' to one where their vulnerability became apparent. The Catholics had been vulnerable all the time, but while the initiative was held by, and all the running had been made by, Catholic groups, many Catholics had failed to realize this. The realization when it came was bound to be a shock. The Protestant community did not react quite so emotionally to the assassinations. After all, its members had felt themselves to be under attack for over three years.

The day after Rosato's death there occurred a double killing that only added to the hysteria in the Catholic community. The victims were Miss Rose McCartney, 27, of Iris Drive in the Lower Falls, and Patrick O'Neill, 26, who lived in the Ardoyne. Both were Roman Catholics and the couple had been going out with each other for only a few weeks previously. There was never much doubt that the deaths were the work of Protestant extremists. There was a suggestion that the IRA could have been responsible. O'Neill was a member of CESA, but he was regarded in IRA circles as unreliable. He was a police and Army informant and had been warned by the IRA a number of times. This would have been sufficient motive for the IRA to have killed him. He was basically a crook. He possessed a criminal record that predated the Troubles, and he seems to have been another of these people who were on the fringe of illegal political organizations through their connections with ordinary crime. But, even if they had a good reason to kill O'Neill, the IRA had no reason to kill McCartney. She was well known as a popular singer in Republican Clubs (a branch of the Official IRA) and despite this connection with the rival wing, it seems unlikely that the Provisionals would have killed her. The only possible reason would be that they were after O'Neill and McCartney just happened to be an innocent victim.

The circumstances of the killing also tend to rule out the IRA and place responsibility in the court of the Protestant extremists. Before midnight on the night of Friday 21 July, O'Neill and McCartney left the latter's house in the Springfield Road area of the Lower Falls to go to O'Neill's house in the Ardoyne. The geography of a city segregated on sectarian lines is of crucial importance in what happened on this journey. To get to the Ardoyne from the Lower Falls, it was necessary for the couple to pass through strong hard-line Protestant areas, for between them and the Ardoyne lay the Shankill and Woodvale. The route O'Neill is known to have regularly used was via the West Circular Road, Ballygomartin Road, and Woodvale and Crumlin Roads. In doing so he skirted the tops of the Shankill and Woodvale, laying himself open to the frequent patrols of Protestant extremists in these areas. It will be recalled that less than two weeks before, the young English Jehovah's Witness, Paul Jobling, had been picked up at a UDA road-block on the West Circular Road and his body dumped on the Glencairn Estate. O'Neill and McCartney were found near by.

On the night they left Iris Drive for the last time, O'Neill ordered a taxi as usual and the couple left to meet the cab ordered. They were found the next morning shot dead inside a stolen taxi, on the Forthriver Road on the Glencairn Estate, off the Ballygomartin Road. As mentioned in earlier killings that involved taxis, during the assassination campaign a number of people were singled out for death because they had inadvertently disclosed their religion when asking for a taxi. O'Neill's order for a taxi to the Ardoyne was probably heard by Protestants tuning into the radio frequencies used by taxi companies, and the stolen cab was dispatched to pick the unsuspecting couple up. The taxi had probably been hijacked earlier in the day for just this purpose and was standing by.

In the early hours of the morning of Saturday 22 July police were called to the site of the bodies. They found O'Neill and McCartney in the back of the vehicle. They had been shot a number of times each in the head and body. At their inquest in May 1973, a witness told that she had seen men get out of a second car and fire six shots into the back of the taxi before driving off in the second car. But the shots the witness saw being pumped into the bodies were not the ones that killed the couple. They had been shot earlier and were taken to Glencairn to be dumped. At this time the area was a very popular dumping-ground for Protestant extremists – a fact that, to their credit, did not go unnoticed by the R U C and the security forces. In the O'Neill and McCartney killing, two men drove a car about 100 yards in front of the stolen taxi containing the two bodies from the actual scene of the killing in case an Army or police patrol was about. When this convoy arrived at Glencairn, six shots were pumped into the already lifeless bodies, just to make sure, and the third man who had driven the taxi escaped with the other two in the first car.

Immediately after the deaths became public, rumours began to circulate in the Roman Catholic community that McCartney had been tortured and mutilated. She was the first female assassination victim – a fact that was in itself regarded as particularly shocking in a puritanical society that saw a woman's place in the home. Despite notable exceptions, women in Ulster did not engage actively in politics at this time and, as a result, both sides had tended to treat them as non-combatants, concentrating their sectarian assassinations on males, even if they were only boys of 12 or 13. McCartney was the exception, and this may in part explain the extraordinary spread of the rumours concerning the manner of her death that had sections of the Catholic community verging on hysteria. It was said that she had been raped and then vilely mutilated. Her breasts were claimed to have been cut off while she was still alive, and her body was said to be covered with hideous stab wounds. There was no truth whatsoever in the rumours. The pathologist's photographs of her body show no sign of any torture or beating. The only wounds are those caused by the bullets that killed her.

As late as May 1973, when the inquest was held, rumours continued to circulate that McCartney had been tortured and mutilated. And, of course, as far as the assassination campaign in July and August 1972 was concerned, this was what mattered.

The rumour was not effectively quashed until almost a year later at the inquest. At the time the rumour was given wide credence and passed by word of mouth throughout the Catholic community in Belfast. One can only speculate on the degree to which it may have led Catholics in this community to feel that it justified the IRA hitting back indiscriminately at individual members of the Protestant population.

Although there was no element of torture or mutilation in the O'Neill and McCartney killings, there was a growing trend towards such practices in the assassinations. In this climate it was only too easy for allegations of this nature to be attached to virtually every assassination, whether it was true or not. Such a killing did take place the same day that O'Neill and McCartney were assassinated, and this may have been in part responsible for the credibility given the allegations about McCartney. Francis Arthurs, 34, a Roman Catholic of Fallswater Road, off the Falls Road, was found dumped at Liffey Street in the River Streets area of the Oldpark the morning of Saturday 22 July. Arthurs had been subject to a severe torturing before his death. He had been shot through the head and mouth, but the body contained numerous small stab-wounds.

Like O'Neill and McCartney the same evening, Arthurs had taken a taxi on Friday night. He was taken out of the taxi in the Oldpark–Crumlin Road area that night, and was not heard of alive again. Local people said they heard shots at about 4·00 p.m., and a witness saw his body being carried out of a UDA club in Ohio Street by a number of men. It was found some hours later in a stolen car in Liffey Street near by. Arthurs was almost unrecognizable. As well as the bullet-wounds, the wounds of the knife covered many parts of the body. He had also been beaten and showed considerable bruising. Significantly, the wounds he bore were remarkably similar to those inflicted on another Roman Catholic in the same area shortly after: Thomas Madden.

Thomas Madden, 48, a Roman Catholic bachelor of Cliftonville Park Avenue, was the brother of Hugh Madden, the greengrocer who had been shot by a sniper operating out of Louisa

Street in June. Thomas outlived him only till Sunday 13 August. Thomas Madden was described by those who knew him as an inoffensive man. He worked as a night security guard at Ewart's Mill, a factory employing mainly Protestants, in the Crumlin Road. Madden lived in lodgings off the Cliftonville Road, not far from the Oldpark. He was a man who never engaged in politics and who appeared to have no enemies. Though a Roman Catholic, his father had been a member of the RUC. The only facet of his character that may have singled him out from others like him was that he had a drink problem. He was a man who spent a lot of his time in bars and pubs, and he apparently did not mind too much where he drank. He was known to visit bars frequented by IRA men, and this may have been just the basis on which his death-warrant was signed.

Three weeks before his death, Madden was picked up by the UDA and held and interrogated in a club in the Shankill Road area. He told his landlady afterwards that on the first day of his detention his gaolers had taken his rosary beads, lighter, cigarettes, and money from him, but that on his release all his personal belongings except his money were returned. He apparently thought the UDA had decided not to harm him. His route to work from the relatively safe Cliftonville Road took him via Manor Street, Oldpark Road and Crumlin Road – all borderline areas.

On the evening he disappeared, Saturday 12 August, he was drinking at the Meeting of the Waters public house in Manor Street. This pub was known to be a regular haunt of many IRA Provisionals and this had led to several bombing attacks by Protestant extremists on the premises. The most recent of these was in June 1973. Madden was in the Meeting of the Waters till 6·00 p.m., and he told his drinking companions that he was afraid to go to work that night. Whether he had a premonition of danger, or whether he had a more tangible warning we shall never know.

He returned to his lodgings and told his landlady that he was too frightened to go to work. Nonetheless, at about 9·30 he did go. He failed to arrive and eight hours later his badly mutilated body was found in a shop doorway in Oldpark Road. A trail of blood led for about sixty yards along Baden-Powell Street to Hillview Street – not far from Louisa Street, where the sniper who had killed his brother had been based. What happened to Thomas Madden during those eight hours is quite clear from the injuries he received. Why it happened is a matter for speculation.

Madden was stabbed approximately one hundred and fifty times. A detective said of these wounds at the time: 'I stopped counting after fifty – there were so many.' These wounds covered every part of the body including the scalp, the face, the arms, the legs, and the torso. They would appear to have been administered by a nine-inch double blade, and none of the cuts was deep. They were in the nature of small nicks, as if someone had cut little lumps out of the body. It is these wounds that bear such a striking resemblance to those inflicted on Arthurs, though Arthurs's body did not contain anything like as many wounds as Madden's. One can only speculate on the purpose of such wounds, but one must surmise that the main motive was to cause pain to the victim, not to kill him. In neither case, Arthurs or Madden, were the knife-wounds the cause of death. Arthurs was shot and Madden was strangled. They suggest either a particularly drastic form of deep interrogation or perhaps simply that the man or men inflicting them derived pleasure from them.

For Madden to receive his injuries he was stripped naked and almost certainly, in view of the fact that the knife-wounds cover virtually every conceivable part of the anatomy, he was suspended from above. Possibly he was suspended in a slowly tightening noose that gradually strangled him while his assailants chipped away at his body with a knife like a sculptor at a block of stone. Down his back were carved a number of deep parallel lines. The wounds from the knife were not immediately fatal, but they would ultimately have proved so without swift medical assistance. Loss of blood must have been considerable and Madden would have lost consciousness a number of times, perhaps to have been revived with a bucket of water by his captors.

Such treatment towards a man as inoffensive and politically

insignificant as Madden is strange. Particularly so as he appeared to have been vetted three weeks before by the UDA. It is possible that the only motive in the killing was the pleasure the killers may have derived from the torture. But, it may have been the case that Madden's injuries were inflicted in the course of deep interrogation about the IRA. Perhaps at his earlier more gentle questioning he had given some indication that he possessed valuable intelligence. He was frightened to go to work that evening. Why? Had he agreed three weeks earlier to act as a spy for the UDA, and had he been told to report back with information on his way to work that night? It is all a matter of speculation.

Another curious aspect concerns the death in June of his brother. Was there any connection between the deaths of Hugh and Thomas Madden, or was it just coincidence? Certainly, neither man was a member of any political organization, but, as was said earlier, Thomas's drinking habits frequently led him to the same bars as known Provisional IRA men. This may not have passed unnoticed in the Protestant community on his doorstep.

With the introduction of the 'romper rooms' and 'rompering'* by the Protestant extremists, much valuable information was now coming into their hands. Such practices had become a feature of UDA rule in the Protestant areas. But although huge amounts of valuable intelligence were gained in this way, how much useless and incorrect information was also gathered? Just how many people, when subjected to a beating or electric shocks to their genitals, confessed to activities and actions that they were innocent of? And perhaps more important, how many people were made the subject of such false information? People under such stress are inclined to make every attempt to save their own skins, even at another's expense. It is a matter of conjecture as to how many people may have died because others falsely attributed to them membership of an illegal organization or personal participation in terrorist activities. But it is known to have happened.

This, at least, is one explanation for why Thomas Madden

*See p. 277.

should have met the fate that he did. The dead man was last heard of alive at 4·30 in the early hours of Sunday 13 August. A woman living in the vicinity of Hillview Street said she heard a man in obvious agony screaming the words: 'Kill me. Kill me.' Madden was granted his request. His body was found one hour later.

Before they dumped Madden's body, for some reason his killers carefully put all his clothes back on him. They then proceded to carry the body into the near-by Oldpark Road and hurl it over a six-foot-high railing into a shop doorway – an exercise that required a number of able-bodied men.

A number of factors are apparent in the Madden case from the nature of the killing. First, a number of men were involved. Second, the amount of blood flowing from the multitude of wounds on the body must have been considerable. Had it taken place in an ordinary house, the blood-stains from the killing would have been excessive and hard to remove completely. It has been suggested from one source that the scene of the killing was not a house, but a lock-up garage in Hillview Street. This would seem eminently plausible. Here the signs of the torture could have been hosed away quite efficiently to leave no trace, and there would have been greater facility in hanging Madden from, say, rafters in the roof. It might also be pertinent to ask why the police did not make an immediate house-to-house search in the vicinity of the spot where Madden's body was found. This would certainly happen were the killing to have occurred in any other part of the western world other than Belfast in August 1972. But no greater comment can be made on the absence of real personal security in Northern Ireland in these times than to reflect that it was possible for a man to be picked up on his way to work, tortured, killed, and then dumped – all within an area of no more than half a square mile, and the police were powerless to apprehend the killers. No arrests were made in the Madden killing, and police were still without a lead in August 1973 when this book was completed.

Another assassination that also involved a number of men came to light just over a week before Madden's death in the country town of Portadown in Armagh. In the month of July the local UDA had set up their own No-go area in Portadown modelled on those in Belfast and Londonderry. By August the UDA No-go area had disappeared, and on Friday 4 August the body of a Roman Catholic factory worker, Felix John Hughes of Granville Road, Killycomain, was dragged out of a drainage channel inside the former No-go area.

The cause of death was later diagnosed as a massive fracture of the skull. The body had been tied to a mattress which had been weighted down. Hughes had been missing from his home since Sunday 15 July – when the No-go area had still been in existence – and the circumstances of his death were revealed in court the following May when a 16-year-old juvenile from Belfast was charged with his murder. The youth admitted to the court that he had been at a house in the Portadown No-go area where Hughes was detained, but he denied the charge of killing him. He said that Hughes had been picked up by the UDA and taken there for questioning about the IRA. He admitted that while he was in the house he had hit the dead man a number of times, but he claimed that he was not responsible for the fatal blow. Detective-Sergeant Ronald McMahon told the judge, Lord Chief Justice Jones, that at least twelve people had taken part in the beatings that led to Hughes's death, and that several of these were more mature than the accused. He added that it was highly probable that the police would not have been able to connect the youth with the offence but for his statement.

Defending the youth, Mr Desmond Boal Q.C. said that two years earlier the youth's family had had to move from their home in one area of Belfast to another through fear. This had been a dramatic and embittering experience for the boy. In the area to which the family subsequently moved, the boy, who was big for his age, had felt obliged to react to community pressures as a man. Boal said the youth was associating with older men, some of whom belonged to the criminal element. The youth was involved in an armed robbery and sent to training school, from which he escaped. After his escape he found himself 'on the run'. He was dispatched by the UDA to their No-go area in Portadown. This put him in a vulnerable position and he was thus made to act in a way which he would not have been disposed to on his own.

The accused admitted that he took 'a few digs' at the dead man, but, Boal submitted, this was on the fringe of 'the ghastly set-up'. Boal's defence worked. The youth was found guilty of manslaughter, a lesser crime, and his plea of not guilty to a charge of murdering Hughes, while acting in concert with person or persons unknown, was accepted by the prosecution. On Wednesday 16 May 1973 at the Armagh Spring Assizes he was sentenced to eight years detention. Though he may well have been only on the fringe of the 'ghastly set-up' that was responsible for the death of Hughes, he certainly knew who was at the centre of it. But he kept this information to himself. The day after the youth was sentenced, a charge of failing to give information to the police about the Hughes killing was dropped against another youth, George Preston, 17, of Ardgart Place, Rathcoole, near Belfast.

The facts that emerged at the Hughes murder trial are interesting for a number of reasons. They show quite clearly the practice of the UDA in interrogating Catholics about the IRA. Hughes was not connected with either wing of the IRA, and his interrogators probably knew this. But they were after information about the IRA, and coming from a Catholic area, Hughes probably knew something that would have been of interest to them. The polarization of the two communities in Northern Ireland at this time was such that both communities were ignorant of the most simple intelligence about their rivals. Such information that would be common knowledge to everyone living in an area could only be obtained by the extremist organizations through interrogations like the one Hughes suffered.

Hughes, therefore, was on the wrong end of the standard UDA 'rompering'. He was tied to a chair and questioned, and to loosen his tongue his questioners beat him – took 'a few digs' at him. The number of people involved is of interest, because it confirms the theory that a large number of people – in this case at least a dozen – are usually involved in 'romperings'. The age of the juvenile convicted also confirms the prevalence of very young people in such activities. Detective-Sergeant McMahon said that of the twelve people involved, several of them were more mature than the accused. It follows that several others were just as immature as the 16-year-old youth who was 'big for his age'.

The defence to murder that Boal put forward is also worthy of comment. It is not the authors' intention to question in any way the law on this, but one could logically infer that it is a defence that might be applied by many youths of a similar age from an identical background, in this case or in any other – that is to say it could be applied to a large number of the young men taking part in the assassinations that we are dealing with. It was claimed that because the youth was in a vulnerable position he was made to act in a way which he would not have been disposed to on his own. He took a few digs at Hughes because others were doing so, and he did not want to lose face. He was big for his age, and had to act as though he was a man in the community in which he found himself. How many young men in this age group, one wonders, have acted in concert with others in ways they would not have been disposed to on their own, in recent years in Northern Ireland – on both sides – to prove their manhood? It is a matter of speculation, but it is a matter also of much concern if Ulster is ever to return to any semblance of normality.

Another aspect of the Hughes case is the light it sheds on the organization of the UDA. The youth was sent from Belfast to Portadown, which presupposes at least a rudimentary structure of centralized command. The need at that particular moment in July was for men in Portadown, and the youth was dispatched there for that purpose. There are indications that he was not the only outsider sent in by the UDA in Belfast. There have been a significant number of assassinations that have taken place outside Belfast that have borne the mark of previous killings inside the city. If men could be sent to different areas of Northern Ireland, as this youth was to Portadown, it follows that assassins could be sent out to country areas for specific tasks.

Just over a week after Hughes's body was found, and a day

before Thomas Madden's killing, another Roman Catholic was killed in Belfast. The body of Frank Wynne, 37, a labourer of Elizabeth Street in the Lower Falls, was found dumped in a stolen car in Jaffa Street off the Crumlin Road. Wynne was a quiet man who lived alone with his mother. She said that she had last seen him when he went out at 5·30 p.m. on Saturday 12 August. She told Belfast's coroner in May 1973: 'As usual he did not tell me where he was going or when he would be back, but he never stayed out later than 10·30 p.m.'

Wynne worked in Mackie's Foundry, a factory in the Springfield Road with a largely Protestant work force. His body was found at 9·50 p.m. His movements till that time are unknown. He was shot in the head, but before death he had been severely beaten. He had suffered numerous injuries in his beating, and they drew comment at the inquest from the coroner Mr James Elliot, who dealt with five assassination victims that day (17 May):

These are really incredible and horrific stories we are hearing today of man's inhumanity to man. Mr Wynne seems to have been a very quiet and inoffensive man who lived at home with his mother. This unfortunate man seems to have fallen into the hands of some monsters who gave him a severe beating-up. He suffered the most severe injuries, so much so, that it is unlikely that he was conscious when he was shot. One can only think that this was a mistake. They wanted someone else and they tortured him until he confessed that he was someone else and then they shot him.

The coroner's last statement was pure conjecture. No evidence was ever produced to indicate that the Wynne killing was a case of mistaken identity. But though Mr Elliot may not have necessarily been accurate in his analysis of the causes of this particular death, in the context of the assassination campaign as a whole and the frequency of severe beatings the victims received before death, he hit the nail directly on the head. Just how many victims had preferred the certain death of a false confession to the agony of their interrogation? How many, like Thomas Madden, pleaded with their killers to put an end to the torture and kill them?

One of the other assassinations that Mr Elliot had to deal with was that of Thomas John Boyd, 28, of Carlisle Street, Belfast. It will be recalled that Boyd was mentioned earlier as one of the men responsible for the killing of UDA man Ingram 'Jock' Beckitt in the Shankill Road in March. Boyd was shot dead by intruders at his home in the early hours of Sunday 27 August. He had outlived his companion in the Beckitt killing, William Spence, by just eleven days. Both men were Protestants.

Spence, 32, a barman of Blackmartin Parade, Springmartin, was shot on the night of Wednesday 16 August as he was clearing the glasses from the Long Bar in the Shankill Road after closing-time. Two men came into the bar and asked for Spence by name. When Spence replied they beat him over the head, produced revolvers and shot him four times in the head. Spence was a member of the UDA, and as well as being responsible for the Beckitt killing he may have incurred the wrath of other Protestant extremists by giving police information on their activities.

The killing was not unexpected. Both Spence and Boyd had lived on borrowed time since killing Beckitt. He had described the group of men these two belonged to as 'not men at all, only a bunch of thugs and gangsters'. They were an element in the UDA that saw the Troubles as a chance to feather their own nests by carrying out illegal activities under the cloak of patriotism. For both Boyd and Spence had police records for petty crime that predated the Troubles. What men like Beckitt found most distasteful in their activities was that they were conducted at the expense of average working-class Protestants, whose shops were robbed, or who had to pay levies each week, ostensibly to finance 'the cause' but in reality to line the pockets of men such as Boyd and Spence.

Involvement in the shady side of the Protestant organizations – thefts and extortions – had previously caused Boyd to be rompered in May. In this early attack, Boyd had received a broken skull, which had forced him to go on to social security benefit – though, as the coroner was to remark, he was never to lack for money.

At the inquest Mrs Sarah Boyd gave a vivid account of her

husband's death. She began by explaining that the flat in which she and Boyd were living in Carlisle Street – off Carlisle Circus at the foot of the Crumlin Road – was not theirs:

I was squatting in the flat with my husband and five children. We had moved there from 58 Malvern Street. We had to leave because of the rats. My husband was on the sick with a fractured skull he got in May 1972. He had recovered fairly well and was working in the Horseshoe Bar on the Shankill. I was expecting him home that morning at about 2 o'clock and would not go to bed till he came home.

She explained that she then went up to her bedroom and lay on the bed with her clothes on waiting for her husband to come home. When she heard him come home she looked at her watch and saw it was 5·00 p.m. exactly. She went downstairs and demanded to know where he had been till that hour:

I knew my husband usually goes to one of the wee bars in the Shankill Road after the Horseshoe closes. I know he went to one in Agnes Street, Aberdeen Street, and another one off the Crumlin Road. [In fact he had gone to the Oak Bar, Oak Street, in the Donegal Pass area of the city, quite a distance from the Shankill Road.]

I heard him come in at 5·00 a.m. I started to give off to him and as soon as I spoke I knew that he had a lot of drink in him. I asked him if he had locked the front door. He said 'no' and I got the impression that he was going out again. I told him I was worried with him coming in home so late.

The next thing, two armed and masked men burst into the flat and came into the living room where Boyd and his wife were talking. Mrs Boyd described the intruders:

Both men carried guns and both wore black stocking masks with slits for the eyes and mouth. One of them did something with his gun and it made a clicking sound, and something dropped on to the floor. At the same time, Homer – that's what I called my husband – got up and made a grab for the other one. I heard a loud explosion and Homer fell to the floor. Homer tried to say something, but only sounds came out.

One of the attackers was aged about 30. He had a thin build and wore jeans and a dark anorak, and was about 5 ft 10 ins in height. The other was about the same height but stouter with a broad build. The second man appeared to be older than the first. Mrs Boyd was asked if she could think of any reason why the men should have burst in and shot her husband.

I have no idea why this should have happened to my husband. I know he had been upset by Billy Spence's murder as he had been a good friend of his.

She then related the circumstances in which Boyd had received his broken skull in May. She said it had occurred after he had been picked up by some men who had dumped him on the corner of Malvern Street (where the Boyds had earlier lived) and the Shankill Road.

Why my husband got his fractured skull was also a mystery to me. It seemed he had been dumped from a car on the corner of Malvern Street and the Shankill.

Boyd had discussed the incident with her, and, she told the coroner, he also could not think of why it had happened. Nor did he know who was responsible. She added:

I do know that he had been terribly nervous and only the week before he had talked about going to Liverpool and getting a place for us there.

Boyd obviously knew that he was in danger. As well as the death of Beckitt, there was also another motive for his death, and that of Spence. Spence's death had obviously shaken Boyd deeply, and probably with good reason. Spence was the driver of the getaway car used by a UVF squad at a robbery in Serpentine Road earlier in the year. While his colleagues went into the premises and carried out the robbery, Spence drove off. It is not clear whether he did this because he heard police arrive or whether it was a calculated manoeuvre. When the UVF men emerged from the building they found their getaway car had vanished, and they were apprehended by the police without much trouble.

It was widely believed in Protestant circles that Boyd and Spence had tipped off the police about this operation. Two of the men apprehended later escaped before the trial. Spence was killed the day after the others were sentenced. This may well have accounted for Boyd's nervousness in the period before his death. At the inquest, a man in his twenties who was being held in custody at Crumlin Road gaol, James Rossborough, admitted being with Boyd till 4·40 on the morning of his death. He said he had met Boyd in the Oak Bar, in Oak Street, in the Donegal Pass area of Belfast at 3·15 a.m. in the company of another man, Billy Murdine.

'At around 4·20 we decided to go home in Billy's car. In the car was Billy, Homer, and myself. We went to a garage in Chichester Street, but it was closed and we came back and ran out of petrol at Donegal Street.'

They then stopped a passing Army patrol and Billy Murdine went off with the soldiers to get petrol. Rossborough last saw Boyd walking off up Donegal Street towards Carlisle Circus, which was little more than 100 yards away. The report of the state pathologist on Boyd said that he had been killed by a bullet-wound in the head from a single shot. He added that Boyd had been severely intoxicated. Mr Elliot commented:

'This is another one of these cases that occur with senseless frequency. There seems to be no motive. Why he could afford to drink to the extent that he did when he was unemployed is a matter for speculation.'

Where Boyd got his money from is a moot point. Both he and his friend and partner Spence were people attracted to the organizations that had sprung up in the Protestant communities during the troubles less for political motives than for what they could get out it for themselves. For just as there were people in both communities who were men of action, and who responded to the unique political circumstances in Ulster with policies of direct action, so, too, there were those who saw in the turmoil of a province in virtual civil war the opportunity to further their careers as criminals under the guise of patriots and soldiers. Such men were Boyd and Spence, though only at the foot of the ladder of such activities.

In both communities, men lined their pockets, bought themselves colour TVs, new homes and furniture. And all of these new-found material possessions were financed through the operations of the extremist organizations which were ostensibly political. Extortion of individuals and small businesses went on unchecked in both communities, because over vast areas of Belfast and elsewhere in Ulster the rule of law ceased to exist. Justice was meted out by those very organizations – I R A and U D A – that were responsible for the rackets.

It was precisely this sort of practice that Charles Harding Smith, one of the founders of the U D A, tried to curb in the Protestant communities on his return to Belfast in December.* He believed there was a level of extortion that would be accepted in the Protestant areas to provide funds for the U D A. He realized that public opinion in these areas would turn against the extremists when too much was demanded from ordinary people and owners of small businesses – who knew, moreover, that only a small fraction of what they gave ever went to finance the 'cause'.

The killings of Boyd and Spence in August – both Protestants – by Protestants, can be seen in this context. The conflict between the elements in the Protestant community – the one which was strictly political in outlook, the other more closely resembling the Mafia – was to reappear from time to time, often with a direct bearing on the assassinations.

*Harding Smith is discussed more fully on pp. 146–9, and in Chapter 14.

7. Two Catholics killed for every Protestant: September and October

As we have seen, in the preceding months when the number of assassinations had risen rapidly, almost as many Protestants were killed as Catholics. In August, nine Catholics were killed and five Protestants. Of the five Protestants, Spence and Boyd were executed by Protestant extremists. In the months that were to follow the assassinations continued, but instead of the victims averaging out more or less evenly, there were to be slightly more than two Catholics killed for every Protestant.

September began as a quiet month for assassinations. There were none until the end of the first week, when there were two, and there were to be no more for another week after that. As in the past, those responsible for the killings appear to have been inactive. When they resumed their activities, it was the IRA who struck first.

Samuel Boyde, 20, a Protestant who became a Roman Catholic, was a well-known footballer in Northern Ireland. He played as outside left for Irish League club Glenavon, and lived in the Springfield Road, in the Lower Falls. On Wednesday 6 September his body was found at 7·30 p.m. in a deserted alley behind Celtic Park not far from where he lived in the Falls. He had been shot in the head, killed by the Provisional IRA after a kangaroo court had passed sentence on him as an informer. Weeks before his death he had been remanded on bail at Belfast Magistrate's Court on a hijacking charge. The police were looking for other people connected with the charge.

It was highly unusual for a magistrate to grant bail on such a charge at this time. But neither the Crown nor the investigating police officers opposed bail in the Boyde case. This brought him under immediate suspicion in IRA circles. It was believed that Boyde's freedom had been gained in return for information on the others involved. This sealed his fate. After the IRA court had passed sentence, Boyde was taken to near-by Celtic Park, where he had once played football, and was given the standard execution. A telephone call to the Royal Victoria Hospital for an ambulance for an injured man brought detectives and soldiers to the scene, only to find that the injured man was quite dead. No death notices appeared in the *Irish News* for Boyde from the IRA, though he was known to be a Provisional – a clear sign that he was the recipient of the IRA's form of justice.

On the same night that Boyde was killed, a Protestant, William Moore, 20, of Highcairn Drive, East Belfast, was shot dead by a sniper as he walked along Castlereagh Road, East Belfast, with a friend. Moore was hit in the head by a single bullet, but there were conflicting reports on how the shooting took place. One report suggested that the victim had been shot from a passing car, while another claimed that the fatal shot had come from the near-by Mountpottinger Road, in the Catholic Short Strand. At whose door responsibility is to be laid is not clear. But if the shot did come from the Short Strand, it could only have been the work of the IRA.

Though the week that followed did not contain any assassinations, it certainly was not free of violence for Northern Ireland. This week saw the Protestant paramilitary organizations in open conflict with the British Army. This may possibly explain the absence of killings. The IRA were no doubt content to see such a state of affairs, and could afford to watch its two main enemies attacking each other.

The evening that Boyde and Moore were killed, trouble broke out in the Shankill Road, unconnected with these killings. At the heart of the troubles lay the Parachute Regiment – one of the crack units in the British Army. The Paras were sent into the Shankill shortly before, and, according to the local people immediately adopted a 'get tough' policy. This did not go down well with the loyalist population, who felt they were being treated in exactly the same way as the Catholics – as indeed they were.*

*There is a story that dates from about this time about the British commander of land forces in Northern Ireland, General Ford, who is

During the night of Thursday 7 September, the UDA in the Shankill brought out their guns and opened up on the Army. The situation in the area was described in the *Belfast Telegraph* as 'at boiling point'. A number of civilians were killed in the exchanges and others were wounded before the situation returned to normal. But the UDA could console itself that it had made its point to the authorities. The loyalists were prepared if need be to take on the British Army if they felt threatened by it. The next month in East Belfast, when similar disturbances broke out, two Protestants were killed when an Army vehicle crushed them against a wall. The UDA spokesman, Tommy Herron, issued a formal declaration of war against the Army. The declaration was rescinded within forty-eight hours, but it only served to underline a change in the political situation in Ulster. The honeymoon between the Protestant militants and the Army had ended, just as that between the Army and the Catholics – who had greeted them with tea and sandwiches in 1969 – had earlier ended. In the Shankill in September, people were ruefully remarking that the complaints of the Catholics about the paratroops after Bloody Sunday in Londonderry had not been without foundation.

But the Army had also made its point. There was to be no turning the blind eye to Protestant extremism any more. Fighting a war on two fronts is every military man's nightmare. In the early stages of the Ulster crisis, the Army had tended to concentrate its attention on the threat from the Catholic community in the form of the IRA. This had been wise and practicable so long as the Protestants did not themselves go on the offensive against the Catholics. But once the Protestant backlash emerged with real teeth to it, no matter how much it disliked the idea, the Army was forced to deal with the threat from the Protestants too. The twin threats to peace and stability from the extremists in both communities caused the Army concern, but there was some satisfaction for it in the new situation. At least now soldiers were

alleged to have asked a soldier whether he would be prepared to fire on Protestants. 'Just so long as they're Irish, sir,' the soldier is supposed to have replied.

no longer in the position of not knowing who was the enemy. The Protestant extremists had made it easy – everyone in Ulster was a potential enemy to the average soldier 'just so long as they're Irish'.

The September assassinations resumed a week later when on Wednesday 13 September a man was shot down in a bar in the Springfield Road. The Springfield Road is a continuation of the Grosvenor Road and crosses the Falls area till it joins Monagh Road in the Upper Falls at Whiterock. However, about half way along its length the Protestant West Circular Road runs into it, at the edge of Woodvale, and this border-zone between the two heart-lands of the two rival communities had been a source of much tension. The West Circular Road also affords easy access into and out of both areas for the extremists of either camp. The Catholic-owned Divis Castle bar was situated in this zone.

On the night in question, two young men from the Shankill drove down the West Circular Road into the Springfield Road in a car which had been hijacked earlier in the day. They were armed with submachine-guns, and they burst into the Divis Castle and pumped five bullets into Patrick Doyle, 19, the son of the owner. Doyle died later in hospital.

This killing was the latest and most serious act of aggression aimed at the bar by Protestant extremists. One month earlier a 50-lb bomb had been left in the bar, but a barman had carried it outside and the bar had not been damaged. The Doyle family had been subject to a calculated campaign aimed at forcing them to leave the area. But they had resisted this intimidation. The Divis Castle was their livelihood, and they were not going to leave it without a fight. The killers would appear to have singled out Peter Doyle in particular, as they did not shoot anyone else in the bar at the time.

The killing was symptomatic of the attitudes that were prevalent in Northern Ireland at the time. A favourite slogan among many people on both sides of the fence during the Troubles had been 'Get out or get burnt or shot out.' Those unfortunate enough to find themselves in areas dominated by the other side were often faced with this stark choice – to leave

121

Whiteboy style' intimidation

behind all their possessions, houses and businesses, or to risk injury or death. The Doyle family had paid the full penalty for remaining in the face of intimidation.

In the weeks that followed this killing, the IRA continued its campaign of bombings of shops and factories, and its killings of members of the security forces. The Protestants also stepped up their campaign. The day after the Doyle killing, on Thursday 14 September, a 200-lb bomb was left in a parked car at the Imperial Hotel in the Cliftonville Road. The hotel was known to be the frequent haunt of IRA men and their sympathizers, who often sang republican songs in the bars and on leaving. But this was not an exclusively Catholic area. It was mixed, and such happenings could not and did not go unnoticed in certain quarters. Their answer was left in the car in the car-park this night. As luck would have it, the car was noticed, and the hotel was evacuated before a huge blast destroyed the building and caused extensive damage to a near-by nursing home and old people's home.

Several hotel customers caught in the building suffered minor cuts and bruises, but a man driving past the building at the time of the blast was killed. The man, a Protestant, was engulfed in a ball of fire immediately and had no chance to escape. His charred body was found in the vehicle after the car had burnt itself out. The police and Army on the scene busied themselves with the living – the old and the infirm from the near-by homes who were suffering from shock, cuts, and bruises. One of the injured, a 43-year-old woman who had been helping to evacuate the hotel when the bomb went off, died two days later in hospital. Two more victims of the campaign. And to these was added a third. An elderly Protestant spinster who had been in the old people's home died of shock. The three victims of the blast were: Andrew McKibben, 28, of Sunningdale Gardens; Mrs Anne Murry, 53, of Cliftonville Park Avenue; and Miss Martha Smilie, 91.

The car used in the bombing had been hijacked earlier that night on the Shankill Road. The owner was forced at gunpoint to drive into side-streets in the area to a house where three men were waiting. He was taken to a room in the house with no lighting where he was told that he was free to go, but that if he reported his car missing before 9·00 the next morning, he would be dealt with. He obeyed, walked out of the house and called a taxi which took him home. That night he went to bed and slept while a few miles away his car was used to bomb the Imperial Hotel and kill three people. In the morning he told the police as instructed. This shows the degree of power the extremists wielded in their areas. It puts in its proper place also the degree to which the security forces were unable to guarantee the safety of ordinary citizens such as the car-owner in this case. He had little doubt that the men who took his car were both willing and able – '*volens et valens*' – to kill him if he disobeyed their instructions. He obeyed and was safe to sleep in his bed that night and for succeeding nights.

At this time tension was on the increase in Belfast. On Saturday 16 September, 7,000 masked and uniformed UDA and UVF men marched through the city centre in a massive show of strength. By Thursday 21 September, it was being widely predicted that internment without trial for terrorists would be phased out in the immediate future. 'INTERNMENT – THE END IS IN SIGHT' was the page-one headline in the *Belfast Telegraph* that Friday. Such a change in policy would hardly have been welcomed in the Protestant areas.

The previous day in the town of Larne on the Antrim coast, 3,000 UVF men, dressed in black leather coats, sunglasses, and black berets, marched at the funeral of a man killed two nights earlier in fierce rioting in the town. The dead man, Sinclair Johnston, 27, a Protestant of Wellington Green, was shot by troops during an attack by Protestants on a small Roman Catholic housing estate in the centre of the Protestant town. Overwhelmingly outnumbered by the surrounding Protestants, the Roman Catholics looked at one stage in the riot to be in danger of being swamped by their attackers, until the Army and police intervened to head off the trouble. The death of Johnston occurred at this point. But Sinclair Johnston was not just a member of the UVF. He was the intelligence officer of the East Antrim Brigade. His death was not an action likely to soften the hearts of the UVF towards the security forces nor, indeed, towards the Roman Catholic population.

That night in Belfast Protestant extremists killed a middle-aged Roman Catholic. William Mathews, 50, lived in the Lower Falls in Divis Towers. He was a bachelor, and was an insignificant little grey-haired man who took no interest in politics. He took a drink, and this probably cost him his life. He left his home in the early hours of the evening to go to a bar and never returned. He was found the following morning dumped on the Glencairn Estate. He had been stabbed in the back and the chest, and the body showed signs of torture. It was a killing similar to that of Francis Arthurs in July who was dumped in Liffey Street, except that after his torture with the knife, Arthurs had been shot.

Four days later, on Tuesday 26 September, another Catholic was murdered. Paul McCartan, 52, of Park Avenue, East Belfast, was found shot through the head beside the Connswater river in East Belfast. This was the first killing in East Belfast for a number of weeks. Three Protestant men were later charged with this killing.

The following evening, An army plain-clothes patrol shot two Roman Catholic youths in the St James area of the Falls, killing one of the youths and seriously wounding the other. This killing was to create much public outrage in the Catholic community. The circumstances surrounding the death of the youth Daniel Rooney, 18, of Rodney Parade, will be dealt with in a separate section on Army involvement in Chapter 15.

That same night two more victims were added to the assassins' list, one Protestant and one Catholic. Alexander Greer, 54, of Leslie Street, Legoniel, a suburb of Belfast on the road to the airport, was standing with a Catholic friend when gunmen opened fire at close range. Both men were hit, Greer fatally. Like the Orr brothers these two men would have been regarded as legitimate targets by extremists on both sides. Extremism does not tolerate friendships that cross Northern Ireland's sectarian boundaries.

At almost the same time, in the Upper Falls at Flush Lane,

not far from the Divis Castle bar where Doyle had been killed, a Roman Catholic schoolboy was shot dead. James Joseph Boyle, 17, of Glen Road, was not involved with either wing of the IRA. He was shot by a single bullet and his body was found near a polluted stream, the Flush, behind the Divis Castle, close to the Protestant West Circular Road and Woodvale.

The following evening, Thursday 28 September, a young Protestant was shot dead at the door of his house in East Belfast. William Edward Pavis, 32, of Glenvarlock Street, East Belfast, was on parole from prison where he was serving a sentence for having firearms illegally. He was staying with his parents and was due to return to prison the following day. He had been convicted in February 1971 of possessing a Luger pistol and ammunition. At the trial a Crown witness had said of Pavis that he was 'willing to sell guns to anyone'. This was his undoing. Pavis is something of an enigma. He had an IQ in the region of 140 and 150 – more than most of us have. He was obsessed with guns. After his death he was described in the press as an 'arms dealer'. This was not true, but it referred to a curious matter that had brought Pavis before the courts with a Roman Catholic priest.

Pavis played the drums, and in the 1960s he had played regularly at weekends at the Clonard Hall in the Roman Catholic Lower Falls at dances. There he had become friendly with Fr Eamon McGorrian, the local curate. The two discovered a common passion for guns and went out shooting together. On one of these trips the priest is alleged to have asked Pavis if he could get him any guns, and Pavis alleged to have said that he could. The result of this bizarre arrangement between a Roman Catholic priest and a Protestant from East Belfast was that eventually the police got to hear of the deal. Pavis was sentenced to three years for illegal possession of arms and ammunition, but Fr McGorrian was fined only £20 on a charge of possessing an unlicensed shotgun in February 1971.

Shortly before his death Pavis was sent by a magistrate to Purdysburn Mental Hospital. The reason for this was that he was said to be suffering from 'delusions' that men were out to kill him. Armed guards were secretly placed in the grounds of the hospital to protect Pavis, who was regarded by the police as a potential source of valuable information on illegal arms shipments. The medical authorities at the hospital insisted that Pavis was not mentally sick and sent him back to the magistrates with a certificate stating that he was fit to undergo his prison sentence.

On the evening of his death, two young men on a motorcycle arrived at Pavis's home. One stayed outside while the other went into the house and spoke to Pavis. The two apparently knew each other because they had a long conversation. Pavis escorted his visitor to the front garden gate where the youth drew a pistol and shot him at close range. The killers escaped on the motorcycle.

The motorcycle used in the Pavis killing was stolen on the Ballygomartin Road near the Glencairn Estate just before the youths called at the Pavis home. Several months later, another cycle was stolen in the same area and used in the murder of a Roman Catholic on the Shore Road, James Joseph Reynolds. Two men were later charged with the Pavis killing: Mervyn John Connor, 20, of Mayo Street, and Leonard Thompson Murphy, 21, from Percy Street, both from the Shankill Road area. Murphy was alleged to have fired the fatal shots, and Connor was said to have been the driver of the motorcycle.

On 24 April 1973, while still in custody awaiting trial, Connor died in mysterious circumstances. Warders who rushed to his cell early that morning in Crumlin Road gaol found him unconscious. Despite immediate attempts to revive him with mouth-to-mouth resuscitation and a cardiac machine, Connor died. A post mortem examination the following day failed to reveal the cause of death, but a part of the stomach was sent to forensic experts. The cause of death has at the time of writing (August 1973) yet to be made public, but the authors have been informed by an impeccable source that it was cyanide poisoning.

On 18 June, Murphy went on trial charged with the murder of Pavis. Several Crown witnesses identified him as the man who had shot the deceased. But the jury also heard that at an earlier identification parade in a police station, Murphy had created a scene. He had stepped out of line and complained that he did not want to take part in the identity parade. It was in this atmosphere that the witnesses had picked out the accused. Thus a seed of doubt existed that could bear fruit in the minds of the jury. Was Murphy chosen by the witnesses because he was the killer, or because he had stood out at the identity parade?

Murphy claimed in court that he had never known Pavis, but admitted that he was unable to give a statement of his movements on the night of the killing. He said it was possible he had been working somewhere, but he could not remember. At that time he often helped a number of car engineers whom he knew well. On this defence, and in the face of the sworn evidence of eye-witnesses who testified that he was the man who pulled the trigger on Pavis, Murphy – the Protestant with a Catholic name – was acquitted.

Murphy's trial ended on 20 June, late in the evening. When the verdict of the jury was returned, the judge told Murphy that he was a free man and could go. As he left the dock, Murphy was met by police officers who arrested him under the Special Powers (NI) Act. He is now in detention, and can be held as such indefinitely, without any charge being laid against him, or any further court hearing.

The last day of September saw the killing of a Roman Catholic student who lived in a mixed area at the top of the Crumlin Road. Francis Peter Lane, 23, of the Crumlin Road, had just finished his studies in medicine at the Queen's University, Belfast. His death was almost certainly linked to the activities of his father. Dr Patrick Lane was a celebrated surgeon at the Mater Hospital in the Crumlin Road. Dr Lane was an ex-member of the British Army Medical Corps and served in France and the Middle East with distinction during World War II. He also spent fourteen years in the Colonial Service. But what marred his record, or verified his integrity, depending on one's point of view, was that Dr Lane had been an outspoken critic of the British Army's techniques of interrogation in Northern Ireland.

After internment began in 1971 he attempted to raise the

medical aspects of the treatment of men at the Army interrogation centre in Holywood and at Long Kesh before the British Medical Council.* His attempts failed but he continually reprimanded medical men and Army doctors in the province for their silence, and in so doing he found his name frequently in the press. In addition, he was an excellent surgeon, but he continued his hostility to the military in this area too. He was responsible for the treatment in the Mater Hospital of men with gunshot wounds – both IRA and UVF – whom he invariably reported as suffering from some other ailment, thereby breaking the law that stated that all such injuries must be reported. He refused the police and Army access to such patients for questioning on innumerable occasions.

But perhaps his worst offence in the eyes of loyalists was that he was one of the main people behind the case of the Government of the Irish Republic at the Commission on Human Rights at Strasburg. This case was initiated by the Eire Government in 1971, and alleged that the rule of law had ceased to operate in Northern Ireland and that British troops there were behaving in a manner that violated the basic human rights of many of the inhabitants.

Dr Lane was a sincere but eccentric man in the context of Northern Ireland at the time. Living as he did in probably the worst flashpoint in the whole province – the Crumlin Road – his activities were an open invitation for trouble. The surprise was that trouble, when it came, came not to the doctor himself but to his son.

On the night of Saturday 30 September, Peter Lane had been watching television with his parents when he decided to go out. He changed his clothes and his parents assumed he was going to visit a friend next door. When his son did not return home before midnight, Dr Lane was not unduly worried. Peter had

---

*The report of the Compton Commission on allegations of brutality towards prisoners stated that though they were hooded and subjected to continual noise like that of a generator, deprived of food for long periods, and made to stand with their arms and legs outstretched against a wall for long periods, this might constitute 'ill treatment' but it was not 'brutality'.

often been out late to dances, and he usually stayed till the early hours when he visited the people next door.

But the next-door neighbour whom Peter used to visit, Henry Taylor, did not see him that evening. At 3·00 the following morning, Peter Lane's body was found in a derelict house on the Protestant Glencairn Estate – a ten-minute journey on foot from his home in the Crumlin Road. A Land-rover patrol from the Parachute Regiment had been on duty at Glencairn that night. An observant corporal in this patrol had noticed a red Vauxhall Victor car go down Glencairn Road past him after midnight. He took the number of the vehicle, but it has never been traced.

The car had been travelling from the direction of the derelict house in which the body was later found. The corporal later explained that at the time the car passed him he had no reason to stop it, and so had let it pass. A UDA vigilante patrol subsequently approached the soldiers and told them they had heard a shot in the vicinity of the derelict house. After a search, Lane's body was revealed. He had been shot once in the head by a 9 mm. pistol. The fatal bullet had travelled down through the head and neck and lodged in the chest, indicating that he had been kneeling at the time of death. His head and hands bore the marks of a severe beating, which the State Pathologist later suggested could have been caused by pistol-whipping. No evidence exists to explain how Lane came to get to Glencairn from his home the night of his death. No clues were found by the police. The Glencairn Estate had claimed yet another victim.

The night before Lane vanished, a company of Paratroopers and a police task-force were placed in hiding around the Protestant estate. Police believed that the killings taking place here were possibly the work of a single group. They also believed that if they lay in wait long enough they could catch the killers in operation. For one week the estate was staked out by scores of troops and police after dark. But nothing happened, and the manpower involved could not be justified. The troops were needed elsewhere in the city, and the day Lane was killed the operation was called off, and only the usual patrols were left at Glencairn.

One reaction to the Lane killing in police circles was to see it as bad luck. If only the troops had been kept there for a further twenty-four hours the Glencairn killings could have been cracked. But this is probably to confuse cause with effect. The police and Army were not dealing with an ordinary hunt for killers. This has to be said, even though it is obvious, because the standard detection procedures in this situation were not adequate to deal with it. The massive influx of manpower, all of it uniformed, might have proved successful in another part of the United Kingdom where the authorities were seeking a lone killer, or one with a few accomplices. But this was not the case in Glencairn. The authorities were not dealing with lone killers, but a highly organized paramilitary body – a body which patrolled the area in uniform, and which had at least the tacit support of virtually everyone in Glencairn. The killers knew exactly when the police and Army moved in, and they knew when they moved out. They were, understandably enough, not disposed to carry out further assassinations while the security forces were encamped throughout the area, but once these forces evacuated, they went into action once again.

The only way Peter Lane's death in Glencairn might have been averted would have been for the police and Army to have encamped there indefinitely – something quite impracticable from the military point of view. But even then, this probably would not have been sufficient to save Lane's life. The killers would have found another dumping-ground near by. The climate of opinion was such in most Protestant areas that people were reluctant to talk to the police about the killings, whether from fear or from political conviction. The Scotland Yard Officers who returned home in the autumn of 1971 complaining about the lack of assistance from the Roman Catholic community about the Kavanagh killing, should think themselves fortunate they were not faced with the enormous task of their colleagues in the RUC. These men had over 100 killings to solve from the beginning of the Troubles. They knew that within both communities there were thousands, probably tens of thousands, of people with vital information on the killings. And they also knew that there was little or no chance of these people coming forward to assist the police while the existing security situation continued.

We have seen that the courts of law were often unable to convict in Northern Ireland. This failing, that of a peacetime legal system trying to cope with a state of civil war and armed insurrection, was recognized in the report of the Diplock Commission. It recommended that the existing system should be replaced for the duration of the Troubles by one in which the jury should be dispensed with, and a single judge should be responsible for the determination of both law and fact. In a normal free society such a system would be unacceptable. But Northern Ireland during the Troubles was not a normal free society. It was a society at war with itself, and a drastic situation called for drastic measures.

So, too, with the system of law enforcement. The failure to trap the killers using the Glencairn Estate as a dumping ground underlines the difficulties the security forces had in their attempts to track down the killers. For one week they had virtually unlimited manpower, and yet could do nothing. The killers watched and waited till the Army and police went away before resuming their activity.

October began with the death of a Roman Catholic. William Bonner, 37, of Iveagh Street in the Falls area, was shot dead in a pigeon club, yards from where he lived, by the Provisional IRA. Pigeon racing and breeding is a major occupation and hobby for countless thousands of men on both sides of the fence in Northern Ireland. With the onset of the Troubles, the pigeon clubs gained an added popularity, which may be due in part to the fact that drinks were sold in these establishments without recourse to the licensing laws.

On the night of Monday 2 October Bonner was in the Iveagh Street pigeon club when a car drew up outside containing several masked men. There were a number of young boys outside the club but the masked men told them they would not be hurt. Two men then went into the club carrying guns, while a third stayed at the car.

Inside the club there were about twenty men enjoying a drink when the gunmen entered. They lined everyone up against a wall with their faces towards the wall, and walked along the line of men till they came to Bonner. One of the men then put his gun to Bonner's head and shot him at point-blank range. The two men then ran to their car and made off.

Bonner's was not a random killing. The killers knew exactly who they were looking for. Earlier in the year Bonner's son, a member of the Provisional IRA, had been shot dead by the army when he failed to stop his car at a military check-point. Bonner blamed the Provisionals for his son's death. He was, as we shall see, a man who was not by temperament prone to restrain his emotions. The Provisionals regarded him as too talkative, and took seriously his threats to give information about their activities to the security forces – he was considered unreliable, and had to go.

Immediately after the shooting, however, the residents of Iveagh Street, and the Provisional IRA in the area, claimed that those responsible for Bonner's death were members of an Army undercover SAS (Special Air Services) murder squad. The substance of this allegation rested on an incident that had taken place earlier in the week. The Army had carried out a search of Bonner's home. Such searches, it must be added, are a frequent occurrence in areas such as the Lower Falls. The Army is not renowned for its respect of privacy or personal possessions in such searches. Nor are the residents in these areas renowned for their loyalty towards the British Crown or for adamantly refusing to allow the IRA to use their homes to store arms.

Neighbours after his death said that at the Army search earlier that week Bonner had been very uncooperative and had claimed he was being harassed. No doubt the soldiers who conducted the search were aware of the political affiliations of Bonner's dead son. Bonner is alleged to have challenged the soldiers to a fist-fight in the street, and one of the soldiers is supposed to have replied: 'We will get you, Bonner.'

On this rests the claim that Bonner was killed by the Army. For their own reasons the local Provisionals helped fan the emotions of the local people on this. But there is hardly any doubt that the responsibility for Bonner's death lies with the Provos. Bonner was not important enough for the Army to have bothered with him. Abuse from people whose houses are being searched is an occupational hazard for the British Army in Northern Ireland – an occupational hazard infinitely preferable to being shot at and bombed. The only organization Bonner had ever belonged to was his pigeon club. After the death of his son he became a broken man. He began to drink heavily – a fact that shocked the neighbours who had previously known him as a quiet and inoffensive man.

Bonner certainly had no love for the Army, and his challenge to the soldiers for a fist-fight was no doubt in some way connected with his son's death. He is very unlikely, feeling as he did, to have given information to them. But the Provisional IRA are not a body famous for giving people the benefit of the doubt. Bonner had vented his misery on both the Army and the Provos – the two groups he held responsible for his son's death. The Army had better things to do than pay attention to Bonner. The Provos took him seriously.

The Provisional IRA were also responsible for the death the following night of a Protestant, Geoffrey Walter Hamilton, 23, in the Lower Falls. Hamilton was a native of County London-derry who lived in a quiet middle-class residential area near the Queen's University. He had lodgings in Stranmills Road, and was a bank clerk. However, it was his hobby of photography that was to cause his death.

Shortly before his death Hamilton had become friendly with a number of American newsmen who were in Belfast to cover the Troubles. On the evening of Tuesday 3 October, a Catholic bar on the Grosvenor Road in the Lower Falls, Lynch's Bar, was bombed by Protestant extremists. The newsmen went to the scene of the bombing, and Hamilton accompanied them. Hamilton drove his friends to the bar, situated in the heart of an IRA stronghold. He became separated from the Americans, and his body was found the next morning in near-by Murdoch Street. He had been badly beaten and then shot four times through the head and neck. Two brothers were later charged with conspiracy to murder Hamilton, and with kidnapping one of the Americans. Both were acquitted of these charges on the direction of the judge. However, much of the evidence at the trial of Daniel Martin Butler, 21, and Anthony Gerard Butler, 20, of Venice Street, off the Grosvenor Road, indicated what happened to Hamilton after he was separated from his friends.

Robert Moore Jones, an American journalist, told how he and two colleagues had met Hamilton by chance in a bar in Belfast's city centre. On the night of the explosion he had driven them to the bombed bar at Distillery Street on the Grosvenor Road. The Americans left the car, and when they returned later Hamilton was missing and a group of young men were standing near by. Jones alleged that one of these men, whom he identified as Daniel Butler, said: 'Hamilton is being taken care of.'

Jones said that one of the other men tried to start the car with a bunch of ignition keys, and when this failed the group began to push the vehicle. He claimed Daniel Butler then said to him: 'We will show you where Hamilton is.' Jones was then taken to a house in near-by Venice Street by Butler and another man dressed in a leather jacket. When they entered the house, Jones claimed he was confronted by Anthony Butler who was carrying an Armalite rifle, which he pointed at Jones's head. He was then taken into a room where he was interrogated. His captors accused him of working for British Army intelligence, and at one point in the questioning he said a woman entered the room and identified him using the words: 'Yes, that's the bastard. I saw him with the troops taking photographs.' Jones thought he was going to be shot. The man in the leather jacket came into the room and took the Armalite rifle away with him. Jones at this stage told his captors: 'If you think I took a film of you, I will give it to you.' The other two Americans were also picked up and brought to the house in Venice Street. But all three were released in the early hours of the morning.

The Americans almost certainly owed their lives to the documentation they carried on their persons verifying that they were pressmen. The IRA is very adept at propaganda, and is well aware of the power of the press, particularly the foreign and American press. Once satisfied as to the real identity of the newsmen, they were prepared to let them go.

But Hamilton was a different matter. He was not a journalist, and consequently did not carry any press documentation. It was a common practice at such incidents as the Lynch Bar explosion for the Army to photograph the people in the vicinity. These photographs were later used to pick out and identify known terrorists in the area. Hamilton was regarded by the IRA as an Army spy. The authors have no evidence to substantiate this, but it is plausible that he was a spy and had struck up a friendship with the Americans for this purpose. Certainly, to venture into the Lower Falls late at night with a camera, and to proceed to take photographs of the people there, was an act of consummate folly that a man of normal intelligence in Belfast would not have undertaken. The explanation that he was a keen photographer is not convincing, and it certainly failed to convince the Provisional IRA who, as mentioned earlier, were not prone to give the benefit of the doubt to those they suspected as spies or informers. If Hamilton's story was genuine, he was a very foolish man indeed, and such people who dabbled in the serious business of the Troubles in Northern Ireland at this time had a very short life-span.

When the two other American journalists were having their ducuments checked by an unknown man he told them not to worry about Hamilton, and said: 'He has been taken care of.' Before all three were released, the man in the leather jacket said: 'If you want to find the body, go down that street, to the first small street, and turn left.' Police and troops followed these directions and found Hamilton's body, as predicted, in Murdoch Street.

At their trial, the Butler brothers had the services of Desmond Boal Q.C. Boal, a Protestant, had been a Stormont MP and a co-founder with the Rev. Ian Paisley of the Democratic Unionist Party. He was considered the party's most powerful political thinker. He was also the most brilliant barrister in Northern Ireland, and probably in the whole of the United Kingdom.

Despite his strong political convictions, his services were used with equal effect for extremists on both sides of the sectarian fence. His services were, and still are, much sought after.

Mid-way through the trial, Boal made a legal submission to Mr Justice McDermott that on the basis of the prosecution evidence there was no case to answer on the charges of kidnapping and conspiracy to murder. He claimed that it had not been proven that there had been prior knowledge and agreement on the part of the two accused to kill Hamilton. He further claimed that if there were interlinking activity between the two groups of men – the one which had held the American photographer (to which the accused admitted he belonged), and the other which had taken Hamilton – this activity in itself did not amount to conspiracy to murder. The words Daniel Butler had used to the American, that Hamilton 'was being taken care of', were not to be construed to have a sinister meaning.

The judge accepted the submissions and said: 'I am not satisfied there was evidence to prove that there was prior knowledge and agreement on the killing.' He also dismissed the kidnapping charges, and directed the jury to acquit the accused on both charges.

Both men, however, still faced charges arising out of the incident of possession of an Armalite rifle with intent to endanger life and of having it with the intention of imprisoning Jones. Anthony Butler denied the charge of possessing the Armalite with intent to endanger life, but admitted possessing it with intent to imprison Jones. Daniel Butler denied both charges.

Daniel Butler told the court that he did not know the man in not leather jacket who was with his brother after the explosion in Lynch's bar. He saw Jones later in a house in Venice Street in the custody of the man and his brother, who had an Armalite. He claimed that he tried to mediate on behalf of the American, but was told by the unknown man to 'mind my own business'.

Both men were found guilty of the charge of possessing an Armalite with intent to imprison Jones. Daniel Butler was found not guilty of possessing the Armalite with intent to endanger life, but his brother Anthony was found guilty on this charge.

Anthony Butler was sentenced to eight years in gaol for his part in the incident and his brother David was given five years. The Armalite rifle referred to in the charges was never produced in court as it had not been found. The man in the leather jacket was also never traced. At the time of writing, no further charges in the Hamilton killing have been brought against anyone.

The evening following the Hamilton killing, Wednesday 4 October, Protestant extremists in East Belfast killed another Catholic. James McCartan, 21, of Holywood, was found at some waste ground at Mersey Street, beside the Connswater river, at 1·30 in the morning. McCartan was a barman and may have been followed as he made his way home after work. He was found bound and hooded, and had been shot through the head. Three young Protestants were later charged with this killing. They were also charged with that of Paul McCartan on 26 September and Philip Fay on 18 August – both in East Belfast – but these charges were later dropped.

A week after the killing of James McCartan, the IRA struck again. The target was a Roman Catholic magistrate, Mr William Staunton, 46. Staunton lived in the middle-class Deramone Park, in the Malone area of Belfast – an exclusive and expensive neighbourhood that had seen nothing of the Troubles. Staunton had been Crown Prosecutor before he became a magistrate in 1971. He was known as a magistrate, and earlier as Crown Prosecutor, to take a particularly hard line towards IRA men who came before him. This was taken exception to by the IRA, principally because Staunton was a Catholic, and consequently, in their eyes, a traitor to his own kind. A few weeks before he was shot, Staunton was bitterly attacked in the *Republican News*, an organ of the Provisional IRA.

He regularly drove his two young daughters to their convent school in the Falls Road every morning. He made his last trip with them the morning of Wednesday 11 October. Two youths on a motorcycle drove up to Staunton's Citroën car as he neared his daughter's school. The pillion passenger opened fire on the magistrate from close range, hitting him in the head and body. Fortunately for the lives of the two girls in the car, Staunton remained conscious long enough to pull the car into the kerb and stop. He then collapsed over the steering wheel. He was rushed to the Royal Victoria Hospital, and put in the intensive care unit. He remained alive for several weeks, but he never regained consciousness, and he died early in 1973. This killing was well planned. The killers must have known that Staunton took the same route every day, and were lying in wait for him.

Three days later, Protestant assassins in East Belfast killed a young Roman Catholic. Terence Maguire, 23, who lived in Andersonstown, had worked in East Belfast on the Castlereagh Road since before the Troubles began. Like many Catholics in similar positions who had to cross the sectarian boundaries to go to work, Maguire would have been known to the extremists in the area where he worked. He was last heard of on the evening of Friday 13 October when he left his work to go home with his weekly wage packet. His half-naked body was found the following morning at near-by Clandeboye Street in an alley. His body bore the marks of a considerable beating. A woman living in the area told the press that the alley where Maguire was found was regularly patrolled by UDA vigilantes.

The night Maguire's body was found, two more Catholics were shot dead in an off-licence on the corner of Tate's Avenue and the Lisburn Road. Thomas Marron, 59, of Gransha Avenue, and Leo John Duffy, 45, of London Street, were employees at the Catholic-owned off-licence. On the night of Saturday 14 October two young men wearing balaclava helmets and combat jackets burst in. In the shop at the time was a 21-year-old student who was a customer. The intruders ordered the three to lie on the floor behind the counter. They then walked up to the victims and shot each of them several times with .38 and .45 revolvers. They then rifled the cash register, and at first the motive for the killings was thought to have been robbery. But masked robbers would not have needed to shoot three men in order to rob a till, and a sectarian motive appears more likely.

The student recovered from his wounds, but Duffy died instantly and Marron two days later. The killings were carried out in a professional manner. This was not the first attack at the store. On Saturday 5 August the owner's son had been shot in an identical attack. He had been a member of the Catholic-dominated Civil Rights Association. The store was situated on the fringe of a predominantly Protestant area, close to the so-called "Village" – a hard-line Protestant area in which a number of assassination squads were based. The activities of the owner's son, plus the fact that here was a Catholic-owned off-licence continuing to operate in an area close to Protestant areas, would have been sufficient motive for the Protestant extremists. The store was later destroyed by a bomb.

On Tuesday 24 October the assassins moved their activities outside Belfast to the border, when two Roman Catholics were killed in retaliation for the death of a UDR man a few days previously in the area. Michael Naan, 35, was the owner of a farm a short distance from the border with County Cavan in Fermanagh. Andrew Murray, 25, was a farm labourer who worked for Naan. The farm was situated two miles from the spot where Private John Bell of the UDR had been shot dead by the IRA earlier in the week.

When police were called to the Naan farm on the morning of 24 October, they found the owner lying dead in a byre where he had been tending to his animals. That of Murray was in a haystack. Both men appeared to have been stabbed to death with a pitchfork, but an autopsy later revealed that the wounds could only have been inflicted by a double-edged knife – the weapon used in the Madden and Arthurs killings.

8. A brief pause, but the killings continue: November and December

The new month that opened, November, was to be the quietest month for assassinations since April, with only eight people killed. All of this month's victims were Roman Catholics. But for the first ten days there were no killings at all, and, as often in the past, people began to wonder whether the assassins had finally hung up their guns. They were answered on Saturday 11 November when a newsagent on the Crumlin Road was shot dead by two men who came into his shop. The victim was Gerard Kelly, 58. The white Ford Escort used by the killers was hijacked on the Shankill Road. Kelly's shop was in a flashpoint area, and had been attacked on previous occasions.

On Monday 27 November a Roman Catholic schoolboy was killed on his way to school in a killing reminiscent of that of the magistrate William Staunton the previous month. Rory Gormley and his brother Paul, 17, of Windsor Park, Belfast, were being driven to school by their father with two friends when the car was riddled with bullets as it passed through the Shankill Road. Rory was killed in the attack, his brother was injured, and so too was their father, Peter.

Peter Gormley, 52, was a distinguished ophthalmic surgeon at Belfast's Mater Hospital. But, like his Colleague Dr Lane, he was involved in the Troubles in other ways, being one of the leading lights in an organization called Campaign for Social Justice. Like William Staunton, who had lived in the same area of Belfast Peter Gormley took a regular route to his sons' school every day. This involved crossing the Shankill Road, and his killers, who were not too happy at his activities in the CSJ, were ready and waiting for him on the morning of the attack. However, they failed to kill their target and killed his son instead.

All four boys were wearing the school uniform of the Roman Catholics St Malachy's College, and just before the killers opened fire one of the surviving boys said he heard a shout: 'There's a car full of Taigs.'* Rory Gormley died in his father's arms seconds after the assassins struck. The first person on the scene was a Protestant housewife from near-by Downing Street. She said afterwards that she recognized the religion of the boys immediately by their school uniform, and said: 'That's what I hate about Northern Ireland – the school uniforms.'

A few days after the Gormley killing, a Roman Catholic barman was shot dead as he took a taxi home after his night's work. Gerry Gearon, 22, worked in McGlades public house in Donegal Street – a public house used by journalists from Belfast's three newspapers, *Irish News*, *News Letter*, and *Telegraph*, and situated just behind the *Telegraph* offices, within easy reach of all three newspapers. Gearon had been working in Dublin for several months but returned to his old job in McGlades a few weeks before his death. He lived in the Roman Catholic Ardoyne. He was known to the customers of McGlades as a likable though talkative young man. He held strong republican views and expressed these openly and often in the bar – perhaps too often. He had been warned by pressmen that it was unwise to express such views in public, and the advice was ultimately shown to have been sound.

On the night of Thursday 30 November Gearon left McGlades as usual after closing time. He declined a lift home from a colleague, and walked about two hundred yards to a taxi office in Clifton Street. The office he went to was that of Arkle Taxis. It will be recalled that an earlier victim of the assassins, Gerald Patrick Donnelly, had been a taxi-driver for Arkle. He had been killed by passengers who had asked for a taxi to the Ardoyne the previous April. Gearon's death was to be almost a carbon-copy of this earlier killing.

When Gearon got to the taxi office there were two young men sitting there waiting. The receptionist later said that these men

*'Taig' is a slang word for 'Catholic', used by Protestants in Northern Ireland.

141

had asked for a taxi to Ligoniel. The Ardoyne is on the route to Ligoniel, and when a cab arrived, Gearon and the two men got into it. Gearon sat in the front seat, and the two men in the back.

The driver of the taxi was John Breen, and at the inquest on Gearon in May 1973, he explained what took place next. He said he had driven past Carlisle Circus and along the Crumlin Road only a few hundred yards when one of the men in the back seat appeared about to be sick. He told him to open the window if he was going to be sick, but his companion told him to stop the car. Breen obliged, and the man who was not sick said they would walk and asked how much they owed. Breen saw him fumble in his pockets and assumed he was looking for his money, and turned away. But instead of money, the man was searching for a pistol:

'As I turned away I heard four shots in quick succession. One was fired through the rear door and the others through the front passenger window. I think it was the elder of the two who did the shooting.'

Gearon slumped sideways onto Breen's shoulder with blood gushing from his mouth and head. He was dead by the time he reached hospital at 1·15 a.m. It was not until an hour later that Breen realized that one of the bullets that had hit Gearon had also hit him in the arm.

The Belfast coroner, Mr James Elliot, described the assassination as a 'cold-blooded killing' and said: 'I can see absolutely no reason for the murder. The only reason may be that they heard he was going to the Ardoyne. Of course, his occupation was barman, and they may have known more about him than he knew about them.'

The killing took place within a short distance of the Army post of Belfast's Crumlin Road gaol, but the killers were able to make good their escape quickly through the maze of small side-streets leading off the Crumlin Road into the safety of the Shankill.

A few days after Gearon was killed, assassins struck in East Belfast in a killing that was reminiscent of that of the Roman

Catholic UDR man, Henry Russell, in July. The victim of this latest killing was a Roman Catholic, Patrick Benstead, 23, of Kilmood Street in the Short Strand. At daybreak on the morning of Saturday 2 December, a man walking his dog along Templemore Avenue came across a bundle lying in an alley at Crossley Street. Upon examination the bundle was found to be the badly tortured body of a young man. Police were called, and forensic experts soon came to the conclusion that the dead man had not been murdered where he was found. Death had been caused by a single bullet-wound to the head. The body had probably been dumped from a car shortly before it was discovered. It was found barely 200 yards from the spot where another Roman Catholic, Terence Maguire, had been found the previous month, down the same alley, but at Clandeboye Street. Benstead's body bore the marks of severe torturing. His killers had used a red-hot poker to brand a cross on his back. They had also branded the figure 4, and IRA on him. It is unclear why the figure 4 was used, though it is possible that his killers thought him to be their fourth victim connected with the IRA. Detectives covering the case described it as 'one of the most vicious' killings they had dealt with.

Henry Russell, who was found on 13 July in Larkfield Drive, East Belfast, had also had a cross branded on his back. Both he and Benstead had been 'romper room' victims. The beatings they had received and the torture indicated that a number of people must have been involved in their deaths.

Patrick Benstead had been missing from his home in the Catholic Short Strand area of East Belfast for twelve hours when his body was found. The only thing that is known for certain about his movements that evening is that he got off his bus on the way home from work a few stops before his regular alighting point, which left him in Protestant territory.

Patrick Benstead was a grown man, but he was well below average in intelligence. He was very childish in his manner and speech. He often did the shopping for his family, and enjoyed being trusted with the money for this chore. It may be that his simple nature was in some way responsible for the treatment meted out to him by his killers. He lived in the Short Strand, a hard-line IRA area, and this may have been enough to convince his captors that he possessed vital intelligence for them on the activities of the IRA in that area. Of possibly greater significance, a relative of Benstead's had been involved in an arms trial, and the killers may have assumed that Benstead too was an IRA man. Such, in fact, is a common characteristic in Catholic areas – allegiences to the IRA tend to be family-based rather than individual. Fathers, brothers, and uncles tend to be members together, and so it may not have been such an incorrect assumption for Benstead's killers to have made that their man knew a lot about the IRA in the Short Strand.

Several days later the Provisional IRA in the Short Strand took their revenge for the Benstead killing. The victim was a 32-year-old Protestant man, and he was treated to a degree of torture unusual for an IRA killing. Samuel White lived in the quiet town of Newtownards outside Belfast, and travelled to work through East Belfast every day. On Wednesday 6 December he made the journey for the last time. Shortly before midnight his body was found at Lisbon Street in the Short Strand. He had been shot in the head, which was hooded. But before this he had been stabbed several times in the head and the chest. These wounds were described by a detective as 'horrible gashes'. In addition, White had been badly beaten. In this killing the IRA showed that they too could wield the knife. White's death was a clear message to the men who had killed Benstead. 'What you can do, we can do,' is how a Provisional from the area spelled it out.

The day after White was found, Thursday 7 December, an abandoned car was spotted in a street off the Protestant end and of the Donegal Road near Tate's Avenue. The police and Army were called, but they were cautious in case a large cardboard box in the rear of the mini-traveller contained a bomb. The box did contain a bomb of sorts, but it was not made of explosives – it was a political bomb. An army explosives expert placed a small charge to the rear doors of the car and blew them open. Then a rope was carefully placed round the cardboard box and it was dragged out of the car onto the street. As the box fell from the car it revealed its contents to be a body. On closer examination, the victim was seen to have been killed by a blast from a shotgun fired at close range to the head. Police immediately knew who the victim was. They had already been informed that Ernest 'Duke' Elliot, a Lieutenant-Colonel in the UDA and one of the Protestant paramilitary organization's top men, had been 'kidnapped'.

The previous night Elliot had been kidnapped along with a second man. The morning of the 7th the second man was found wandering along the Protestant Ainsworth Avenue between the Springfield and Shankill Roads. He had been badly beaten. He told police that he and Elliot had been drinking in UDA clubs in the Shankill area the previous night, when they had decided to go to Sandy Row for a drink.

To get to Sandy Row, it was necessary to cross the Lower Falls at Millfield, near the Divis flats complex. According to the story given by Elliot's unnamed companion, he and Elliot had taken the official car of the Woodvale Defence Association – a paramilitary body of which Elliot was a leader. This was the car in which he was found. As they crossed the Lower Falls, they stopped at traffic lights. Three masked men approached the car and produced guns. The man claimed these men were IRA men, who then separated him from Elliot.

But this claim was at the time, and has always ever since, been treated with something slightly more than the utmost scepticism. The whole story is highly implausible. To capture Elliot the IRA men must either have been aware by some prior knowledge that he would be at that particular spot at that particular time – something that would seem to be implicitly ruled out by the mystery man's statement that he and Elliot had decided to go to Sandy Row on the spur of the moment. Or else three masked IRA men were loitering with intent to pick someone up at that spot. Once again, we have to return to the sectarian geography of Belfast. The spot where Elliot was alleged to have come across his captors is one of the most dangerous in the city. After dark, very few law-abiding citizens would have the courage to stop at a red light there, for the junction stood close to both the Lower Falls, heartland of the IRA, and the Protestant Sandy Row, equally solid for the UDA and UVF. If the IRA men had hung around there for very long, it would not have gone unnoticed to local Protestants, and if it was not unnoticed, action would have been taken against the IRA men, because their intentions would have been quite clear. It would also seem quite absurd for us to believe that Elliot, one of the highest-ranking UDA men, would have scrupulously observed a red stop light in such a dangerous spot as the Lower Falls late at night. As well as this, near by was Hastings Street RUC and Army barracks. To have planned to kidnap anybody here would have required a remarkable audacity on the part of the IRA. It could have been done, but it would have required split-second timing – the masked men could not have hung around waiting for their victims, because they would have been spotted. But what makes the whole story most implausible of all is the simple fact that Elliot's companion ever lived to tell the tale. If the IRA killed Elliot – and there can be no doubt but that they most certainly would have done if they had got the chance – why did they release the other man? Perhaps he had 'set up' Elliot in the first place and told the IRA the route they would take? But if this was so, his life-expectancy from the Protestant side would not have been too high – yet he was not harmed by his colleagues. It just made no sense at all for the IRA to kidnap two UDA men, kill one of them and free the other. If this is indeed what happened, the man who escaped enjoyed a privilege similar UDA men in this predicament had not enjoyed before, nor were to do so thereafter.

There is little doubt that Elliot was killed by his own side in the midst of a very serious internal upheaval in the Protestant camp. This upheaval had a name: Charles Harding Smith. Harding Smith had been one of the founders of the UDA. But he had been out of circulation for many months as he stood trial in London on charges involving the smuggling of large quantities of arms into Ulster for the UDA. In December, having been acquitted in England, Harding Smith returned. Exactly what happened next is slightly muddied, but the broad general terms are quite clear. Harding Smith did not like what he saw in the Protestant areas. When he had been arrested he had left behind a large paramilitary organization, political in motivation, and possessing genuine grassroots' support of the local inhabitants in the Protestant areas. What he found on his return was markedly different. The new heroes in the Protestant community had become drunk with power. People had gravitated into the UDA less to further its political aims than to feather their own nests through acts of common illegality given the flavour of respectability by membership of the Association. Harding Smith found the Protestant areas in virtual anarchy, with powerful 'robber barons' ruling their independent fiefs throughout the city, and with only a loose and ineffective overall structure of command. Robberies had escalated alarmingly. Hijackings of liquor lorries for UDA shebeens had become a serious worry. Harding Smith knew that if the lawlessness continued it would eventually lead to the banning of the UDA and the internment of many of its leaders. Another source of concern was the growth in the level of extortion exacted on local people and shopkeepers. Harding Smith had sanctioned weekly levies on individuals and shopkeepers, but he had shrewdly kept the demands in proportion. As a consequence, the local people – hard-working but not rich – were not bled dry. There was an acceptable level of demand where the people would pay gladly, knowing that the money was genuinely going to further the Protestant cause. All this had collapsed while Harding Smith was away. And with it had plummeted the popular support of the UDA among working-class Protestants. Also contributing to this was the breakdown in the UDA's police services. The RUC feared to patrol many Protestant areas on foot at night, and the UDA were the real police force to many Protestants. Yet this service too had been allowed to break down, and the people felt unprotected. It also seemed that those they needed the greatest protection against were the men who were supposed to be their protectors.

Into this background Harding Smith emerged after his London

acquittal. He had been the leader of the Woodvale UDA of which Elliot was now the number two man. On his return a number of UDA men dissatisfied with the situation approached Harding Smith and asked him to take over once again and clean things up. He agreed on one condition: that he would have complete control. This was accepted, and he set about repairing the damage. Elliot was part of the spring-cleaning. He had a criminal record. Harding Smith had been known, when he had been in charge of the UDA, to drag petty criminals to RUC stations to be dealt with. Moreover, Elliot also had a sharp left-wing philosophy. He read Marx and Guevara but worst of all from Harding Smith's point of view, he had engaged in discussions with representatives of the Official IRA, who shared similar ideological views. Both his political deviations and the fact that he had at least condoned the lawlessness in the Protestant areas were sufficient for Elliot to receive the wrath of Harding Smith. It is highly unlikely that he and his colleague ever left the Shankill area on the night of his death. The companion was not a partner in Elliot's guilt, and therefore was not killed. He was, however, severely beaten, and released later with the story of the IRA kidnapping. Had the IRA been responsible for the Elliot killing, one can be sure that this man would not have lived and, also, that those responsible would have made the maximum propaganda capital out of the deed. As it happened, neither was the case. Hours after Elliot's body was discovered, the RUC made it prefectly plain to newsmen that so far as they were concerned the IRA story was not true. Either the police had received new information from a source other than the beaten man, or they just did not believe him. The Elliot killing was the first act of a drama that was to continue in the UDA and the Protestant areas throughout 1973. The shock-waves set in motion by the return of Harding Smith and his resumption of power were widespread. The following month, the top UDA man in Woodvale, David Fogel, who had taken over from Harding Smith earlier, fled the country. Fogel claimed that Harding Smith was trying to integrate the UVF – 'evil men', Fogel called them – into the UDA. This smacked of the truth, though not in the way Fogel would have liked it understood. The UVF was a dedicated political organization. Once discredited, it too, like its leader, Gusty Spence, had become something of a legend – a legend in the Robin Hood mould. For the UVF was known to gain its money, not from the people, but by daring bank raids and the like – robbing the rich, as it were. The UVF, one can be sure, were not happy at the degeneracy seen in the Protestant areas under UDA control while Harding Smith was away, and he certainly had their support in his clean-up operation. Elliot was the only notable fatal casualty in the operation but the clean-up had much success. In West Belfast, the power-base of both Harding Smith and the UVF, the clean-up was complete, and Harding Smith was in total control. In the East, however, he did not have it all his own way. On this side of the Lagan stood Tommy Herron, a man frequently dismissed as a lightweight, but, significantly, not in UDA circles. Herron was only the Association's vice-chairman, but this belied the fact that in the East he was the number one man. He was not so easy to get rid of. So a compromise was agreed in January. Herron would rule the East and Harding Smith the West. It was an uneasy alliance. Harding Smith disliked the way the UDA ran rackets in the East – operations which increasingly lost it popularity in the overwhelmingly Protestant area – and Herron was suspicious of Harding Smith and the militants in the West, whom he knew would oust him at the first opportunity, if it came. Elliot's death, then, stood as a reminder to all involved in the power struggle in the loyalist camp. The strain had begun to show in the unity that had existed in the early days of the UDA. Just like the IRA, it was beginning to crack along differing lines. Policies and ideologies, personalities and suspicions, were all combining to divide rather than unite those on the loyalist side. The New Year 1973 was to see these frictions tested to breaking-point.

The immediate effect of the Elliot killing came the following day. Across the Lagan in East Belfast, many Protestant militants were inclined to believe the claim that the IRA had killed the Woodvale man. Their immediate reaction was to assassinate a

Catholic in revenge. Joseph Kelly, 47, a Roman Catholic of Monagh Place, Turf Lodge, in West Belfast, travelled each day by bus to work in East Belfast. Like other Catholics in this position of commuting through Protestant areas every day, this had not passed unnoticed. He was probably one of those who were on the 'lists', so often talked about earlier in the year, of IRA men and their 'sympathizers'. In the early evening of Friday 8 December, Kelly was one of two men riding on the top of a corporation bus when it stopped at Castlereagh Street in East Belfast. He was on his way home. As the driver of the one-man-bus watched, a youth ran upstairs carrying a gun. Another youth levelled a pistol at the driver and told him he would be 'alright'. As he spoke the second youth shielded his face with his hand from the driver's gaze. Unaware of this, Kelly was sitting upstairs reading a book. The other youth came up behind him and emptied the contents of his revolver into the victim's head at close range. The other passenger was left unharmed and undisturbed. Kelly, a married man with children, was killed instantly as his brains spewed out onto the bus seat. At the subsequent inquest the coroner asked the bus-driver why he had not driven off when the first gunman had boarded the bus. 'It wouldn't have been worth my life,' was the straightforward reply. And it was undoubtedly true. The youths knew who they wanted. They had no desire to harm the bus-driver or any of the other passengers. Kelly was a marked man, a man known to the men who killed him as a vulnerable target. He could be picked off whenever the occasion demanded it. Like so many people in his position he obviously did not believe he was in danger when he travelled through East Belfast. As a Catholic, he would almost certainly not have made this journey after dark, but in broad daylight he must have felt he was safe. He was wrong. The tragic thing about Ulster in the Troubles is that such mistakes can be cruelly punished. Kelly paid the full price.

Just under a week later, a Roman Catholic youth, who was standing with a group of friends on the fringe of the Catholic Bawnmore Estate on the Shore Road, North Belfast, also paid. James Joseph Reynolds, 16, was standing at Dandy Street talking when a motorcycle with two youths on it drove by. The pillion passenger was carrying a Sterling submachine-gun, and opened fire on the group. Reynolds fell dying in a hail of bullets. Police later discovered that the motorcycle used in the murder had been taken from a youth in the Ballygomartin Road, in a Protestant area near the Glencairn Estate. They also learned that the owner of the motorcycle had been standing at a street corner with a number of other youths when the machine had been taken. It appeared, therefore, that there would be a large number of witnesses to identify the killers of Reynolds. However, the police were to find that theirs was to be no easy job. The wall of silence effectively shielding the killers in most of the other assassinations was to prove just as inpenetrable here.

The group of young men at the Ballygomartin Road had been approached by a young man who had got out of a mini car. He had asked the owner to lend him the motorcycle for 'half an hour'. The owner refused, and the young man produced a revolver and said that he was taking the machine, but would return it later. The promise was kept, the motorcycle was returned, and the police then apprehended the owner and informed him that it had been used in Reynolds's killing. The owner made statements to the police on the events that led to the machine being taken. So did the other youths around at the time, but the curious thing was that none of the statements matched. For example, on such a major point as the colour of the car the killers had used, each of them gave a different reply. However, despite this, and despite the obvious fear of the witnesses, the police believed they knew who the killers were and thought they had a case against them. The suspects were under police surveillance when one of the key witnesses, a boy of 16, was picked up by armed men. He was taken by them to an alleyway off the Shankill Road and a hood was placed over his head. He was told that he was about to be shot, and he began to plead for his life. He was subsequently released – he had got the message. The same message was conveyed to all the other witnesses. One was taken to a club and beaten. But one escaped the treatment, and this was the principal witness. Ian Woodside, 18, was the owner of the motorcycle, and police were counting on his evidence to convict their two suspects. But when he heard of the incident involving the 16-year-old-boy, Woodside immediately left Belfast. One may see his exit as timely, for it was reliably reported that all the other potential witnesses were later taken to a club in the Shankill Road and pistol-whipped. Woodside, whose evidence would be crucial, may have had a different fate reserved for him had he stayed. As it is at the moment, the police have made no progress in solving the Reynolds case.

Two days after Reynolds was killed, Saturday 16 December, a Roman Catholic butcher was found dead in the huge refrigerator of his shop at Main Street, Derrylin, in Co. Fermanagh. Louis Leonard, 26, had been in his shop late the previous night when his wife had gone out to make some deliveries to outlying farms. She expected him to lock up and go home, but he never got home. Another shopkeeper in the street saw two men, one well dressed and the other in labourer's clothes, get out of a car at 11·00 p.m. and go into Leonard's shop. The shopkeeper thought nothing of this at the time, and did not get a good look at the men. The following morning Leonard's brother called the police and then climbed into the shop through a rear window. He found his brother's body in the fridge. He had been shot through the head twice and once in the chest with a .45 revolver. He had been killed shortly after midnight, according to forensic evidence. Leonard had not been involved in any organizations connected with the Troubles. He lived in a quiet agricultural area which had been spared the greater part of the disturbances of the previous few years. Police could only speculate that the motive had been purely sectarian. It was recorded as another 'apparently motiveless murder'. The only people who could provide the answer are the two visitors to Leonard's butcher's shop that night, and they have never been found.

The same day that Leonard's body was found, two masked youths walked into a Roman Catholic-owned off-licence at York Road in Belfast and shot the man behind the counter. Joseph Blaney, 38, the brother of the parish priest of the near-by St Patrick's Church, was serving a woman and her daughter when the raiders arrived. The youths ordered the woman and her daughter into a back room and then shot Blaney several times. At first police considered the possible motive of robbery for the killing. But this would seem to be belied by the fact that, after shooting Blaney, the youths did not rifle the cash register. There would also have been no point in putting the two women in the back room if the object of the exercise was to rob the till. It would appear more likely that the motive was simply to kill Blaney, a Catholic who was, despite the dangers involved, running a business on the fringe of a predominantly Protestant working-class area.

Two days later, on Monday 18 December – a week before Christmas – the Provisional I R A demonstrated that it was having nothing to do with the season of goodwill to all men when it killed a Protestant councillor. William Johnston, 48, as well as being a Unionist Party councillor, was a member of the Armagh Police Authority. He owned a carpet firm and had agreed to sell some carpet to a friend who lived in the predominantly Catholic Drumarg Estate in the city of Armagh. He went to his friend's house on Sunday evening, the 17th, to help lay the carpet but he was spotted by some I R A men entering the estate and kidnapped by them. He was held for twenty-four hours and then executed. The Provisional I R A considered Johnston a legitimate military target because of his connection with the Armagh Police Authority. They considered ordinary R U C men as legitimate targets, and as far as they were concerned, Johnston was in the same category. He was found shot in the head in a car near where he lived. Several men who were identified by Johnston's friend as being responsible for kidnapping him, were subsequently charged with the killing. All are members of the I R A.

Two days later, Protestant extremists struck back in a revenge attack on a Roman Catholic bar in Londonderry city for the killing of Johnston. The Top-of-the-Hill bar was frequented by members of both communities, although most of the customers were Roman Catholic. On the night of Wednesday 20 December, the bar was crowded as usual. Shortly before closing time the front doors were thrown open and two masked men strode in, one armed with a revolver, the other with a submachine-gun. As the drinkers froze in horror at the sight of the intruders, the gunmen began to spray the bar with bullets. When they rushed out seconds later they left five dead – four Catholics and one Protestant – and many others injured. A third man waiting outside in a Ford Zephyr car drove the two killers from the scene. The car had been stolen earlier in the day in the city. It was later found abandoned, a burnt-out shell, after it had been set on fire by the assassins.

The killings shocked the province. The death toll was the largest in any one assassination so far: Charles McCafferty, 32, of Anderson Crescent; Frank McCarron, 52, of Strabane Old Road; Bernard Kelly, 28, of Mimosa Court; Michael McGinley, 37, of Anderson Crescent; were the four Roman Catholics. Charles Boyd Moore, 31, of Spencer Road, was the lone Protestant. All were from Londonderry. Police in the city were convinced that Protestant assassins were responsible. The following day they mounted major searches in the Protestant areas of Londonderry. The killings had been carried out with cool efficiency. It had only taken a few seconds for the assassins to rake the bar with thirty bullets. Hitherto, the city of Londonderry had remained relatively free of sectarian killings. Though it was the second city of Northern Ireland, it had a Roman Catholic majority and, as well as this, the two communities were segregated more efficiently than in Belfast. This killing stunned both the city's communities. They had not experienced anything like it since Bloody Sunday eleven months before.

Two more people were to die within twenty-four hours and then, perhaps because Christmas was approaching, the killings stopped. There was one more on 30 December. Hugh Martin, 56, a Roman Catholic and member of CESA who lived in the Ardoyne, was the last man to fall a victim of the assassins in 1972. The year that had begun in so much hope had ended in gloom. Instead of being a turning-point, a new beginning, the year had been one of unending disaster. The situation had gone from bad to worse, and then worse still. The bombings of civilian targets by the IRA had not only continued, but had increased. So too had the attacks on the security forces. 1972 had been the worst year in the history of Northern Ireland for violence and terror. It had seen the emergence of the assassins. There had been 121 victims – an average of ten per month. In the first six months only twenty-eight had been killed. In the second half of the year the killings were running at an average of fifteen per month, or one every two days. In a population of 1½ million these figures may appear small, but the amount of fear and bitterness these killings caused is the more realistic evaluation. People no longer felt safe on the streets. Indeed, they were beginning to realize that even their own homes were not safe from the assassin. More people died on the roads in Northern Ireland in 1972 than at the hands of the assassins. But no one who lived in the province during those twelve months would have any difficulty deciding which was the more frightening statistic. The real casualty figures of the assassinations are not to be found in the body counts of killed and injured. They are to be found in the minds of 1½ million people, most of whom lived in terror of their lives.

Part Three

The Killings: January–June 1973

9. The UDA call off the assassins: January 1973

Unlike the previous year, the New Year 1973 found Ulster in deep gloom. The false hopes of previous new beginnings had engendered a climate in which it was widely felt that things could only deteriorate – that some horror even worse than those already suffered lay just around the corner. They were no fine words of hope to greet this New Year.

On 1 January Great Britain and Northern Ireland, together with Eire and Denmark, officially joined the Common Market. This was the subject of the leader of the *Belfast Telegraph* that evening, and it wrote, more in sorrow, perhaps, than in anger:

> One of the worst faults of the Irish people is their obsession with the past. They continue to fight the old battles while the world passes by. The EEC is the best hope for the future if it makes people realize that the world is bigger than Northern Ireland or Eire, and that 1973 is vastly more important than 1690 or 1916.
>
> Sir Winston Churchill in an eloquent passage once referred to the effects of the Great War and its enormous significance for the future map of Europe. 'But', he wrote, 'as the deluge subsides . . . we see the dreary steeples of Fermanagh and Tyrone emerging once again.' As the map changes once more we can only hope that such a passage will not be justified again.

This was not a very optimistic outlook for the New Year. The mood of depression was characterized well in a cartoon on an inside page of the *Belfast Telegraph*. It depicted an aged 1972 passing the sands of time to a youthful 1973, with the words: '– and you must learn of the horrors and shootings in Northern Ireland where, incidentally, about ninety-seven per cent of the population want only to live in peace with each other.' This indeed was the tragedy of Northern Ireland. The

159

overwhelming majority of the people of each and every religious persuasion only wanted to be left to lead their lives in peace. And yet the violence and the killings increased.

The front page of the *Belfast Telegraph* on 1 January brought home the stark fact that nothing had changed for the Ulster people. Under the headlines 'GIRL'S SCREAM LEADS POLICE TO GRUESOME DISCOVERY' and 'ENGAGED PAIR FOUND SHOT IN AN EIRE LANE', they found the detailed story of 1973's first assassination.

'A girl's scream in the night led police to a lonely Donegal road early today where they found the bodies of an engaged couple, believed to have been the victims of Eire's first assassination,' the story began.

Oliver Boyce, 25, and his fiancée, Breige Porter, 21, were two Roman Catholics. They had been stabbed and shot a number of times in the early hours of the New Year just across the border from Londonderry at Buncranna, County Donegal. They had earlier been to a dance, and were the victims of a Protestant assassination squad sent from Northern Ireland.

In the early hours of the following morning, Tuesday 2 January, another Protestant assassination squad in Dundonald, a suburb of Belfast a stone's throw from Stormont, opened fire on a car containing Roman Catholic workers travelling to the near-by Rolls-Royce factory. Jack Mooney, 31, a father of two from the Whiterock Road in the Falls area, was killed. Mooney's father had been among the men who escaped the attack. Later the dead man's Westminster MP, SDLP leader Gerard Fitt, claimed that Mooney's predominantly Protestant workmates must have set him up for the killing. Mooney had been sent to Coventry by these men because, in common with most other Roman Catholics in the province, he had observed a one-day strike at the time of Bloody Sunday – almost one year before.

Clearly the assassinations were continuing unabated, and the *Belfast Telegraph* was stirred, on the evening of Mooney's death, to devote its whole leader to the subject. Under the heading 'DEATH IN THE SHADOWS' it said:

The U D A call off the assassins

Mr Whitelaw returned to Stormont Castle today with public morale at a low ebb. The reason is not hard to find. It is the assassinations.

At a time when spirits should be lifted by the apparent success of the security forces in limiting the I R A's bombing campaign, fears are increased and a feeling of hopelessness induced by the continual killings. It is the dictatorship of events.

Last night another man was gunned down on his way to work. That he was the only victim is miraculous. Five companions in his car could so easily have been added to the death toll. All were Roman Catholics. On Sunday gunmen opened fire from the Protestant Highfield estate on a corporation bus travelling to the Catholic Turf Lodge estate. Two passengers are still detained in hospital. On Saturday a Catholic bakery worker, a man who had been a German prisoner-of-war, was murdered after finishing a night shift.

Even after 122 assassinations it is impossible to place responsibility with certainty. They are put down as motiveless murders. Many appear to be sectarian killings. Protestants too have suffered grievously. But the majority of the victims have been Catholics and the proportion is rising. As well, there is evidence in last night's murder, and that on Saturday, of organization. The killers in these two cases clearly knew about the identity and movements of those whom they condemned to death.

Whoever they were, the effect of their actions must be to give aid and comfort to the I R A. While Catholics are murdered they can masquerade the easier as protectors. Ending the cycle of violence, as much as the pursuit of justice, now requires that searches for Protestant guns and ammunition in Protestant areas are mounted as vigorously as for I R A guns in Catholic areas.

And there are clear grounds for questioning all those in both communities who, whether through the written or spoken word, could be regarded as contributing to a climate in which intimidation becomes commonplace and murder unexceptional.

The public's duty is to place every scrap of available information before the police and to make full use of the confidential telephone service. That would be a helpful step – in sharp contrast to the call by the Catholic Ex-Servicemen's Association for Catholic workers to stage a token strike. This could only increase sectarian tension on the shop floor.

But the Government and the security forces also have a duty to the public. People need reassurance. They appreciate the difficulties of the Army and the police. But they deserve to be told more about what is being done to combat the assassins. Mr Whitelaw and his advisors should not delay in making a public statement.

There can be no doubt that morale among the population in Northern Ireland had hit rock-bottom because of the assassinations. What the *Telegraph* called 'the dictatorship of events' had affected everyone. The shock and the horror at the seemingly indiscriminate sectarian killings had reached every quarter of the population – including, as we shall see shortly, one where it was possible to do something to remedy the situation.

The fourth victim of the new year was killed on Friday 5 January. William Trevor Rankin, 18, a Protestant from the Ravenhill Road in East Belfast, was shot dead by Provisional IRA men in the Ben Madigan filling station on the Shore Road. Rankin's death was the result of a cruel irony. The Provisionals were waiting for a UDR man who used the station every day. Rankin had the misfortune to drive the same colour car as the intended victim, and this was enough for his killers to believe he was the the UDR man and kill him. He was a young man who had no contact with any illegal organization, and his death illustrates yet again the ease with which an innocent civilian could fall a victim of the assassins.

Against this background of gloom and increasing pessimism the day after the *Belfast Telegraph*'s leader on the assassinations, Wednesday 3 January, the heads of the four main churches in Ulster made an effort to cool the situation. In a joint statement, signed by the Church of Ireland Primate, Dr George O. Simms, the Methodist President, the Rev. Edward Lindsay, the Moderator of the Presbyterian Church, Dr Victor Lynas, and the Roman Catholic Primate, Cardinal John Conway, they said:

We appeal to the whole community to root out this evil – tell the murderers and assassins they are on their own. The horror of recent assassinations haunts our minds. We are conscious of the multiplying numbers of women and children who are being robbed of the men they love and who are nightly in fear. These sectarian and political murders, whether of civilians or security personnel, have brought shame to our land and tragedy to countless homes. They are a crime before God and are a disgrace to our common Christian heritage.

As usual, the church leaders meant well, but – again as usual – it took more than their moral authority to affect the situation. But that situation was dramatically affected the same day when a statement was issued by a body that could back up whatever moral authority it had with real physical power.

On Wednesday 3 January and Thursday 4 the UDA circulated all its members with a statement that bluntly said that the assassinations were to stop or else the killers themselves would be dealt with. Thursday evening, the UDA vice-chairman and spokesman, Tommy Herron, announced publicly that the UDA had ordered the assassins on both sides to stop the killings. He added that if the warning went unheeded, those responsible would be 'eliminated'. He said that the 'wrath of the UDA' would be quick to swoop on those men who killed for sectarian motives, as more could be achieved by talking to the British government than by killing. Herron disclosed that the UDA had compiled a dossier on the motives behind the murders and had concluded that there was now a group of Protestants who believed that they could achieve their ends by adopting the same bomb-and-bullet tactics as the IRA.

Herron's statement was a bolt out of the blue and led immediately to wide speculation that the UDA had called the killers off. But the *Belfast Telegraph* was not too impressed. In a leader entitled 'PRIME DUTY' it argued that if the UDA had information on the assassinations it should pass it on to the security forces:

The first reaction to today's statement from the UDA will be to welcome its condemnation of sectarian killings ... [but] Ulster, as evidenced from the kind of grisly justice meted out by the IRA, has had enough of kangaroo courts. The law must take its proper course and the UDA should be prepared to play its part ... Public opinion is sickening of violence from any quarter. Perhaps the time is coming when even the most militant in this community will lay less emphasis on force. A frightened public earnestly hopes so.

The day after Herron's statement, Friday 5 January, newsmen besieged the Association's headquarters in the Newtownards Road in East Belfast. Herron was this time accompanied by members of the UDA inner council, and the council in a statement reiterated Herron's words of the previous evening: 'Unlike the powers that be' it had traced and assessed the root of the killings and looked for an answer in an attempt to establish motives.

We firmly believe we have the answer and will strive to administer the antidote immediately. Our work in this field was hampered by vile accusations and by the continued harassment of the Army . . . We make this statement loud and clear to all those involved in these murders to stop now or face the wrath of the UDA.

Herron was closely questioned as to what exactly the 'wrath of the UDA' might entail. What did he mean when he said that the assassins themselves would be 'eliminated' if they did not comply with the order to stop the killings? He replied that this was not to be taken out of context:

What the UDA statement meant to convey was that the assassinations will be eliminated by way of educating those responsible of the futility of their course. UDA, which believes it has a very big influence, and can drastically reduce, if not completely stop, the killings, will tackle the question of why murders should stop, and also from the angle why, through ill-advised Government action, the situation should never have arisen.

Herron said that the UDA did not claim to have specific knowledge as to who was responsible, but they were certain that there was a small number of extremists involved. The UDA, he explained, understood that these people themselves were acting out of fear and because they saw their future in jeopardy. But if persuasion did not work, physical force would be used, though this would stop short of killing. The UDA would concentrate on preventing future killings and would not concern itself with solving past ones. They would not help the police–Army task-force in its investigations into the murders, because, he said: 'We are working for the people of Northern Ireland and not the Westminster government and Whitelaw administration.' But he quickly added that this was not to be understood to mean that the UDA would deliberately hinder police inquiries into past killings.

It was a masterly piece of double-talk, but the message was clear: the UDA was telling the Protestant assassination squads to stop the killings. And the message was heeded. From the death of Jack Mooney on Tuesday 2 January there was not a single assassination of a Roman Catholic until four weeks later on Monday 29 January. The only killing in the intervening period, that of William Trevor Rankin, was the work of the Provisional IRA.

The UDA called off the assassins, and it worked. The motives behind the move, and the reasons why it collapsed, are essentially part of the power-struggle in the Association which had come to light in December 1972. As we mentioned in the preceding chapter in that month, Charles Harding Smith, 41, one of the UDA's founders, returned to Belfast. He had been in custody in London facing charges of trying to smuggle large quantities of arms into Northern Ireland. He was acquitted and made an immediate return to Ulster. His arrival was a surprise to the UDA.

On 7 December, as we have seen, Ernest 'Duke' Elliot, a Lieutenant-Colonel in the UDA, and number two in Woodvale to Dave Fogel, had been killed by elements in the UDA loyal to Harding Smith. On Wednesday 10 January Harding Smith officially resumed control of the UDA. He became joint chairman, superseding both Herron, the vice-chairman, and also, *de facto*, Jim Anderson, who had been sole chairman while Harding Smith was away, and who now became the second joint chairman. In actual fact, this move was merely a recognition of the new realities in the balance of power within the UDA. Harding Smith had been in effective control of most of the Association for a month.

Three days later, Fogel, still the Woodvale commander in name, was taken to East Belfast where he was brought before Harding Smith as a virtual prisoner. He was questioned about the deterioration in law and order in his area. He claimed that this was untrue and that outsiders had recently been engaged in a campaign to discredit himself and Elliot by causing incidents. Cars had been set fire to and robberies committed so as to create the impression that the UDA in Woodvale was unable to protect the people. Elliot, of course, had been killed, and Fogel was quite clearly a very frightened man as the charges of dereliction of duty were put to him. According to Fogel, Harding Smith told him that he was taking over the UDA. Fogel could be a puppet chief in Woodvale, if he wished, but the real power would rest with Harding Smith. Harding Smith had been the commander in Woodvale, a pleasant working-class residential area at the top of the Shankill Road, before he went to England and Fogel took over. He had a personal attachment to his own area that put the edge to his annoyance at the degree to which anarchy had developed there during his absence. Fogel saw the writing on the wall – he was only too aware just how close he was to receiving Elliot's fate – and on Monday 22 January he fled to England.

In England Fogel sold his story to the *Sunday Times*. He claimed that the turmoil in the UDA was due to the return of Harding Smith. Harding Smith wanted, according to Fogel, to integrate the UDA with the more militant UVF and was set upon eliminating the men who had come to prominence and gained power in the UDA while he had been in gaol in England.

'There is a power-struggle going on and I don't want to have any part of it,' Fogel said. 'We are mixing with dangerous and evil men out for their own gains and not for the interests of the ordinary working-class Protestant people of Ulster.' He referred to what he termed a 'cruel and vicious' smear campaign that had been directed against Tommy Herron, the UDA vice-chairman in January. He said that people had been telephoning Belfast newspapers with the information that Herron was about to go.

This was, indeed, true. For a number of weeks at this time it did seem that Herron was about to topple. He had become identified with the new 'soft line' in the UDA that had been instrumental in calling off the assassins. There were phone-calls claiming that he was no longer in charge. Rumours began to circulate about him. His Roman Catholic connections – he was baptised a Catholic in St Anthony's Roman Catholic Church in East Belfast – became the subject of comment and discussion. It was claimed that some of his relatives were in the IRA, and that one was a prominent member of the Provisionals in Andersonstown. It appeared that Herron was being discredited prior to his swift removal from the scene.

On Sunday 21 January, the day before Fogel fled, 200 local UDA commanders met and reaffirmed their support for Herron and publicly refuted the rumours circulating about him. In a statement issued afterwards, Herron said that the rumours were being spread by a man who was 'seeking to break up the organization and take power for himself'. The man, he added, was not even a member of the UDA.

There is little doubt that the man referred to was Harding Smith. It is interesting that this statement from Herron came ten days after Harding Smith officially resumed the post of chairman of the UDA. It illustrates the confusion and turmoil then existing within the ranks of the organization. The UDA had grown up spontaneously – a rare birth for such a large and powerful paramilitary body – and this to a very large extent explains much of the later stress and strain. Because of the spontaneous development, the UDA tended to be a loosely structured body. Local commanders wielded virtually unchecked the total power at their disposal. They came together as a body only in the UDA inner council, a democratic organ, where overall policy was thrashed out on a majority basis. It is no surprise, therefore, that the major positions in the UDA should be that of chairman and vice-chairman. These positions denote that, initially at least, they were intended for purposes of debate and discussion. Unlike the military structure of the local units, Lieutenant-Colonel, Major-General and so on, the posts of chairman and vice-chairman did not carry any implied executive authority. Those in these positions were not expected to give orders, merely to chair meetings of the inner council and act as a spokesman for the UDA to the outside world. They were intended to be *primus inter pares* – and no more.

It was this devolution – and as he saw it, weakening – of power in the UDA that Harding Smith was determined to crush. When he returned to Belfast in December he had found the organization he had helped to build up in a shambles. The local commanders had either been unable or unwilling to check the decline, and the UDA's central structure had been too weak to do anything about it. The UDA was out of control, and Harding Smith was determined to bring it back under control and give it a centralized structure, governed by an iron discipline, with himself at the head.

But this policy was not pleasing to everyone in the UDA, and certainly not to those local commanders who had profited from the absence of a strong central authority to check their excesses. There was resistance to Harding Smith, and it formed up behind Herron.

Harding Smith had been the commander in Woodvale, in West Belfast. Fogel claimed that he wanted to integrate the UVF into the UDA. The UVF was strong in West Belfast. It detested the corruption and lawlessness of UDA rule in the Protestant areas and was a natural ally for Harding Smith in his attempt to clean up the situation. Harding Smith's own personal power base also lay in the West. The West too, was more conscious of the personal threat of the IRA in the surrounding Catholic areas. The lack of political concern on the part of the local UDA leaders, who preferred to line their own pockets at the expense of the people, gave Harding Smith the popular support he needed. But the East was another matter. There the threat from the IRA was slight because, apart from the small Short Strand enclave just across the Lagan, there were no Catholics. In the overwhelmingly Protestant East, Herron and his henchmen were in charge. Extortion and racketeering were at a higher level than in the West, and went unchecked. In the East Harding Smith had little natural support, and the UVF was weak.

In the preceding chapter it was explained how the conflict between the East and the West was resolved in a compromise. This compromise left Herron in charge of the East and confirmed Harding Smith's control in the West. Also part of the agreement was that the UDA lift its prohibition on the assassinations. This was a concession by Herron to the West, and marked a return from a line of policy that Harding Smith found as abhorrent as the laxity with which the UDA ruled the Protestant areas.

This line of policy was the attempt by certain UDA men, including Fogel, Elliot and Herron, to reach an accommodation with the Roman Catholic working class. This attempt inevitably led to discussions with the Official IRA, and to Harding Smith this was anathema.

It is to be remembered that the Official IRA had not terminated the truce with the Army in July 1972 along with the Provisionals. Since then it had maintained its position, impressing the Army and many Protestant extremists alike with its integrity and discipline. Its political philosophy had consistently been one of opposition to sectarianism, and it had stated time and time again that its wish was for a unified working class in Northern Ireland to fight for social justice and eliminate inequality on both sides of the religious barrier.

It was of paramount importance to the Protestants that the Officials made it clear that the first priority was this working-class unity, transcending religious differences. While they were committed to an eventual reunification of Ireland, this came second in importance to working-class solidarity in the North. Furthermore, the Official IRA believed that it would be futile to achieve unity through force, and thus attempt to integrate into an all-Ireland republic 1 million resentful and unwilling Protestants. The Officials claimed they only used force in self-defence. Their ultimate aim was a 32-county all-Ireland socialist republic, which they hoped to see achieved by political, and not military, means. These were the fundamental points of difference between the Officials and the Provisionals. The Provisionals believed it was possible to bomb and shoot the North into the republic. They tended to ignore the existence of the 1 million Protestant Unionists in Ulster, and could not grasp the fact that these people possessed a genuine and legitimate patriotism for the state equal to their own for the 32-county republic.

In many important respects the Official IRA had more in common in its aims and outlook with the working-class Protestants in the UDA than with the Provisionals. In its outright condemnation of the Provisionals' terror campaign of bombings and killings, it had the respect of many in the UDA, who were similarly shocked by the rise of the Protestant assassins. Here was a genuine basis for agreement between two moderate elements on either side. Both had a commitment to the defence of their own communities. Both were working class, and both wanted to see an end to the violence that was, in different ways, destroying their respective communities.

The decision to call off the Protestant assassins was at least in part prompted by contacts the existing leadership of the UDA had had with the Official IRA. This is not to say that there was any 'deal' involved. But it is to say that the decision to call the killers off the Roman Catholic community was a conscious response by people in the UDA inner council to the belief that there was a common ground of social discontent and genuine grievances that was shared by both the Catholic and Protestant working classes in Ulster. These grievances transcended the sectarian devides, and to many on both sides were an issue of more burning importance than the border.

James Connolly, the Irish socialist and trade-union organizer who had been shot by the British Army in 1916 for his part in the Easter Rising, once said:

The man who is bubbling over with love and enthusiasm for Ireland and yet can pass through our streets and witness all the wrong and suffering, the shame and degradation wrought by Irishmen upon Irish men and Irish women, without burning to end it, is, in my opinion, a fraud and a liar in his heart.

The Official IRA regarded itself as the legitimate heir of Connolly, and stressed, as he had done, the links between the working classes on both sides. By 1972, Augustus 'Gusty' Spence, Protestant hero and leader of the UVF, could claim to be the legitimate heir of the working-class Protestants who had flocked to the standard of the old UVF in 1912. In June Spence, who had escaped temporarily from gaol, gave a television interview where he said:

One has only to look at the Shankill Road, the heart of the empire that lies torn and bleeding. We have known squalor. I was born and reared in it. No one knows better than we do the meaning of slums, the meaning of deprivation, the meaning of suffering for what one believes in, whatever the ideology. In so far as people speak of fifty years of misrule, I wouldn't disagree with that. What I would say is this, that we have suffered every bit as much as the people of the Falls Road, or any other underprivileged quarter – in many cases, more so.

These were remarkable sentiments from the man who had been trying to kill Roman Catholics in 1966, long before the Troubles began. But Spence in 1972 was a different man. He had matured politically in gaol, where he had met and got to know, for the first time in his life, people from the Roman Catholic community. Official IRA men told Spence of the dreadful social conditions in their areas, and Spence began to understand why the Catholic working class had never accepted Unionist rule. He questioned too the automatic support the Protestant working class had given the Unionists – middle class and aristocratic – for fifty years. He became aware through his discussions that there was much to unite the working class on either side against the establishment that had, in different ways, oppressed them both.

Spence was not the only Protestant working-class leader to have undergone such a political transformation. In his *Sunday Times* story Fogel told how the UDA mistrusted both Faulkner and Craig. Both were middle-class politicians from the old Unionist Party, and both were only interested in their own personal interests. They were not friends of the working class. Fogel ascribes his political development explicitly to the assassinated Elliot:

Ernie had helped me train the Woodvale men. He had been our press officer. He had been the man who always encouraged me to think in terms of politics. When I first met him I was a Conservative, but he made me more left-wing. He used to walk around Woodvale with Che Guevara books stuffed in his pockets.

Such a philosophy had contributed to Elliot's death, but his subordinate's views had clearly made a strong impression on Fogel. In terms reminiscent of both Connolly and Spence he described the political situation in Belfast as he then saw it. The Marxist interpretation is quite evident:

171

The two communities have been completely separated since 1968. On the factory floor and in the shipyards, where Prods and Catholics work together well and have strong trade unions, they avoid politics like the plague. But when they get back to Woodvale and the Ardoyne, a thick wall drops down. The only solution is for Catholics to come and live in Woodvale and Prods to cross the Crumlin Road and live among the Catholics in the Ardoyne.

But it's separate schools that's dividing the communities. As long as the Catholics insist on going to church schools, they will be cut off from us. The British government should pass a law forcing them to mix with the Protestants. There would be fighting for a wee while in the school, but after a time they would get sick of knocking heads in and settle down. And there would be parents in both communities who would not let their kids go to school with the others. But most would accept it eventually.

Fogel also discussed the sub-standard social conditions in Protestant areas, and then disclosed that contacts had taken place with socialists on the Catholic side and the UDA in the form of himself, Elliot, and Herron.

The lack of amenities in the Woodvale area is scandalous. Hugh Smyth [a Belfast City Councillor], Ernie Elliot and I saw a corporation official a few months ago and warned him that we would start passive resistance like stopping traffic if things didn't get better. As a result the pavements outside bombed buildings were tarmaced and street-lighting was improved. *Here again, we know it is just as bad in the Catholic working-class areas.*

My men will be surprised to learn that the late Ernie Elliot and I were engaged in talks with Two Nations. That is the only Marxist group that recognizes Ulster. *It wants Catholics to come out categorically for the continuation of the border. It's this which keeps the Catholics and Prod working class apart. Once the Prods lose their fear of Dublin then the way is open to a united working class.* Well, these fellows came up from Dublin, one with a big black beard, and we had a couple of meetings in my house. Tommy Herron met them and was quite interested.*

Such contacts would have been unthinkable only a few years earlier, but times had changed. Fogel, Elliot, and Herron,

*Italics ours, in this passage and the next – M.D. and D.L.

however, were too advanced for many of their colleagues. Fogel continued in his interview to expound further views that showed the degree to which he and the element in the UDA he represented had moved towards the idea of a united non-sectarian working class in Northern Ireland. He attacked middle-class Unionism, which he saw represented in the Whitelaw administration.

It is easier for Whitelaw to understand the Unionists than the working class. He lives in that environment and talks to them at their smart dinner-parties and they have more opportunity to plug their line.

I thought Gerry Fitt, the SDLP leader, was a very sincere man. Nobody in the UDA actually hates him. He is the sort of man who could build a bridge between the communities. The UDA is not anti-Catholic, only anti-IRA. Unfortunately, it has no Catholic connection at all. When Herron called for Catholics to join us, we only got two, both in Derry.

This is where the Catholic Ex-Servicemen's Association, CESA, could act as a link with us. I consider them the counterpart of the UDA, though they are sometimes a front for the IRA. *I tried to make contact with the CESA fellows in the Ardoyne next door to Woodvale, but Harding Smith was against it. Now he has plumped for working with the UVF. That could get the UDA banned, leaving the ordinary Prod without anyone to speak for him.*

Fogel's views are very interesting. Though they may appear fairly tame to the outsider, they are quite extraordinary in the context of Northern Ireland at this time. His views on social conditions in both communities and his hostility to the Unionist Party are identical to the Official IRA's. So too is his attitude to a united Ulster working class.

But Harding Smith was opposed to this ideology, and he was a formidable opponent. He was appalled by the signs of an accommodation between the Official IRA and the UDA. He saw this as another sign of the decline and degeneracy in the ranks of the organization he had helped to build. He set himself to eradicate the malignancy, in all its forms, that had set in while he was away, and introduce a rigorous discipline throughout the Association. The lawlessness and racketeering would be curbed, and so too would the dangerous flirtation with the other side.

Herron remained in East Belfast, but under pressure. Within the UDA as a whole, he was isolated and out-flanked by Harding Smith and the hard men in the West, who were backed by the UVF. He was not strong enough to resist Harding Smith on his own. He agreed to a compromise. He accepted Harding Smith's takeover of the UDA's central structure. In return he retained the vice-chairmanship and his control in the East and he agreed to reduce the level of extortion in his areas to an acceptable level.

The hard men in the West had been champing at the bit of enforced inaction. At the end of January, they were unleashed. On Monday 29 January with the killings of 14-year-old Peter Waterson, and James Trainor, 22, both Catholics, they showed that they were in business again. Twelve people were to die in the next seven days as the assassins, idle for four weeks, returned to their task.

On Wednesday 31 January the UDA made it official. Five people had been killed in the previous two nights – four killed by Protestant gunmen, and one by the IRA in retaliation – and Herron issued a statement in which he said it was now futile for the UDA to clamp down on Protestant extremists. The UDA would no longer make a special effort to stop sectarian killings because this was impossible in view of the continued attacks by the IRA on soldiers, policeman and property.

We cannot control Protestant extremists in the face of IRA killings of UDR men, policemen, and civilian Protestants, and in the face of the attitude of Republican M Ps who are not happy unless they are talking about oppression and injustice.

Only four weeks ago we made an effort – we said the killing must stop and it did. But now the bombings by republican rebels have provoked them.

The message was clear. The 'moderate' element in the UDA had tried to achieve peace. It had made a gesture – at considerable personal risk to those behind it – to the Catholic working class by calling off the assassins. The only response from the Catholics had been for the Provisionals to step up the campaign of bombings and killings of members of the security forces.

One should not undervalue the significance of what had happened. The olive branch was there, if only someone on the Catholic side had clasped it. Just as the Provisional IRA had been given an opening in June 1972 by the British government, so, too, in January 1973 the Officials were given a chance by the UDA. It was not enough for the UDA to call off the assassins. It required a *quid pro quo*.

Immediately after the announcement by Herron that the killings would stop, the executive of the Republican Clubs – a front for the Official IRA – issued an invitation to the UDA to take part in joint patrols to stamp out the killings. A spokesman said that he had always been confident that the UDA was representative of the Protestant working class. The offer was tersely rejected by the UDA which said in a statement: 'Under no circumstances will we meet the IRA. These people can praise us all they like, but we will never meet the IRA.'

The Officials had made a blunder, and their offer can hardly have helped Herron and his followers in the power-struggle. The UDA needed no help from the Officials in keeping the assassins quiet. What it did need, however, was a similar move by the Officials to keep the Provisionals inactive. The response that the moderates in the UDA wanted was quite simple. They could hold back the hard men on their side if the Officials could stop the Provisionals' campaign of bombings and shootings.

But the Provisional IRA not only continued its activities, it increased them during the pause in assassinations. Just as the truce with the British government had been incorrectly interpreted as a sign of weakness in Whitehall by the Provisionals, so too the UDA's decision was also dismissed as weakness. There was no thought of a ceasefire.

But the Official IRA might have had sufficient moral authority within the Catholic community to compel the Provisionals to stop. It is also more than likely that by this time the Officials had more men and greater firepower, had they wished to use it, than their rivals. Yet they used neither moral authority nor physical force to make the Provisionals end a campaign which they themselves regarded as useless and counterproductive. This is puzzling. But the answer may lie simply in the fact that the Official IRA did not understand what was taking place in the Protestant community, and distrusted the UDA and its leaders. The offer of joint patrols – rejected out-of-hand as ought to have been realized beforehand, in view of the state of mind in the Protestant areas caused by the Provisional IRA campaign – may have been a genuine attempt to get a dialogue going. Once accepted, the Officials might have been sufficiently sure of the UDA's good faith to move against the Provisionals.

That the Official IRA will eventually move to eliminate the Provisionals is, to most observers in Ulster, beyond doubt. Left alone in wary respect by the British Army, the Officials have retained intact their numbers, weapons, and command structure. At the date of writing (August 1973) the Provisionals have been decimated, with young girls of 16 or 17 in command positions. Public opinion in the Catholic community, sickened by the ceaseless, and apparently motiveless, violence, has swung round behind the Officials and away from the Provisionals. The question now is not will the Officials move against the Provisionals, but when?

But in January, the Official IRA made no move, and the Provisional IRA's campaign of terror continued unchecked. In the face of this, the moderates in the UDA were forced to give way to the hard-liners led by Harding Smith.

Gone were the attempts at working-class solidarity – for the time being at least. UDA officers no longer walked down the Shankill and Sandy Row with Che Guevara books sticking out of their pockets. Talks were not held with Republicans and, incidentally, lawlessness was dramatically curtailed in Protestant areas, especially in the West.

The rifts in the UDA leadership that emerged in this crisis were contained, but they were not eliminated. They were there as a constant potential for conflict between the East and West Belfast sections. They had essentially different philosophies – not necessarily social or political, but rather personal and practical – towards the role of the UDA. These rifts were to emerge again less than six months later.

10. The assassins unleashed:
29 January to 28 February

The first victim of the assassins after the pause was a Roman Catholic petrol-pump attendant. James Francis Trainor, 22, of Lisburn, was working at the Speedline garage in Kennedy Way, Andersonstown, on the night of Monday 29 January. A turquoise 1100 car pulled into the forecourt at about 8·00 p.m. Trainor walked out casually to serve petrol to the car, but he suddenly paniced as he saw several men in the vehicle and a gun protruding from a side window. He tried to return to the garage office, but he never made it. A hail of bullets ripped into his back sending him sprawling and dying onto the concrete forecourt.

The car used by the killers was seen making off down Kennedy Way towards the M1 motorway. This killing and three others within the next twenty-four hours were the work of a single assassination squad. In order to understand how these killings were executed, it is necessary to appreciate the geography of the small area in which they took place.

The M1 motorway, as referred to previously, begins at the end of the Donegal Road, South Belfast. In its first few miles it divides the Roman Catholics in the Falls area of the city from Protestants in an area known as the Village. The assassination squad that killed Trainor and three other Catholics on 29 and 30 January came from the Village.

Kennedy Way leads from the first exit on the M1 to the Falls. On the other side of the exit roundabout is Stockman's Lane. This road leads to Balmoral, a quiet residential and non-sectarian middle-class area astride the Lisburn Road. Across the Lisburn Road from Stockman's Lane is Balmoral Avenue which leads to Shaw's Bridge and across the Lagan into East Belfast. The journey by car from Kennedy Way into East Belfast can be accomplished in a matter of minutes by car.

The Village is a small pocket of working-class Protestants cut off from the surrounding areas. On one side the M1 divides it from the Catholic Falls. On the other the Belfast–Dublin railway-line cuts it off from the Protestant Windsor area. Access to the Village can be gained at the north end through the Donegal Road, and at the South by Stockman's Lane. These two roads are the third and fourth side of a rectangle that encloses the Village. They are about two miles apart, and this ensures the isolation of the area.

Access to the Falls from the Village was possible by three routes. The first was to go to the M1 roundabout on the Donegal Road, but to continue on the Donegal Road – which then became Roman Catholic – and reach the Falls via Rockville Street. The second route was to take the M1 as far as the first exit and then leave it and use Kennedy Way. This route was faster than the first. But the third route was far less conspicuous, hardly ever patrolled by the security forces, and ideal for the assassins. This was Boucher Road, and this was the route they used on 29 and 30 January.

Boucher Road is a virtually unknown and little-used road that runs from Stockman's Lane into the Village. It is mid-way between and parallel to the Lisburn Road and the M1. On either side there are no houses, only an industrial estate. The road is deserted at night and there are no street lights. Trainor's killers used Boucher Road as their escape route. Leaving the Speedline garage they headed for the M1 roundabout at the foot of Kennedy Way, but instead of joining the motorway, they continued round to Stockman's Lane. After barely 100 yards they turned left into Boucher Road. The journey from where they killed Trainor to their base in the village took less than five minutes. The police and Army believed they had used the M1. This was to prove a fatal error.

Three hours later Peter Watterson, 14, a Roman Catholic schoolboy, was standing outside his mother's newsagents on the junction of Rockville Street and the Falls Road. A number of other youths of the same age were with him. A car approached travelling down the Falls Road from the direction of Kennedy

Way towards the Donegal Road. As the vehicle neared the Donegal Road one of its occupants opened up on the standing youths with a submachine-gun. Peter Watterson and a 12-year-old friend were cut down by the bullets. The friend later recovered. Waterson was dead before the ambulance arrived. The assassins made their escape into the Village – only seconds away. A number of eye-witnesses noted the registration number of the car used.

The killing was well planned. The squad had driven up Boucher Road, Stockman's Lane, and then down Kennedy Way onto the Falls. It was the reverse direction of the circular route used to kill Trainor hours earlier. The killers were obviously supremely confident to operate a second time that night, deep in hostile territory. Had they been stopped by an IRA patrol – as they so easily might have been after the Trainor killing – their fate would not have been pleasant, as is clearly illustrated by what happened next.

The assassins had struck deep inside Catholic territory and claimed two victims within hours of each other. The local Provisional unit was furious. The witnesses to the Watterson killing passed on the description of the car used and its registration number to the Provisionals within minutes of the incident. After making inquiries, the Provisionals believed they knew who was the owner of the car.

Francis Smith, 28, was a Protestant who lived in Benburb Street, off the Donegal Road – in the heart of the Village. He was a member of the UDA. He was known in the Falls area to the IRA because he had married a Roman Catholic girl before the Troubles began, and had lived in Ballymurphy – a Catholic area – before he moved to the Village. He was known to make frequent visits to Catholic friends in the Falls area even after the Troubles began.

After Watterson's death, the Provisionals sent two volunteers to pick up Smith. The following morning, Tuesday 30 January, Smith's body was found in an alleyway at Rodney Parade – only 200 yards from the scene of the Watterson killing. The body wa found by a woman and her 9-year-old daughter at 8·00 a.m. as they were bringing out a dustbin for collection. The woman said she saw a man lying face downwards only yards from her back door. At first she thought he was drunk and walked towards him.

'I asked if he was alright and lifted his arm to help him,' she said. 'And his face – Oh my God! his face – it was covered in blood and I ran back into the house dragging my daughter with me.'

Neither this woman, nor any of the other neighbours, recalled hearing any shots fired the previous night, though forensic evidence suggested Smith had been killed where he was found. He had received the standard I R A execution of several bullets through the face and forehead at close range. He had been interrogated.

The I R A accepted responsibility for Smith's death. They claimed that he was a U D A gunman and that, as well as being involved in the Trainor and Watterson killings, he had shot two Provisional I R A volunteers. Whether this is true or not – and Smith was given a U D A funeral with full military honours – the Protestant assassins retaliated for the killing fourteen hours after Smith's body was found.

Philip Rafferty, 14, of Tullymore Gardens, Andersonstown, was, like Watterson, a schoolboy and a Roman Catholic. At 10·00 p.m. that night, he left his band practice on the Upper Falls Road to walk home, heading in the direction of Kennedy Way. It was a cold wet winter's night and the few street-lamps that survived the riots earlier in the Troubles provided just the circumstances for the assassins to strike again.

There were few people on the street as Rafferty, a frail youth, made his way home. A car drew up alongside him coming from the direction of the Donegal Road. Rafferty was not able to put up much resistance against the car's occupants, and he was swiftly bundled into the car, which drove into Kennedy Way, barely 300 yards away. From there, the car travelled via Stockman's Lane, Balmoral Avenue, and Shaw's Bridge to a deserted tourist spot known as the Giant's Ring. The kidnapping had taken place so quickly that nobody had seen it happen. Within minutes the killers and the victim were at the Giant's Ring.

There Rafferty was made to kneel on a grass verge. His anorak was pulled over his head, and he was shot in the head at close range, dying instantly. The body was not found for several hours, and during this time the assassins returned to the Falls to pick another victim. As the previous night, their confidence must have been high, for though no one had witnessed Rafferty's kidnapping, he was soon missed, and after the previous night's killings, the IRA were on the look-out for strange cars in the area.

While Rafferty was being killed, a 17-year-old Roman Catholic was seeing his girlfriend for the last time. Gabriel Savage lived in lodgings in the Lower Falls. He was an orphan and was working as an apprentice mechanic. He had only met his first girlfriend a few weeks before. At 10·30 p.m. the two young lovers walked along Andersonstown Road, not far from Kennedy Way, to a taxi-rank. Savage usually took a taxi home after seeing his girlfriend as the buses did not run in the Catholic areas after dark. As a consequence a lot of people had become freelance taxi-drivers to fill a need and make themselves some money.

As the two stopped to kiss goodnight a car approached them. It was just over half an hour since Rafferty had been kidnapped less than a quarter of a mile away. Savage thought the approaching car was a taxi and walked towards it. As he did so, a man got out from the back of the car and ordered him to get in. Savage became alarmed and the man produced a gun, and tried to force him into the car.

The girl began to struggle with the man to save Savage, but then the assassin threatened to shoot her. Savage agreed to go quietly if the girl were left behind unharmed. The girl abandoned her efforts and the car made off down Andersonstown Road towards Kennedy Way.

The girl was distraught. She ran down the middle of the road and, as luck would have it, within seconds came came upon a passing Army patrol. However, she was hysterical and the soldiers could make no sense out for her for a number of precious minutes. By the time she could relate all that had happened it was too late. The killers only needed one or two minutes before they were safe.

Instead of taking the victim to the Giant's Ring or a similarly lonely spot, the assassins took him to their base. They realized that the girl they had left behind would give the alarm within minutes, but they were confident enough to believe they had sufficient time to get home. They travelled down Kennedy Way, around the roundabout and into Stockman's Lane, and then via Boucher Road into the Village.

Within minutes of the kidnapping Savage was taken to a house in the Village while soldiers and police combed the M1 motorway, and set up road-blocks far from the small area within which the kidnapping had occurred. The following morning at 7·30 a motorist found his body on a grass verge near the end of the M1 adjacent to the Village, and not far from where he had been held. He had been shot through the head.

Had the routes the assassins must have taken in the previous two killings on 29 January been considered, those the following day might have been avoided. No ramps or check-points were in operation at either end of the M1 and the Falls. Police chiefs believed at the time that several squads were involved in the four killings, but this is not true. A close study of the circumstances of each would make this highly improbable.

The four killings illustrated the high degree of organization and intelligence behind the assassinations on the Protestant side. Somebody had clearly worked out routes to a split second. And those actually carrying out the killings were possessed of a large amount of courage and confidence. The Falls is not an area to enter lightly late at night, even in a car. The killing of Smith demonstrated just how ruthless the IRA could be. The men from the Village who took part in the Catholic assassinations must have been aware of the risks they were taking. To drive in and kill not once, but twice, within a few hours, on consecutive nights requires men possessed of extraordinary qualities.

A few days later, on Tuesday 1 February, Protestant assassins in East Belfast showed that they could match their colleagues in the West for planning and daring. Early in the morning a bus containing Roman Catholic building workers from West Belfast was attacked. The bus was making its daily trip to the site of a new Catholic school in the exclusive suburb of Cherryvalley on the outskirts of East Belfast. The school had been the target for Protestant bombers the previous year.

There were about twenty men on the bus, most of them from Andersonstown, and the vehicle was owned by a Falls Road firm which employed the men. It was driving through the middle-class Cherryvalley residential suburb when a man wearing a hat and carrying a walking-stick began to limp across the road in the bus's path, forcing it to slow down. Two men in blue anoraks then appeared, and in what must have been a pre-arranged plan, one smashed one of the bus windows while the other tossed in a hand-grenade.

The live grenade landed under Paddy Heenan, 50, a foreman joiner of Innishmore Crescent, Andersonstown. Sadly for Heenan, a married man with five children, that morning he had broken a long-standing habit and not sat in his accustomed seat. He took the main force of the blast, and was killed almost immediately. His fellow workmen were injured by pieces of flying shrapnel.

The three assassins were seen making off in a car which had been stolen the previous night in East Belfast. It was later found abandoned in the near-by Protestant Tullycarnet estate, two hours after the bombing.

Hundreds of extra soldiers and police poured into the East. The killing of Heenan and the attack on the bus had shocked the province – even after so many killings, it seemed, people could still be shocked. Tracker-dogs were used in an effort to find the killers. For once the police were to be successful in detaining suspects, and the results of their success were to be far-reaching.

The police investigation led them to two Protestant men. But the evidence – as had proved the case before – did not seem sufficient to assure a conviction in the courts. But instead of letting the men go free as in every other case before, security chiefs took a decision of immense importance: they decided to invoke the Special Powers Act and detain both men without trial.

This was a momentous decision. Since August 1971 over 1,000 Roman Catholics had been either interned or detained in Ulster under this act, which gave the Government a blanket power to lock up anyone it thought was a danger to the State. But till this time no member of a Protestant organization had been imprisoned in this way. The decision to use the Special Powers Act against Protestants in the aftermath of the Heenan killings produced shockwaves in the Protestant community that reverberated around the province.

The day after Heenan's death, Friday 2 February, the Provisional IRA hit back. Angered by the attack on Roman Catholic workers, it ordered the death of a young Protestant who was employed in Campbell Brothers glass and paint firm at the lower end of the Springfield Road, near the Catholic Kashmir district. The victim was James Greer, 21, of Clovelly Street, in the Protestant end of the Springfield Road.

Two young Provisional volunteers were sent to Campbell Brothers at 4·30 p.m. that day armed with a submachine-gun and a revolver. They held up staff at the reception desk and then lined about twenty employees up against the wall, with their backs facing the intruders. The IRA men asked who was Greer, and as he stepped from the line, one of the gunmen walked up to him and shot him in both legs and then in the head. The victim was dead before his killers had left the shop.

Greer was not a member of any organization, but he was known to the Provisional IRA in the Springfield Road area. Like many others in the same position of working in an alien area, albeit only a few hundred yards or so from where he lived, he was vulnerable and could be eliminated by the opposing side for its own reasons whenever it so wished. Clovelly Street where he lived was Protestant, but it will be recalled that a few months earlier Tony Davidson, a Catholic Ex-Serviceman, had been shot dead at his door in this street by Protestants.

The local IRA later said that Greer had been involved in cases of intimidating Catholic families out of their homes in the area where he lived. In Greer's case this is untrue, but there is a distinct possibility that the IRA mistook him for a younger brother.

This brother was described by his mother, Mrs Eleanor Greer, as a tearaway, and she admitted that he might have been involved in some of the sectarian 'rioting in the area'. If this is true, then James Greer would not have been the first person to have died at the hand of the assassins after a case of mistaken identity. The Greer family had, according to the mother, previously received letters purporting to come from the IRA threatening them with death. The dead man was engaged to be married, and had intended leaving Ulster to make a new life for himself and his bride after the wedding.

Whatever the personal motives involved in the Greer killing, the overriding one on the IRA's side was one of vengeance. The killing fitted the pattern of the time. Revenge now came swiftly in Belfast from both sides. Only hours after the IRA executed Greer the hooded body of a Roman Catholic Ex-Serviceman was found in the boot of a car in the Protestant part of the Springfield Road – where Greer had lived. Patrick Brady, 28, of Rosapenna Square, Andersonstown, had been beaten and then shot in the head. The car in which he was found had been hijacked earlier at Fleetwood Street near the Protestant Old Lodge Road.

That night Protestants, reacting to the detention of the two Protestants in connection with the Heenan killing and to the large-scale Army searches, took on the security forces in gunbattles in East Belfast. For six hours snipers raked the narrow streets with gunfire. Meanwhile, across the Lagan in North Belfast, Provisional IRA men, using a stolen mini car, shot down five young Protestants who were standing outside a café in the Oldpark Road. A sustained burst of automatic fire wounded four of the youths and killed Robert Burns, 18, of Sunningdale Grove, off the Ballysillan Road. Burns was a sergeant in 'C' Company of the UDA. The youths had often stood at that corner talking in the evening – a fact that probably did not go unnoticed in the near-by Catholic areas.

February was only two days old and four civilians had died, but the coming weekend was to see violence of an intensity in Ulster only equalled at the time of internment eighteen months before. The morning of the following day, Saturday 3 February, the largest bomb ever seen in Northern Ireland was left outside the offices of the *Belfast Telegraph* in Library Street. A petrol-tanker had been hijacked by the Provisional IRA. It contained 5,000 gallons of petrol and a 7-lb. charge of explosives to set the whole thing off. However, the timing mechanism was faulty and an Army explosives expert was able to defuse the bomb. Had it gone off it would have annihilated the centre of the city and caused damage to everything within a quarter of a mile radius of the centre of the blast. It would also have wiped out virtually the entire editorial staff of the *Belfast Telegraph* who worked for some time in their offices before the alarm was spread. The tannoy system in the building that alerts staff of bomb attacks had that morning broken down. While the rest of the building and the neighbouring shops and offices within a 400-yard radius had been evacuated, the editorial staff worked on in ignorant bliss. Only a sharp-eyed reporter who spotted the empty tanker outside – the street is in a controlled zone and vehicles are not permitted to park without someone remaining inside them – finally alerted the journalists of the peril in which they were working.

Tension was high that evening throughout the city, and especially in the Protestant areas. Catholic areas were reported to be quiet, according to security forces. At about 7·00 p.m. a Protestant assassination squad entered James Fusco's café in York Street, near the New Lodge Road (Catholic) and Tiger Bay (Protestant). The 58-year-old Italian-born Roman Catholic was in the café with his wife. The couple was alone when two young men burst in, one armed with a submachine-gun, the other with a semi-automatic pistol.

While the man with the machine-gun held Mrs Fusco at gunpoint, the other ran behind the counter and shot Fusco in the head. Mrs Fusco said later that she recognized the killers as customers of the café on several occasions, though she did not know their names.

At the same time trouble broke out in the near-by Roman Catholic New Lodge Road, and six people were shot dead. The Army claimed that all six victims were IRA gunmen who had been shot by soldiers. But the Army version is not accepted by either the IRA or the local people. What gives some authority to the latter is that the IRA acknowledged that four of the dead were gunmen, but vehemently deny that the two others were.

Local residents claimed that these two men, Brendan Maguire and John James Loughran, were shot from a passing car within the sight of the Army post at the junction of the New Lodge Road and the Antrim Road. They claimed that this incident led to the subsequent gun-battle between the Army and the IRA in which the four other men were killed. The residents were so certain of this that many of them made statements to this effect to solicitors later.

These claims were later corroborated to some extent by forensic evidence. Tests were made on all six dead men to see if they had been in contact with weapons before their deaths. On the four acknowledged IRA men the tests proved positive, but on Maguire and Loughran they were negative – they had not handled any weapons.

The refusal of the Army to admit that these two men were not IRA gunmen led to a belief in the area that they had been killed by an army plain-clothes patrol with the deliberate intention of provoking a confrontation. Such a clash, it was argued, took the heat off the Army elsewhere in the city as the Protestant extremists would be expected to think twice about taking on the Army at the same time as the Army was fighting the IRA elsewhere. There is no evidence to support this theory, no matter how nicely it fits IRA propaganda. But it is clear that the two men were not gunmen, and it is almost certain that they were killed by Protestant assassins.*

East Belfast was quiet that night, but an assassination squad did torture and kill a man not very far from the headquarters of the UDA in the Newtownards Road. This killing took place in the Connswater area of East Belfast, and was almost certainly carried out by the same people who had earlier killed Patrick Benstead, Henry Russell, and Terence Maguire. But this time the

*This incident is discussed again in Chapter 15.

victim was not a Roman Catholic like the other two, but a Protestant, John Boyd, 35, of Knockmore Square, Lisburn.

Boyd had been drinking in Belfast late that night. He was a well-known figure in East Belfast because of his drinking habits. But though he was a Protestant, Boyd held strong republican views and would describe himself as an 'Irish national'. Such views were not conducive to a long and healthy life when held by a Protestant in Belfast at this time. It was unwise in the extreme for men holding such views, even though he was a Protestant, to frequent bars in East Belfast.

Children playing on the banks of the Connswater river at lunchtime on Sunday 4 February saw a naked corpse in the water. It was Boyd. A police patrol arrived on the scene and dragged the body to the bank. Boyd had been brutally beaten and then stabbed a number of times before being shot in the head. His injuries were similar in nature to those of the three earlier victims in East Belfast that have been mentioned above.

Ulster's weekend death toll reached thirteen later that day when a Roman Catholic, Seamus Gilmore, 18, of Rosscoole Park, in the Ballysillan area, was shot dead while working in a filling station at Ballysillan Road in the north of the city. Although he was a Catholic, Gilmore lived and worked in a predominantly Protestant area, and had been a close friend of the young Protestant UDA man, Robert Burns, who had been killed two days earlier. Gilmore was killed within sight of the café where Burns died.

Two youths entered the Mountpleasant filling station, and while one sat in the forecourt in a stolen car, the other walked up and executed Gilmore. As the killers made off they crashed the car, but made good their escape on foot. Once again there were several witnesses to the shooting, but at the time of writing no one has been charged with the killing.

The weekend of violence had claimed ten Roman Catholics and three Protestants dead – eight of whom were assassination victims. But what escaped much of the attention was the number of attempted killings. Just as the gun-battle began in the New Lodge Road, a carload of Protestant gunmen, armed with submachine-guns, opened fire on a group of ten people standing on a street-corner in the Falls Road. The gunmen fired burst after burst at the group as men and women dived for cover. Surprisingly, although nine of the people were hit by the bullets, none of them received fatal wounds.

Elsewhere in the city, on the Ormeau Road, a Roman Catholic youth was shot down as he drove his motorcycle along the road, and in the north, at Ligoneil Road, a man walking along the pavement was shot from a passing car. Both survived. But for chance, the total of killed this weekend could have been as high as twenty-four. The weekend – which was the first since the Protestant extremists had abandoned the assassination pause – shocked Northern Ireland. The province was in a state of high tension as claim and counter-claim was made by the three protagonists, the Catholics, the Protestants, and the Army, about what had happened. The funeral of the four IRA men killed in the New Lodge Road gun-battle, scheduled for Wednesday 7 February, seemed to be a likely flashpoint.

If Protestant gunmen were responsible for the two non-IRA men killed on the Antrim Road – and it seems unlikely that the Army were the killers – then their tally of victims, both dead and wounded, this weekend is formidable. Clearly Herron had not been talking idly when he said the UDA would no longer use its restraining influence to halt the assassinations.

In the aftermath of these few short days the Catholics mourned their losses and the Protestants seethed in anger at the detention of the two men for the killing of Heenan on Thursday 1 February. While the IRA and the Army had been engaged in the New Lodge Road, 1,000 masked and uniformed Protestants had protested outside the RUC headquarters in the city. Loyalist groups threatened that if the men were not released immediately thousands of Protestants on stand-by in the province would engage in confrontations with the security forces.

One of the two UDA men held by the police was Leonard McCreery, 18, from the Tullycarnet estate, where the car used in the Heenan killing had later been found abandoned. McCreery had worked on the building site at Cherryvalley where the workmen travelling in the bus that was bombed had also worked. Various loyalist groups, including the banned UVF, combined to call a one-day general strike for Wednesday 7 February to protest at the detention orders. Trouble was guaranteed.

Unlike a similar strike the previous year to protest at the suspension of Stormont, the strike called for on 7 February did not have widespread popular support. Despite this, it was virtually 100 per cent effective, as few people dared be seen to break it lest they suffer an all-too-obvious fate afterwards. In retrospect the strike, with its widespread use of intimidation, both covert and overt, did the loyalist cause irreparable harm. It was called under the auspices of Ulster Vanguard, yet the Vanguard leader, William Craig, perceived the damage that it would do. He tried desparately to get it called off in secret meetings with the UDA and LAW leaders in the hours before, but he was overruled, and publicly supported the call to strike. Craig was like the revolutionary leader during the French Revolution who said on seeing a rampaging mob go by: 'There go my people. I must find out where they are going so that I can lead them.'

The Northern Ireland Committee of the Irish Congress of Trade Unions condemned the strike beforehand and urged all its members to go to work as usual. On Tuesday 6 February, the *Belfast Telegraph* leader took the same line. The detention of two Protestants had come as a rude shock to the loyalists, it said, but: 'The nettle has been grasped, and Mr Whitelaw must have been prepared to get stung.' The paper advised people to take a good look at the groups behind the strike before joining in. The following day the greater part of the paper's mainly Protestant workforce chose to stay at home – particularly the printers who are Protestant to a man – and the paper did not appear.

The night before the strike began tension was very high in Belfast in anticipation of more violence on the streets. Even so, despite the highly charged emotional atmosphere, two young Protestants decided to cross the city, and sectarian lines, on foot late at night. Glen Clarke, 18, of Beechland Drive, Lisburn, was a UDA member. He and his companion made their way past the Roman Catholic Unity Flats complex heading in the Protestant Millfield direction. They were close to an Army post on the corner of the flats and the Shankill, but this was to be of no assistance to them. They were approached by two youths outside Unity Flats. Clarke's companion managed to escape, but Clarke himself was taken. The youths were Provisional IRA volunteers. The Provisionals, aware that the alarm would be soon raised by the escaping man, transferred Clarke swiftly from the flats to the New Lodge Road area. Here Clarke was interrogated. The following morning he was found in an alley in Halliday's Road, off the New Lodge Road. He had been shot in the head at close range. His death passed by virtually unnoticed as Ulster ground to a complete halt with the loyalist strike. UDA men were on the streets in every area, armed not with guns or cudgels but with notebooks and pencils, jotting down the names of those who dared to break the strike. Belfast Corporation bus-drivers had an early taste of what might be expected should anyone defy the loyalists. At 6·00 a.m. the buses were running normally. An hour later uniformed UDA men threatened a number of drivers that they would be shot if they continued. The buses stopped running. But in most cases such overt intimidation was not necessary. Most people had a fairly good idea by now what exactly, to use Herron's phrase, was the meaning of 'the wrath of the UDA' and there were very few brave or foolhardy souls willing to bring it upon themselves for the sake of a day's pay. In Catholic areas, to be sure, like the Falls Road, or in the Catholic city of Londonderry, life went on fairly normally. But almost all of Ulster's Protestants stayed at home.

The Army was certain that trouble would break out but was not sure where. The funeral of those killed in the New Lodge Road was winding its way up the Falls Road in West Belfast, watched by thousands of people, when a Protestant sniper opened fire at the mourners. A young boy and an elderly man were wounded, neither seriously, but the incident sparked off trouble in the area. Elsewhere in the city, Protestants and Catholics were engaged in gun-battles with each other, particularly in the Oldpark area where two IRA men, armed with an

Armalite rifle and a submachine-gun, fired into a crowd of loyalists, injuring several of them, but causing no fatalities.

In East Belfast, Protestant gunmen opened fire on the Army after two women claimed they had been deliberately run down by a military vehicle. Fierce rioting broke out, and during the gun-battle a UVF man was shot dead by a British soldier. In Sandy Row across the Lagan in West Belfast the UDA sent out several armed men to engage troops during riots. A shop on the corner of Sandy Row and the Lisburn Road was bombed and caught fire. In the gun-battle that followed the Army used Browning heavy machine-guns mounted on armoured cars against the Protestants. In the midst of this battle, fireman fought to control the blazing shop fire, and one of these men, Fireman Brian Douglas, 18, of the Shore Road, was shot dead by the gunmen. Douglas was the only son and sole support for his blind widowed mother. The firemen withdrew immediately from the scene and the shop burned to the ground as the shooting continued. Fireman Douglas was the first fireman to be killed on active duty during the Troubles.

The following day, when Ulster awoke to count the cost of the previous day's violence and general strike, the mood was grim. The loyalists had shown their strength, but their tactics had been counter-productive. The violence and the confrontations between the Army and the Protestants in various parts of Belfast shocked most of the population, on both sides. 7 February came ultimately to be regarded as a crushing political defeat for the loyalists and their cause.

The strike had been called to demonstrate against the detention without trial of Protestants. Two days later, on Friday 7 February, troops and police in pre-dawn swoops on East Belfast arrested seven more Protestants. The most prominent was John McKeague. McKeague was charged in connection with a bank robbery and remanded on bail. When he stepped from the dock after receiving bail, he was rearrested and detained under the Special Powers Act. McKeague had been chief of the Shankill Defence Committee, although he lived in East Belfast, and had founded the militant Red Hand paramilitary group. The composition of this group was highly selective, and it was very secret in its operations. Its membership was composed in the main of Protestant youths – the Tartans who roamed the streets at night looking for trouble. These youths longed for action, and McKeague let them have it. It would not be straying too far from the mark to implicate the Red Hand in the ritual killings in East Belfast such as those of Russell and Benstead.

The events of these few days were a traumatic experience for the Protestant militants. Harding Smith and the UVF in West Belfast were extremely annoyed that Protestants had engaged the Army in open confrontation. Harding Smith feared that such a course could only lead to the banning of the UDA, and give Whitelaw the excuse he needed for the wholesale rounding-up and internment of Protestants. Herron was considered responsible for the mess, and this was added to the list of other errors he had committed in the eyes of the men in West Belfast.

The Protestant militants went underground for a week fearing an Army crackdown. The chairman of the United Loyalist Front, the Rev. William McCrea, of Magherafelt, claimed that he had proof that the Army had plans to round up all middle- and top-ranking members of loyalist organizations. He said that he had received this from intelligence officers working with the security forces, and said that the plan was to lock the men up to prevent trouble when Ulster voted in a plebiscite on the border on 8 March, leaving the organizations with no command structure. No such action was taken, but in the climate of the time Mr McCrea's warnings seemed to have the ring of truth.

Against this background, on Thursday 15 February, a UDA member, Albert Edward Browne, 21, of Waverley Avenue, Glengormley, was sentenced to death for the capital murder of a police officer. Browne had been one of a three-man squad caught in a car by the police in January. Browne possessed a revolver, and rather than surrender to police he shot both police officers, emptying his gun into the dead man. The imposition of the death penalty – it was mandatory for the offence of capital murder: killing a police officer or member of the security forces while in the pursuit of their duty – led to uproar in the Protestant camp. It was claimed that the death penalty was no longer valid as Ulster was now ruled from Westminster, and as it had been abolished there, it could not apply. Roman Catholic political and community leaders supported the Protestants, as they feared the consequences for themselves should Browne be hanged. Overnight Browne became a hero. His wife was besieged by pressmen, and her distraught photographs filled the pages and screens of the province's newspapers and televisions. There were few pictures of, or interviews with, the wife of the dead RUC man. Browne was later reprieved.

On Friday 16 February an incident occurred that demonstrated how effective, in certain circumstances, prompt action by the security forces could be to prevent an assassination.

Two Protestant bakery workers on a routine van-delivery in the Roman Catholic Beechmount area of Belfast were abducted by armed Provisional IRA men and taken to a near-by house where they were held for two hours and severely beaten. They were being escorted back to the van by their captors when one of the men made a break for it, and escaped to a passing Army patrol. After a further two hours the second man was still being held by the Provisionals when the Army issued them an ultimatum. The Army said bluntly that unless the man were freed by 6·00 p.m. they would go into the area in force and tear it apart until they found the kidnapped man. Shortly before 6·00 p.m. the man was released near the M1 motorway. He was lucky. Few of the countless other people who found themselves in similar positions were able to have the benefit of such instant and massive support from the security forces.

The following day, Saturday 17 February, Francis Taggart, 20, a Roman Catholic from Newtownabbey, was kidnapped by Protestant youths in East Belfast. Taggart lived with his mother at Fernagh Avenue on the Catholic Rathcoole estate, but worked in a garage in the Ravenhill Road, and left the firm every night to walk to his Fiat car which he parked several streets away. He never varied this pattern. On the evening in question, as he approached his car, he found two youths waiting who forced him to drive them away at gunpoint. The incident was witnessed by people near by, but this was not sufficient to save Taggart as the bakery man had been saved the previous day. An hour later he was found lying in the back seat of the car with gunshot wounds. He was still alive, but died the following day in hospital. He was yet another victim who worked in a hostile area.

The following day, Sunday 18 February, assassins killed two Roman Catholic postmen as they returned home from work in the afternoon along the lower end of the Falls Road. The killing took place within a few yards of an Army observation post sited on the roof of a disused factory. But unknown to local residents, the post had not been manned for months previously since a soldier there had been shot dead by an IRA sniper. Instead a dummy soldier was put there, and this device was sufficient to fool the Provisionals in the Lower Falls, who had been shooting at the dummy repeatedly – it was later found to be riddled with bullets.

Anthony Coleman, 30, of Colligan Street, and David McAleese, 38, of Ballymurphy Parade, were walking towards the Northumberland Street junction on the Falls Road. A car which had been driven down Northumberland Street from the direction of the Shankill Road turned into the Falls Road and stopped near the two uniformed postmen. A young man armed with a Sterling submachine-gun got out of the car and fired burst after burst of shots into McAleese and Coleman. He continued to fire into the writhing bodies of the two men as they lay on the pavement. A third man was also slightly wounded in the incident. The gunmen returned to the car which drove off in the direction of the Shankill Road along Townsend Street.

The car used in the killing had been hijacked earlier on the Shankill Road, and it was found abandoned later at Conlig Street near the Protestant Old Lodge Road. The attack was very well planned, and it would appear that the killers knew that the Army observation post at Divis Street was not manned. At first Roman Catholic politicians refused to believe that the post was occupied only by a dummy. But once this was realized, it gave credance to a belief, widespread in the area, that the culprits for the killing were not Protestants but an Army plain-clothes patrol. Later a Protestant youth was charged with the killing, but the possibility of Army involvement will be dealt with in Chapter 15.

February's civilian assassination toll was completed by the discovery on the morning of Monday 19 February of the body of a man buried in snowdrifts at a quarry on the outskirts of Belfast. Police who went to the quarry at Ligoniel, on the way to Belfast's Aldergrove Airport, found the head of a man sticking out of the snow.

The body was that of William Cooke, 29, a Protestant of Legan Street, Ligoneil, who had been shot a number of times in the back. He had been dead for about a week. Police had received a number of anonymous telephone calls via the confidential police number over the previous five days telling them that a body was hidden in the quarry. But despite a number of searches, it was not until the 19th, when the snow, which had been piling up in five-feet drifts in some places, began to melt to reveal the body. Police had known that Cooke was missing, but had not connected this to the telephone calls. After the discovery detectives issued a television appeal for the anonymous caller to come forward to provide additional information on the killing. Nobody ever did. Cooke was not a native of Ligoniel, but had moved there only a few months before his death. No one knew very much about him there and his movements prior to his death remained a mystery to police. He was described by his neighbours at Legan Street as a 'lonely character'. He was known in the Shankill area where he had been connected with the UDA. He was considered something of a wild, violent man. He was physically quite big, and it was claimed that he had been involved in a number of brawls in UDA clubs. It was also rumoured that he had been the man who had shot Fireman Douglas on the night of 7 February, and that he had been executed by the UVF for this breach of discipline. This allegation is not corroborated by other evidence at present.

In the days that followed, the initiative passed to the Provisional IRA, who maintained their campaign of violence and terror directed against the security forces. On Thursday 22

February they shot two Coldstream Guards in retaliation for the Catholics killed in the New Lodge Road on 3 February.

However, two days later, the prompt action of an elderly doorman saved many lives when a bomb was thrown into the hallway of a Roman Catholic public house. On the night of Saturday 24 February the man was on duty at the Hole-in-the-Wall bar off the Antrim Road. When the bomb was tossed into the hallway from a passing car he immediately kicked it out into the street and ran inside to warn the customers drinking. The bomb went off a few seconds later, but none of the twenty-three people in the bar received serious injury. Such attacks on bars with no warning given were occuring with increasing frequency. The car used by the bombers, a Ford Corsair, had been hijacked earlier in a Protestant area.

In the next twenty-four hours there was renewed violence in the province. A 9-year-old boy in Londonderry walked into a mine planted by Provisional I R A volunteers in his own back garden. The mine, which was intended to kill an Army patrol that regularly passed near by, blew the child's legs off, and he died later in hospital. In Belfast the Provisionals shot a Protestant youth aged 16 in the leg, and at Donegal Pass two Protestants were shot, but neither received serious injuries. Both men were believed to be the victims of a U D A kangaroo court, modelled along I R A lines.

From the deaths of McAleese and Coleman on 18 February there were no more assassinations until the first of the following month. There are many reasons for this. The first half of the month had seen a huge upsurge in violence, and the pattern of the campaign had been that when this had occurred, the assassins would pause for a week or two. But in February, as well as this, the pause was due to the public reaction to the loyalist strike and its consequences.

The militant Protestants had overplayed their admittedly strong hand. In the strike they had shown, not that they had overwhelming popular support, but that the vast majority of the people feared and was intimidated by them. Their claims thereafter to represent the average working-class Protestant –

taken very seriously by all parties previously – were no longer accepted. The violence that had accompanied the strike, and in particular the sight of British troops being fired upon by Protestants, caused a profound revulsion among most Protestants directed against the militant groups. Vanguard, LAW and UDA were all discredited in the eyes of Ulster's silent Protestant majority. The next month was to see a slight shift in emphasis from the streets to the ballot-box. It was to give the other Protestant politicians – people like Faulkner and Paisley, both of whom had been themselves discredited in the Protestant community not so long before – the chance to take a leading role once again. The transformation was not an easy one, and it did not happen overnight, but it began in the events of February.

11. Plebiscite and new constitution – but the assassinations go on: March and April

As we have seen, after four weeks in January without a civilian assassination, February saw the assassins unleashed. Fourteen victims died in the first eighteen days. From 29 January to 18 February, a total of nineteen people were killed, thirteen Roman Catholics and six Protestants. This average of a tiny fraction under one assassination each day for almost three weeks marked a return to the rates of June and July 1972, when the assassination campaign was at its fiercest. But the pace died down, and there were no more fatalities until 1 March.

On the first day of the new month, a Thursday, there were two killings. The first was that of Daniel Patrick Bowen, 38, a Roman Catholic who lived in the Lower Falls area. He was shot dead from a passing car in Linenhall Street, a back street off the city centre behind the City Hall, and on the fringe of the Roman Catholic Markets area. Almost immediately police were able to announce that the death was not a sectarian killing. Bowen was a man with a long history of mental illness. He was a manic depressive who could one moment be on top of the world and believe himself capable of anything, and the next plunged into deep and dark depression. Someone who knew him and his illness well described him as 'a dapper little man, but one who could not be trusted'. Bowen was brought before an IRA kangaroo court, and sentenced to death for a repeated series of sexual assaults against young girls. The sentence was harsh for the offence, but Bowen was a repeated offender – another aspect of his illness – and he paid the full price for his weakness. His death was another example of the stern approach both sides were capable of taking towards offences of a sexual nature.

The second man to die that day was a Roman Catholic taxi-driver, Stephen Kernan, 56, of Station Road, Whiteabbey. His is a curious case of a Roman Catholic who lived in a predominantly Protestant suburb of Belfast, north of the city, and who taxied in the Protestant Shankill Road area. To do this he had to get the permission of the local UDA command. In addition to this, Kernan also visited the Catholic Ardoyne area, as hard-line on that side as the Shankill was on the other. He was well known in bars in both areas as a man who talked a lot and who tried to give the impression that he knew important people in both communities. He seemed to think that his contacts made him invulnerable, but it is doubtful whether they really existed. Because of his visits to bars in both areas which extremists also frequented, he did know a lot of people engaged in terrorist activities, but he did not have the influence with them he liked to give the impression he had. He was a man who talked too much, too loudly and too often for his own good, and it was only a matter of time before someone got to him. It would have been plausible for either side to have hit him. As it happened, it was the Protestants who got to him first.

A day or so before his death, Kernan's taxi had been hijacked on the Shankill Road. He had been taken by UDA men to a romper room and interrogated about his connections with the Provisional IRA in the Ardoyne. Apparently they were satisfied with his explanations, for he was released a few hours later. He was told, however, that his taxi would be needed for a short time, and that if he did not go to the police he could have it back within a few days. On 1 March word was sent to Kernan from the UDA that he could pick up the car at 9·00 p.m. on the Crumlin Road. He left a bar in the Ardoyne at the appointed time, and he is reported to have sworn that he was going to get even with the so-and-sos who had taken his car and subjected him to the interrogation. He was next seen in Malvern Street off the Shankill Road, bleeding to death in his car from gunshot wounds in the chest. Like the day's other victim, Daniel Bowen, Kernan – the man who thought he was important – had a history of mental illness, and had spent a number of years in a mental institution.

The next day another killing occurred that shocked the province and brought Belfast's buses to a complete halt. Patrick Crossan, 38, a Roman Catholic from the Ardoyne, was driving his one-man corporation bus, route no. 53, from Balmoral to Ligoniel. At the top of the Shankill at Woodvale Road, two men calmly boarded the bus at 3·00 p.m. while it contained a number of passengers, and shot Crossan at point-blank range. The killers made their getaway in broad daylight in a white Ford Anglia towards Woodvale. The car had earlier been stolen from Tennant off the Shankill Road.

The assassination of a Belfast bus-driver at the wheel of his bus was regarded with horror by most people in the province. The dead man's colleagues immediately went on strike until the funeral on Monday 5 March. At first the killing appeared to be totally without motive. Later it was alleged that Crossan had been a prominant member of the Northern Ireland Civil Rights Association. NICRA is a small organization, based entirely among the province's Roman Catholic community. In the early marching phase of the Troubles in the late sixties the association had wielded immense power and enjoyed much prestige; but as the situation deteriorated and the violence developed, it began to wane in importance. It became heavily infiltrated by the Provisional IRA who used it for propaganda purposes. If Crossan was indeed in NICRA it would have been a sufficient reason for him to be the victim of Protestant assassins. In the eyes of most Protestants NICRA was synonymous with the IRA. Crossan's family, however, denied that he had been in the association. If this was not the reason – and, of course, it would have been sufficient that Crossan was thought to be in NICRA – then the killing is puzzling. The killers seem to have known who they were killing. Crossan's movements would have been easy to determine from the bus time-tables, and the killers appear to have lain in wait for him.

The same evening, a Protestant was shot dead as he left an Orange hall not far from where Crossan had been shot. George Walmsley, 52, of Glenbank Drive, Ligoniel, was a bachelor who had lived with his parents since leaving the merchant navy.

He was the secretary of the Ligoniel Orange Lodge, and was described by friends as 'a quiet man who had been a friend to everyone, irrespective of their religion'. He and another man were cut down by a hail of bullets from a sniper concealed on the corner of Limehall Street and Ligoniel Street. Walmsley's companion received only slight injuries, but Walmsley was shot dead. One theory later put forward was that the real target for the sniper had been the second man who was in the UDR, but this appears most unlikely. In the bad light at the time it would have been difficult for the sniper to identify the men, and he could not have known when the target would leave the hall. The more likely explanation is that this was a simple sectarian killing. The killers wanted to kill a Protestant or two, and they could be sure that whoever left the Orange Hall would be a Protestant. It may be that the killing was in revenge for the earlier killing of Crossan. It was, however, Walmsley's misfortune to be the victim. Sadly, the reason for his early departure from the hall that evening lay in a family breavement. His father, William, had died only a week earlier, and this had caused his mother of 83 to become ill. Walmsley was on his way home because he was worried about his elderly mother's health.

The next killing occurred in the early hours of Thursday 8 March. This day was an historic and fateful day in Northern Ireland, for it was the date of Ulster's first plebiscite on the border. At 8·00 that morning a woman living in Summer Street in the Oldpark area was on her way to work when she noticed blood trickling down the street from a grey-coloured Ford Cortina which was parked outside her home. As she had never seen the car before, she became curious and looked inside the vehicle to find there the hooded body of a man, his feet tied, lying on the rear seat. The back of the car was covered in blood, and some had seeped through the floor onto the road. The woman says that she had first thought the blood belonged to a dead cat, but when she saw the hooded body she became hysterical. A neighbour heard her screams and called the police. The woman had to be taken to the Mater Hospital and treated for shock. Her husband later told the police that he had left home to go to work at 5·45 and had seen the Cortina but had not thought of looking inside it. No one in the street reported hearing any shots, either during the night or in the early hours of the morning, so one must assume that the execution took place elsewhere, possibly not too far away, and that the body was driven to Summer Street by the killers. It was dumped only a few yards from a polling-station. Army bomb-disposal experts took no chances with the body. In case it was booby-trapped they first blew open the doors of the car, and then a heavy rope was attached to the body, which was dragged unceremoniously into the street. Children on their way to school watched at this all took place – just another part of life, and death, in Ulster.

The victim was later identified as David Glenon, 45, a Roman Catholic from Ballymurphy. He had been missing for over twenty-four hours, and was last seen setting off to visit a relative in the Ardoyne. Like O'Neill and McCartney the previous July, Glenon had to pass through hard-line Protestant territory; and like them, too, he never made it. The car in which he was found had been hijacked on the Shankill Road the previous day. It is probable that Glenon was intercepted by Protestant militants who detained him for interrogation before killing him. The place where the body was dumped is not far from the spots where Thomas Madden and Francis Arthurs were found.

A week later another killing was to create a stir in the province when a well-known Roman Catholic millionaire was killed by a bomb left at his house. Larry McMahon, 43, was one of Ireland's best-known figures in horse-race betting. In addition he owned a number of hotels and bars. A bomb of between 10 and 15 lb. was placed on his porch at the 'Moorings', his luxury home in the plush Belfast suburb of Jordanstown. The bomb exploded without warning and killed McMahon instantly. His wife and four children were badly shaken, but escaped serious injury.

Within an hour the Royal Hotel at Whitehead, which McMahon had recently purchased, was also bombed and destroyed by an ensuing fire. A barman received severe injuries from the blast. A later newspaper report in the London *Times* claimed that the killing of McMahon was carried out by the UVF. The motive suggested was that some of the dead man's betting-shops had been used as a communications network by the IRA. Certainly this was a strong rumour at the time of McMahon's death. Whether the dead man was aware that such activities took place in his shops, or that he had any control over them, is something that remains unknown.

On 8 March, the day of the Glenon killing, Protestant Ulster voted by an overwhelming majority to remain a part of the United Kingdom. Despite the call by all the Roman Catholic groups, from the IRA to the SDLP, for a boycott of the plebiscite – which was largely followed by the Roman Catholic population – 57·5 per cent of the total electorate of 1,031,633, turned out and voted in favour of the union. There were 591,820 votes cast in favour of the union against a mere 6,463 who favoured an immediate united Ireland, and 5,973 spoiled votes. With 42 per cent of the electorate abstaining, the vote could be said to have gone along sectarian lines. But there would appear to be some justification for the unionist claim that many Roman Catholics had voted in favour of the union. Whether this is true or not, it could not be denied that the vote was a massive triumph for the majority Protestant Unionists, of whatever shade of opinion.

Later in the month, on Tuesday 20 March, the British government published its long-awaited White Paper on Northern Ireland. Its main points had been leaked to the press well beforehand, and nothing it contained came as a surprise. The old Stormont system of majority-rule governments with a cabinet and prime minister were gone forever. In their place was to be a new assembly elected by proportional representation. The new executive would be drawn from as many parties in the new chamber as possible, and from both communities. The principle of power-sharing was to be enshrined in the new constitutional bill that would give the White Paper provisions law.

In his speech to the British House of Commons when he introduced the White Paper, the Secretary of State for Northern Ireland, William Whitelaw, had this to say about the measure:

The proposed settlement is devised for the interests of Northern Ireland as a whole. It cannot meet all the wishes of any one section of the community. It requires the cooperation of all the people of Northern Ireland. A heavy responsibility now rests upon their leaders. There can be no excuses for withdrawal of cooperation or resort to violence ... The proposed settlement, given good will, provides for a reasonable basis for progress.

The White Paper was a reasonable settlement for reasonable people. It remained to be seen just how many reasonable people there actually were in Ulster. But there were to be elections – the first for over four years – and these at least would give the Ulster people, Protestant and Catholic, the chance to show exactly who represented them. But in the meantime the violence continued, and so did the assassinations.

The month of April was only three days old when the body of David Thomas McQueen, 28, a Protestant from the Ballybeen estate at Dundonald, was found by a motorist on the coast road from Portavogie to Ballyhelbert. McQueen had gone missing the previous night from his home in the Protestant suburb on the outskirts of East Belfast. The estate where the dead man lived was opposite the Rolls-Royce factory where the Roman Catholic Jack Mooney had been killed while on his way to work at the beginning of the year. Portavogie, in County Down, where the body was found, is a predominantly Protestant town, and police almost immediately ruled out any IRA involvement in the killing. Their investigations pointed to one of the Protestant organizations, but they were unable to establish a motive.

Two days later, on Thursday 5 April, two Roman Catholic priests narrowly escaped death when a bomb was left at their parochial house in Antrim. Police described the bombing as a deliberate attempt to kill or maim. The following day in the House of Commons at Westminster the Under-Secretary for the Army in Northern Ireland, Peter Blake, said that the IRA was being defeated. He based part of this claim on the increasing use by the Provisionals of young people, and said this showed how badly in need of manpower they were. This sort of claim had all been heard before. Even if the Minister's remarks about

205

the success the Army had had in eliminating the experienced Provisionals was true – and it substantially was – the fact remained that bombs or guns in the hands of a 15-year-old could do just as much damage as in the hands of an adult. Indeed, the growing dependence by the IRA Provisionals on such young people tended to lead to greater and more indiscriminate acts of violence and destruction. Despite the Minister's optimism, on the ground in Northern Ireland it did not look as though things were getting better. Even if the IRA were finally defeated, what would be done about the Protestant extremists? The events of recent months had convinced the security forces that the Protestant paramilitary groups now posed as big a problem as the IRA. Could they be effectively disarmed once the source of the present Troubles was eliminated? After four years of optimistic forecasts and pessimistic consequences, no one wanted to hazard a guess.

The night Blake spoke in the House of Commons, another Roman Catholic parochial house was bombed. This house, at Greencastle on the outskirts of Belfast, was not occupied at the time as it was still under completion.

The days following were quiet. The only sectarian trouble was in Carickfergus where a number of Roman Catholic families were forced to leave their homes. Good news came for the UDA on Monday 9 April, when Whitelaw reprieved convicted murderer and UDA man Albert Browne, the man who had emptied the contents of his revolver into a policeman. The reprieve was a relief to moderates on both sides as well as to the Protestant militants. Had the UDA man been hanged the results could have been catastrophic, a factor which, no doubt, influenced the Secretary of State.

The following few days were so quiet that one issue of the *Belfast Telegraph* devoted its main front-page story to the dangers of smoking cigarettes. Its readers must have been interested to learn that there were other ways to die than by the bomb or the bullet. It was not often in these times that the *Telegraph*'s front page was not dominated by acts of violence.

However, the brief period of tranquillity was not to last.

On the night of Wednesday 11 April two Roman Catholic public houses were bombed, and on the 13th a young Protestant was found dying in the toilet of a public house in East Belfast. James Adair, 17, of Dromore Street, later died in hospital after surgeons had fought in vain to save him. He had been shot in the head and a bullet had lodged in the brain. The shooting took place in the Cregagh Inn, in the heart of Protestant UDA territory. There was never any suggestion that Adair was killed by the IRA. Adair was drinking in the bar, which was moderately full of usual drinkers at the time. He was last seen alive walking to the men's lavatory outside at the back of the premises. His killers followed him outside and shot him. They were almost certainly a UDA punishment squad. Police questioned a number of drinkers who were in the bar at the time of the shooting. Unfortunately, none of them was able to recall much of the incident, or to give any description of the killers. By this time bars in both communities tended only to be frequented by regular customers. Too many bombs had been left in bars by people unknown to the publicans. Strangers were suspect, and in such areas as East Belfast or the Falls in the West, one would be in some personal danger to walk into a bar where they were not known. Yet, according to the witnesses to the shooting of Adair in the Cregagh Inn, those responsible for the youth's death must have been strangers.

The same night Protestant bombers were at work again. This time their target was the Celtic Studies department of the Queen's University, Belfast. Security forces were able to identify from which side the attack came from the materials used in the bomb. The IRA by this time had an abundance of funds – mainly from the United States, though not an inconsiderable amount flowed from England and Eire – and possessed large stocks of gelignite. They also still had the men capable of making sophisticated bombs from other explosive materials, such as chemical fertilizers, if the need arose. But the Protestant extremists did not have an inexhaustible supply of money to buy gelignite, and they were forced to rely on more home-made types of bomb. The Provisional IRA tended to use the explosives at their disposal in liberal quantities, producing bombs containing 50, 100 and 200 lb. of material. The Protestants could not afford such extravagance. Their most common type of bomb was a small amount of explosive packed into a metal casing. The metal would fly off in all directions in the blast and create a lot of destructive and lethal shrapnel. Such bombs did not have quite the same devastating effect as those of the IRA, but they could still cause a considerable amount of damage to both life and property. It was such a bomb that was left outside the university department.

The following night a Protestant IRA man, who had for over a year been on an assassination list, drawn up by Protestants, was finally killed. Robert Millen, 23, of Ormeau Road, was doing vigilante duty at McClure Street, when he was gunned down by killers in a passing car. McClure Street is in a small Catholic pocket off the Ormeau Road. The Ormeau Road runs from behind the City Hall across the Lagan into East Belfast. The area in which Millen both lived and was killed is a short distance from the Catholic Markets area, but is surrounded by Protestant areas, just West of the Lagan.

Millen's parents lived in the Ballybeen estate at Dundonald, a staunchly Protestant area in East Belfast. Millen himself, however, was a member of the Official IRA. Because of his religion, the more sectarian Provisionals had always regarded him with suspicion. But the Markets area and the near-by Ormeau Road enclave were controlled by the Officials. The Marxist and non-sectarian Officials admired and respected Millen for his courage in forsaking his background for his political convictions. The history of the Millen family is typical of many thousands of Ulster families forced to pull up the roots of a lifetime and retreat behind the safety of sectarian barricades. Before the Troubles the whole family had lived among the Roman Catholics in Belmore Street off the Ormeau Road. But with the onset of the Troubles the family moved to Dundonald. Millen, however, chose to remain. He did not want to desert his Catholic friends, through whom he had become converted to the Marxist republican ideals of the Official IRA.

One month before Millen's death he received a letter that had been sent to an address in near-by Lavinia Street. The letter was an assassination list that contained nine names including his own. Below the names was written the warning in printed letters: 'We will get you all sooner or later.' Ten days before Millen was killed, one of the other nine men was shot down by gunmen from a passing car. He survived, but if there had been any doubt as to the authenticity of the 'death list', it was removed. The letter Millen received had contained another warning for him: 'At last I have got my finger on you,' it said. 'Every car or man that comes up to you, look at it. I want to see your face as you die.'

Before the Troubles Millen had been a member of a football team that had drawn its members, of both religions, from the youths of the area. The Bankmore Star soccer team was a casualty of the deterioration in community relations from 1968 onwards, in more ways than just its disbandment. Colin Poots, 21, a Protestant, and Patrick McCrory, 19, a Roman Catholic, were also victims of assassinations. Poots was killed on 12 July, and McCrory on 13 March, both in 1972. It would appear that the Bankmore Star football team had been earmarked for special attention by the assassins – probably because its composition crossed sectarian boundaries and seemed to suggest that Protestants and Roman Catholics in Northern Ireland could live in peace with each other.

Two nights after Millen was shot dead a middle-aged Protestant housewife met the same fate. Mrs Margaret Miller, 59, of Beit Street off the Donegal Road, was working in her kitchen in her nighdress late at night when there was a knock at the door. Her husband Alfred was watching television in the living room, and she walked past him to open the door. She turned on the hallway light and was about to open the street door when four shots rang out. She fell, dying. Her husband rushed to the hallway and carried her into the living room where he laid her on a couch before running over 200 yards in his bare feet to call an ambulance. On his return his wife had collapsed into unconsciousness and she died on the way to the Royal Victoria Hospital. A blue Cortina car was seen speeding away from the house along Beit Street and into the Donegal Road after the killing.

The Millers were a quiet couple who rarely left the house at night because of the Troubles. Beit Street is a small street occupied in the main by elderly couples. Only one Catholic family lived there. It would seem that this couple were the intended victims of the attack. The front door of the Miller's house contains a large glass panel through which the shots were fired. However, the glass was not clear glass and the killers would not have been able to distinguish who had answered their knock, despite the hall light. The attack was clearly premeditated. Alfred Miller later disclosed that the previous night at approximately the same time there had been another knock at the door. But there had been a long delay before the door was opened by his wife, and she found no one there. Presumably the killers had believed the couple were out, and decided to pay their visit the following night. Neither of the couple was in any way connected with political organizations on either side.

There were no further assassinations in April. With only four victims the month was the quietest for such killings since exactly one year before. April 1972 had had just one killing fewer. But the last day of April 1973 saw a killing that, though it was not of a civilian, typified the seemingly unending series of deaths in Ulster. This was the killing of Marine Graham Cox by the Provisional IRA in the New Lodge Road area, and it showed once again the degree to which the Provisionals were unable to grasp the most simple of political realities. This shooting aroused the anger and disgust of both the Army and the Protestant population towards the Roman Catholics in the area, which surely must have been contrary to the aims of the Provisional IRA. It also removed an effective deterrent against Protestant assassination squads killing Roman Catholics in the New Lodge Road, which again one must assume was contrary to Provisional intentions. Finally, it damaged the credibility of the IRA men as defenders of the population in the eyes of the local people, and made them extremely unpopular. Without popular support the Provisionals would not be able to operate, so on this count, too, the killing must be judged contrary to their long-term aims.

The background to the killing was this: After the shootings on the New Lodge Road in March – in which local residents claimed Protestant assassins in fast cars had killed at least two people and wounded others – Roman Catholic politicians and residents mounted a vociferous campaign to get the Army to build ramps at either end of the road to keep the car-based assassins out of the area. The Army reluctantly agreed, and erected ramps at the junctions of the New Lodge Road with the Antrim Road at one end and North Queen Street at the other. All vehicles that entered or left the road were thereafter forced to slow down to 5 m.p.h. to negotiate the ramps. The ramps were thus an effective deterrent against the killers, who could no longer speed in and out of the area at will in a matter of seconds.

But the ramps were not confined in their effectiveness to civilian vehicles. Army vehicles also had to slow down to a crawl in order to cross them, and as such they represented a hazard to troops. The unwillingness of the Army command to present their soldiers as sitting ducks to snipers in a militantly republican area run by the Provisional IRA had been the basis of its reluctance to build the ramps; but after repeated appeals from local people backed up by the Catholic SDLP politicians, the Army believed that there was a tacit acceptance on the part of the Provisionals that they would not take advantage of the ramps. The Army was wrong.

The Provisionals in the New Lodge could not appreciate the subtlety involved in such a gentleman's agreement. They saw the ramp's erection in a very narrow light – it gave them the opportunity to attack the Army. On Monday 30 April a Provisional unit was waiting to ambush troops crossing the ramp at the Antrim Road end of the New Lodge. As two Land-rovers of Royal Marines slowed to cross the ramps the gunmen opened fire, killing Marine Cox and seriously wounding a companion. As the gunmen made their escape through near-by streets, the marine was laid on the pavement, his head supported by an Army pack. He died almost immediately, his blood running down the pavement and into the New Lodge Road for all the residents to see just exactly how the IRA had reacted to the Army's gesture in erecting ramps. Marine Cox was the fifty-first soldier to die in Ulster in 1973. He was not to be the last, but by the standards claimed for themselves by the IRA, his was certainly one of the most futile and counter-productive deaths. The Army was extremely angry at the shooting. The following day they moved in with bull-dozers and removed the ramps. The area was once again open to Protestant assassins. The people there were now as vulnerable and defenceless as they were in March when the assassins had taken a heavy toll. If the IRA believed that by killing Marine Cox they were in some way 'defending' the people in the New Lodge, they were guilty of a gross miscalculation. The killing was a depressing end to a depressing first third of the year.

12. 'We are responsible' – the emergence of the UFF: May and June

The IRA was not responsible for any of the April assassinations, and it was to be the same story in May, when nine people were killed. This trend, noted by the *Belfast Telegraph* in its leader at the beginning of the year, accelerated as 1973 passed on. Fewer and fewer of the victims of assassinations were killed by the IRA. Why this should be so is not entirely clear. Since 1971, when the IRA began the assassinations, most of the running had been made by the Protestants anyway. But as well as this, the undoubted success of the Army in rounding up IRA men was by this time beginning to take its toll on the Provisional's command structure. They were far from finished, but they were severely battered, and perhaps just could not afford the manpower to respond to Protestant assassinations as they had previously. But the Protestants had no such problems.

The first victim in May was Liam McDonald, 18, a Roman Catholic of Carnreah Bend, on the Rathcoole Estate, north of Belfast. On the night of Tuesday 1 May McDonald went to visit his girlfriend in the predominantly Roman Catholic Bawnmore Estate on the Shore Road. The estate is surrounded by a Protestant area and had come under attack a month earlier by Protestant extremists. On one occasion 100 UDA men in a convoy of cars had converged on the estate armed with cudgels and revolvers, but the Army and police had been tipped off and had set up road-blocks *en route*.

McDonald was a regular visitor to Bawnmore. That night he left as usual to walk or hitch a lift to his home after seeing his girlfriend. Before he had gone there his mother had warned him to stay the night at his girlfriend's house. But he ignored the warning and set out to return home at midnight. The decision was to cost him his life. He was last seen heading over the Arthur Bridge near the M2 motorway. Three hours later people living on the Ballyduff Road heard a car stop on the edge of a near-by quarry. Three shots rang out, but though local people suspected that someone had been killed, all were too afraid to go outside their doors and go to the spot – some forty yards away – even after the killers had driven off. Such was the fear produced by the assassinations. An elderly man who had seen the car pull up with no headlights showing said the next day: 'I suppose someone should have gone up to the road to see if they could help the victim because he might have been alive at that time. But people are so frightened when this kind of thing happens that they must be excused.'

Other residents claimed that there was no telephone on the estate and therefore could not call the police to the scene. Eventually a man leaving to go to work at 5·30 a.m. found the body. McDonald was face downward on a gravel path. He had been shot twice in the chest and in the head. He was not identified for thirty-six hours after appeals had been made over the radio for someone to come forward to name the victim. His mother had assumed that he had stayed at his girlfriend's home as she had advised. The body contained no identification. Police broadcast on radio and television that the victim had been fair-haired and had worn a red jacket. Mrs McDonald later recounted how she first realized that the dead youth could be her son:

'I never thought the boy mentioned on the broadcasts could be Liam,' she said. 'But I suddenly remembered he had bought a red jacket. I had warned him to stay overnight in his girlfriend's, and I thought he had obeyed me. I always felt sorry for anyone who had lost someone – soldiers, police, anyone – but when it comes to your own door, it's terrible.'

Almost a fortnight later a killing that was to be immensely important took place. On Monday 14 May a Roman Catholic social security officer, John McCormac, 30, of Ballyoran Heights, Portadown, was shot dead in the Lower Falls. McCormac was a married man with four young children. He was working in the area – an area with a chronically high figure of unemployment

– when late in the afternoon at the junction of Raglan Street and Verna Street a car drove up to him and stopped. An armed man got out and walked up to McCormac and shot him five times at point-blank range in the head and chest. The car was then seen to speed off in the direction of Leeson Street. McCormac was rushed to the near-by Royal Victoria Hospital where he underwent immediate surgery, but he died the following day.

It was immediately assumed that McCormac had been shot by the Provisional IRA. They had declared all people who could be considered as part of the State, such as civil servants, legitimate targets. The killing was bitterly resented by local people, the vast majority of whom depended on unemployment and social security benefits to survive. And it was never really doubted by the local people that the IRA were the killers. It appeared that, as in the case of Marine Cox, the Provisionals had 'cut off their nose to spite their face'. It was not thought plausible that Protestant gunmen would have dared to venture into this part of the Lower Falls, an area full of small streets and containing large numbers of armed IRA men of both wings. This was the heart of the IRA in Belfast. The RUC were never to be seen on the streets, day or night, unless accompanied by large numbers of heavily armed troops. The troops themselves kept out unless they were involved in arms searches, in which case they entered in force. For a single car containing only a handful of Protestants just to enter the area at any time of the day would have required enormous courage and daring. To do this, and then shoot someone there, even more so. If this area was not safe from Protestant assassins, then no part of Northern Ireland was. Yet fifteen minutes after McCormac was shot down, a man called the BBC offices and claimed that Protestant extremists were responsible.

The caller said that the shooting had been in retaliation for the killing by the IRA of a UDR corporal, Frank Cadoo, two days earlier on Saturday 12 May, at his dairy farm near the border at Aughnacloy. Later the same day the *Irish News* received a similar call from a man who described himself as an 'adjutant in an extremist Protestant organization in the Shankill'. As with the other call, the 'extremist Protestant organization' was not given a name. The caller said his name was 'George', and continued:

There was a shooting incident on the Falls today. Our organization, which carried it out, is a very extreme loyalist group. *We were responsible for most of the assassinations last summer*. This attack today was carried out in retaliation for the murder of Corporal Cadoo.

We are issuing a warning to the IRA that *if they keep on murdering members of the security forces and harassing loyal citizens of Ulster we will take very stern action against Roman Catholics*. We were responsible for the bombing of the *Irish News*. We took two cars from near the Mater Hospital and used them for the getaway. It was not a 50-lb. bomb but a hundredweight of mixed chemicals.*

The following day, Tuesday 15 May, Roman Catholic SDLP leader Gerard Fitt openly cast doubts on the authenticity of the calls. He was the Westminster MP for the area in which the shooting took place, and his constituency also includes the Shankill Road. He reflected the views of most people who were sure that the killing had been the work of the Provisionals, who had attempted to deflect adverse public opinion from themselves by making the telephone calls. The Provisionals, it was thought, realized that McCormac was a popular man, who had given local people a great deal of assistance, and wanted to blame the killing on Protestants. With important elections imminent for both the new Assembly in June and the local councils later in May, the last thing Fitt wanted was an increase in sectarian bitterness which, it appeared, the Provisionals, with their alleged impersonation of Protestant extremists, were trying to achieve. Fitt said he found the circumstances of the shooting 'very suspicious', and continued:

I find it extremely strange that the caller did not mention an organization. I do not accept the claims made. I am quite certain that when the facts of this shooting are made known, the claims will prove false. I am convinced that when those responsible realized that they had shot a social security officer carrying out his duties, they tried to lay the responsibility at someone else's door.

*Italics ours – M.D. and D.L.

Fitt was, of course, implicitly blaming the Provisional IRA. It was immediately assumed that his statement, in many ways unprecedented for a Catholic politician, was based on hard factual knowledge from local sources. The fact that Fitt, the local MP and respected Catholic figure, could announce publicly that McCormac had not been killed by Protestants was taken to mean that he actually knew this for certain.

However, it was later to be shown that Fitt was wrong. It is now clear that his doubts were an immediate gut reaction to all the circumstances – the same gut reaction that everyone else had – and were not founded on hard evidence. When he spoke he did not know that the car used by the killers, a beige-coloured Austin 1800, had been hijacked thirty minutes previously on the Shankill Road. And he could not know that within a few weeks a Protestant organization based in the Shankill Road would emerge and claim responsibility for assassinations – an organization certainly extreme, but also composed of men with both the know-how and the daring to venture deep into enemy territory to make their kills. The heart of the Falls was no longer safe from the Protestant assassins.

One of the things that suggested in retrospect that the claim to the BBC and *Irish News* might be genuine was the reference in the statement to the newspaper of a bomb attack at its offices not long before. The details of the size and materials used in the bomb, plus the location of the spot where the cars used had been hijacked, were not common knowledge. Unless the bomb attack was committed by the Provisional IRA – and no one believes this would be likely as the *Irish News* has a strong Catholic bias that makes it at least print most of the IRA statements – they would not have known this information.

In June a new extremist Protestant organization put its name in the headlines. Called the Ulster Freedom Fighters, it claimed responsibility for the assassination of Catholics. This was a momentous event. Before this date, no Protestant body had ever admitted killing Catholics. There were many in the Protestant community, and also, it must be said, in the RUC, who believed that the Provisional IRA was responsible for almost all the dead. McCormac was the first victim to be publicly acknowledged by Protestants. At the time of his killing, the name UFF had not been invented. It was later used as a matter of convenience for the killers, but this is part of a wider subject that will be dealt with shortly. The important aspect of the new situation – where Protestants now openly acknowledge their victims – is that the first statement of the UFF, given to the *Irish News*, admitted that the people behind the McCormac killing had been responsible for similar assassinations in the summer of 1972: 'We were responsible for most of the assassinations carried out last summer,' the statement said. As we have seen, it was in the summer of 1972 that the number of assassinations rapidly increased, and the involvement of Protestant assassins in large numbers began.

On Wednesday 16 May, Joseph McKenna, 24, a Roman Catholic of Fort Street, off the Springfield Road, died in the Royal Victoria Hospital. McKenna had been shot from a passing car on the Grosvenor Road on 11 March. Several others had also been hit in the incident.

The day after McKenna died, Thursday 17 May, the Ormeau Road area of Belfast, where Millen had been killed, again made headlines. Two youths on a motorcycle placed a bomb outside a Roman Catholic bar, the Jubilee Bar, at Ivanhoe Street. The bar was crowded with drinkers and, before they left, one of the youths opened the front door of the bar and shot dead one of those inside. Thomas Ward, 34, a Roman Catholic of Lavinia Street, died instantly as he sat at a table drinking a pint of beer. The youths then made off down an alleyway and up the Ormeau Road into East Belfast. The incident occurred so quickly that the other people in the bar did not notice the duffle-bag containing the bomb the killers had left behind. Fortunately, there was a fault in the bomb's timing device, and it had not gone off when the Army arrived. A soldier discovered it and threw it over an embankment on to a disused railway line where it exploded harmlessly.

A few days later, on Saturday 19 May, another Roman Catholic was killed in the vicinity of Carlisle Circus. Edward

Coogan, 39, of Dunleway Street, in the Falls Road area, worked as a painter and for some time had been working in a school off the Antrim Road. He was seen the evening of his death by his workmates when he left the school to return home. Before midnight he was spotted walking through Adela Street, off the Crumlin Road. Minutes later he was shot down from a passing car. There were several witnesses to the shooting, but none of them came forward despite repeated appeals by the police for assistance. He was dying when police reached him, and was dead before an ambulance arrived.

Coogan is believed to have spent the evening at the house of a woman in the Limestone Road, a road off the Antrim Road, near where he had been working. Just over a week later, the woman, Margaret Hrykiewicz, 24, a Roman Catholic, was also found dead in Adela Street. Hrykiewicz had been missing for several days before her body was found – in a piece of black comedy, she, like Coogan, was found beneath a sign saying 'NO DUMPING, BY ORDER'. Police were convinced that she was killed not far from where she was found. Unlike Coogan, who had been shot, Hrykiewicz had been stabbed to death. Residents in Adela Street said later that she had been making inquiries there about the shooting of Coogan – probably the cause of her own death. The dead woman, as her name suggested, was the daughter of a Polish father. She had been born in England but her mother was Irish. She was married, but separated from her husband, and used her maiden name. She had a number of children from the marriage. The area in which both she and her lover died was the scene of a number of assassinations. Given this fact, it was a most unwise course of action for her to call at street doors in Adela Street in search of information on Coogan's death. Apparently the wrong people got to hear of her inquiries.

Between the deaths of Coogan and Hrykiewicz, the body of another Roman Catholic was found at the Giant's Ring, where young Raffety had been killed at the end of January. The victim was Joseph Matthews, 30, of Abyssinia Street, in the Falls. The body was found on Friday 25 May on a grass verge, only yards from the spot where Rafferty had been found. Matthews bore the marks of a severe beating before being shot. Police investigations were made difficult because the dead man's movements prior to his death appeared a mystery. The Giant's Ring had once been the site of a witches' coven. Apparently it had now become the scene of a more modern form of ritual.

The month of May ended on a violent note. Two men were killed, and many others were injured, when three Catholic-owned bars were bombed without warning. On Wednesday 30 May six people were injured in the Anchor Bar, in the heart of Belfast's dockland area. The area around the city's docks is not very densely populated today because of massive redevelopment, but there remains a small, largely Roman Catholic, population served by several bars. These have come under repeated attack during the Troubles, and in one such attack a 5-year-old girl was killed by a bomb.

The day after the attack on the Anchor, 31 May, two men and a woman hijacked a car on the Crumlin Road and drove it into the dock area to Muldoon's bar on the corner of Tomb Street – an unfortunate name as it turned out – and Corporation Street. While the woman planted the bomb at the front door, one of the men walked into the bar and sprayed its occupants with a burst of machine-gun fire. It was an identical operation to the attack on the Jubilee Arms in the Ormeau Road area of the city exactly two weeks earlier, when Thomas Ward had died, except that this time the bomb went off as planned. However, the one fatal casualty of the attack was not a Belfast Roman Catholic, as the killers must have expected.

An English sea-captain, Thomas Holmer Curry, 50, a Protestant from Preston in Lancashire, was in the bar taking a drink just before his ship set sail. He died in the hail of bullets from the machine-gun, and as the bomb exploded two off-duty British soldiers, about to board ship to go home, were wounded. The bomb consisted of 5 lb. of explosives packed into an empty fire-extinguisher which was ringed with shotgun cartridges. It was clearly a Protestant bomb, and constructed to cause as much death and injury to the occupants of the bar as possible.

It was a crude, but extremely effective, variety of what the Americans developed in Vietnam as an 'anti-personnel weapon'.

A short time later that evening a 20-lb. bomb was thrown from a passing car into the public bar of McGlade's public house in Donegal Street in the centre of the city. Gerard Barnes, 31, a Roman Catholic, of Springhill Crescent, Ballymurphy, who was passing the bar at the time was killed instantly. The bar was severely damaged and several people who were in it were injured. The car used in the attack had been hijacked earlier at Alexandria Park Avenue off the Antrim Road.

It is possible that both attacks that evening were the work of one squad. The attack on McGlades was not entirely unexpected. As mentioned earlier, it was the bar frequented by Belfast's journalists, being within easy reach of all three of the city's daily newspapers. UDA men working in the *Belfast Telegraph* had been told discreetly a short time earlier not to use the bar, as it was going to be attacked. The warning was shown to be not without foundation.

Two nights later, on Saturday 2 June, a young Roman Catholic man went to a discotheque in Belfast's city centre, unaware that he went to his death. Samuel McCleave, 25, of Unity Flats, left home early in the evening and set off for Shelly's Discotheque. He must have thought the city centre would be safe. He was wrong. He lived in a dangerous spot. Unity Flats is well-known today throughout the world because of the Troubles in Northern Ireland. It is an entirely Roman Catholic housing complex, in many ways reminiscent in landscape to the estates in the film *Clockwork Orange*, located at the foot of the Shankill Road. Like the Catholic housing complex in the New Lodge area called Artillery Flats, Unity Flats was rather ironically named before the Troubles began. It was about five minutes' walk at a fast pace from the discotheque that McCleave visited. Shelly's was Catholic-owned, and had been the object of attack earlier, though the precise nature of the attack was not known as the perpetrators were caught before they could do whatever they had intended doing. On that occasion an RUC–Army Special Patrol Group (SPG) surprised

221

three young Protestants, one of them armed, as they made their way towards the front door of the discotheque. The men, from East Belfast, pleaded that they had only intended to rob the owner of Shelly's, who generally stood at the door collecting money. But it is something more than a possibility that the real motive was assassination.

McCleave is reported to have enjoyed himself on his last night alive. He was seen leaving the club in a very drunk condition. Two men were helping him as he staggered along the pavement. He was last seen alive in the company of these two men turning into Skipper Street. Several hours later the members of a showband going home after working till the early hours found McCleave's body hanging from the railings of a car-park in Hill Street, off Skipper Street. Hill Street is hardly a street at all. It is a very narrow cobble-stoned thoroughfare. The musicians were horrified at what they saw. McCleave's body bore the marks of a severe beating. There were bruise-marks about his mouth and one of his eyes. It was obvious that had put up a tremendous fight for his life. The cause of death was strangulation, the same means by which Thomas Madden had been killed in August 1972. A gun would not have been a practicable weapon in this killing, as it would have alerted troops and police who were patrolling within earshot of the scene.

It is not known whether McCleave was a random victim or whether the killers knew who they were dealing with. McCleave had earlier been beaten twice, and he was still off work recovering from the effects of the second beating when he was killed. On both occasions those responsible were Protestant gangs. The day after McCleave's death a police spokesman described the killing as 'a particularly brutal murder' which had 'sickened even detectives who had become hardened to mercilous assassinations'.

Before the police officer had given this verdict on the McCleave killing, assassins had struck again in the Oldpark area. Two youths armed with submachine-guns burst into a house in the Protestant Druse Street at 1·00 a.m. – at about the time McCleave met his death – and sprayed the three occupants of the house with bullets. Killed immediately were Mrs Sadie McComb, 41, of

Ballymena Street, and Alfred Acheson, 48, of Ewarts Row. Both were Protestants, and had earlier been drinking with a Protestant woman who owned the house. This woman survived the attack, and her identity has been kept secret. The three had apparently returned to the house for a nightcap.

Almost immediately the IRA was ruled out as responsible for these killings. Druse Street runs parallel with Louisa Street and is separated from the Catholic Bone area by the peaceline. For IRA men to have killed the two, they would have had to cross the peaceline armed with submachine-guns and pass a manned Army post. The peaceline existed to prevent just this sort of raid, and it would not have been feasible for IRA men on foot. Only people who lived in the area of Druse Street, who could disappear down any one of a number of small side-streets into a safe house, could have committed the act.

A motive for the killing emerged some weeks later. The dead woman, Mrs McComb, though a Protestant, lived across the Oldpark Road from the Bone area in the Catholic area known as the Ballybone. It was this area into which the Protestants Clawson and Fisher had wandered to their deaths the previous July. Mrs McComb had been associating with the brother of a known IRA man. The IRA man, James Saunders, had been shot dead during a battle in which the Provisional IRA had fought with the Protestants in Louisa Street. Mrs McComb had been warned a number of times by the UDA in the Louisa Street area to keep away from the Catholic man. Saunders was something of a hero in IRA circles. He had been shot dead by the Army in February 1971 during the first sectarian riot in the area. It was, therefore, something of a provocation to the militant Protestants in the area that Mrs McComb should consort with Saunders's brother and also make frequent visits to her friend in near-by Druse Street. The principal target for the killers was probably, therefore, Mrs McComb. Acheson and the woman who owned the house were merely innocent victims of a long-standing grudge. It illustrated quite clearly that in this war, like any other, fraternizing with the enemy carries a fearful penalty.

On Tuesday 5 June the IRA got themselves back into the picture. Terence Herdman, 17, a Roman Catholic from Andersonstown, was found shot dead in a ditch on the border between Monaghan and Cavan. He had been shot in the head. The body was hooded and the dead youth's hands and feet were tied. Around his neck the killers had hung a placard which bore the word 'Tout'. Herdman was killed by the Provisional IRA who believed he was an Army informer. They claimed that he had been seen going into Andersonstown Army barracks and that, though unemployed, he was never short of money. It was pointed out that the youth had a new suit. What the Provisionals did not know, however, was that Herdman's mother had bought him the suit, and that she had given him a regular allowance. Herdman had moved to stay with relatives near the border one month before his death, perhaps because he feared for his life if he stayed in Andersonstown. His killing once again underlined just how ruthless the IRA could be when it wished.

But by far the most important event in the month of June was another upheaval within the ranks of the UDA. As in January, the conflict centred on the different attitudes held by the men in East and West Belfast, and revolved round the personalities in the Association's leadership.

Despite the Harding Smith–Herron accommodation at the beginning of the year, crime and extortion by the UDA had continued unchecked. The militants in the West were extremely angry at the corruption within the ranks of the UDA and annoyed too that political action had been side-tracked in favour of large-scale racketeering. They wanted an end to the Mafia-type organized crime and an increase in offensive operations against the IRA and the Roman Catholic population. Organized crime had become a major industry in Belfast in 1973. In 1972 it had begun with the hijacking of liquor lorries to stock the illegal UDA shebeens, but the full potential was soon manifest to those involved. Like the Mafia, the UDA rapidly gained a near-monopoly of all thefts in the city. A well-organized system was developed to maximize profit. One example of this concerns the racket in colour TVs.

The UDA controlled virtually all thefts of colour TVs. Petty criminals were now forced to recognize the Association's authority and seek its permission to operate in the city. Housebreakings were carried out by UDA men in plush middle-class suburbs of Belfast. Many victims of these raids were surprised at the selectivity of the burglars. The raids were expertly carried out. Furniture and personal belongings were rarely damaged gratuitously, and only very expensive items were stolen. The thieves were not interested in small items. Colour TVs were a prime target. These were also stolen from shops and warehouses. The stolen sets were rapidly moved to one of a number of special warehouses in the Belfast area. They were taken to a workshop attached to the warehouse, where they were given a false serial number and the relevant documents and guarantees to match. Once this process was complete, the sets were shipped to a legitimate television dealer and sold as new sets across the counter at cut price. The legitimate dealer was a front for the UDA's stolen goods. He advertised regularly in the newspapers. Once the sets had been 'doctored' in the warehouses, there was no way to prove they had been stolen. The records of the dealer showed that the sets had been bought from a certain person. A cheque from the dealer was signed, sent out, and cashed by this person, and debited from the shop's account. However, the person was fictitious, and the account belonged to the TV dealer himself, who was merely transferring money from one account to another to keep the records of the shop in order. It was a sophisticated operation, and only a thorough investigation would bring the racket to light.

As has been said earlier in the book, the police force in Northern Ireland was too overstretched to deal with all the crime committed in the province. Since the Troubles began, a law-and-order vacuum has developed in Ulster. The most spectacular example of this has been the way in which assassins have been able to kill over 200 people with virtual immunity from capture and punishment. But another, and perhaps in the long-term more significant, example of this vacuum has been the creation of a situation in which normal crime has become a lucrative business. The security forces have been increasingly unable to protect life or property in the province. Hence the rise of the assassins, and the growth of what is to all intents and purposes an Ulster Mafia. There are many men in the UDA who have tended towards the latter, and as a consequence they have come into conflict with those who still want to pursue the political aims that led to the assassination campaign.

Chief among those who favour the political line were Harding Smith and the UVF. Against them was Herron, backed by numbers of former nobodies who had found through the UDA, and the Troubles that had spawned it, the wealth and prestige they had earlier lacked. Harding Smith and the UVF wanted to return Ulster to normality, to the days before 1968 when the province had a 'Protestant parliament for a Protestant people'. Indeed, they wanted greater social justice than before, for Catholics as well as Protestants, but their basic aim was to return to a normal stable society. This meant a society in which rampant crime was eliminated. But Herron and the men like him had no desire to go back to the old days. They had a vested interest in the Troubles and the lawlessness. If peace ever returned to Ulster, the good life would end for most of them. There would be no more fast cars, women, drink, or unlimited supplies of money. The Troubles and the UDA had made these men virtual aristocrats in their own working-class areas. People feared them and obeyed their orders or were punished. A return to normality, which meant either working for a living or being on the dole, existing on £20 a week or less – had no attractions for men such as these.

These two elements in the UDA were bound to clash, for, try as they might to coexist, the activities of Herron were damaging Harding Smith and the militant politicals. And Harding Smith was a man shrewd enough to realize it. At the beginning of June he flew to Canada. Canada has a large number of Scots-Irish settlers, and has been the main source of UDA funds outside Northern Ireland. Though the amounts sent from Canada to the Protestants in Ulster in no way compare to the huge sums of money sent the IRA from the United States, they were correspondingly extremely valuable to a body very short of money. As a result, Canadian Scots–Irish influence was considerable in the UDA. But once in Canada he found his Canadian backers very annoyed at the stories they heard coming out of the province. Shopkeepers and businessmen in Ulster who were suffering the burden of the UDA extortion had been writing to friends and relatives in Canada for several months previously. The Canadians were angry that the Protestant people were being exploited by the very people who were supposed to be protecting them.

The man at the centre of the controversy, Herron, was not unaware of the complaints, and realized that they harmed his position in the UDA, which was once again the subject of open comment. For reasons best known to himself, he had put himself forward as a loyalist candidate for the new Assembly elections to be held on 28 June. According to the UDA's rules he should resign his vice-chairmanship because of this. He said he had, but continued to run the Newtownards Road, East Belfast, headquarters of the Association as before. He made statements to the press as usual and, to all intents and purposes, was as in command as ever.

The nominal co-chairman of the UDA, Jim Anderson, who disliked Herron, resigned in disgust, but when he learned that Herron might indeed resign himself, Anderson announced that he was reconsidering his decision. There was much pressure in the UDA's inner council for Herron to resign. Harding Smith, needless to say, wanted him to go, but Herron was made of sterner stuff than Dave Fogel, and dug his heels in. It was becoming apparent that he was not going to go quietly. A removal from the scene *à la* 'Duke' Elliot was beginning to seem the only way that Herron could go.

The situation in East Belfast had got completely out of hand. Herron charged a 25p weekly levy to each householder for 'protection' of their property – but the only people the householders in the East had to fear was the UDA. Upwards of £50.00 – the highest was £90.00 – each week was charged every publican and bookmaker in the area. Those who did not pay were

227

few and far between. A bomb was the usual response to those who had the temerity to refuse to pay the levy. Small shops were expected to provide food parcels, ostensibly for the loyalist prisoners, and to supply UDA men free of charge cigarettes and tobacco, or anything else they fancied. Local garages and filling stations were required to fill up petrol tanks and service 'UDA vehicles' – a blanket term that covered the private cars of virtually every UDA or Tartan man in the area.

Such practices led to the UDA becoming extremely unpopular. Even old-age pensioners were not exempt from the levy, having to pay 10p per week. The different political situation in the East probably contributed to the unpopularity. With no Catholics to speak of – except for the Short Strand, but this was only just in the East, lying across the Lagan from the Markets, and so for all intents and purposes was an extension of the West rather than the East – and consequently no IRA, there was no enemy for the UDA to defend the people from. Thus the extortion of the Association in the East could not be disguised under the cloak of a necessary evil, one of the hardships of a wartime situation. Across the Lagan in the West it was a different story. There the UDA did have a purpose, and performed a valuable service for the Protestant community. As well as enforcing law and order in the absence of effective RUC presence on the streets, the UDA rehoused people who had to flee from sectarian attacks, and did afford a degree of physical protection against attacks by Catholics. Levies were made here too, and people grumbled at them, but under Harding Smith's rule, the sums were smaller than in the East, and the bulk of the money was spent on the UDA, and did not feather the nests of individual UDA members. Harding Smith was a hard, ruthless man, but he was honest, and he was a genuine Protestant Ulster patriot, like the leadership of the UVF. This was not the case for Herron and his colleagues in East Belfast.

In the East the UDA men flaunted their corruption openly, which only increased the anger of the local people. It was noticed that many men who had never held steady jobs, either before or after joining the UDA, were living well above their nominal means. For example, it was noted that Herron's children would go into shops in East Belfast, where the family lived in a modest council house, and buy sweets with £1 and £5 notes. Herron was officially unemployed and in receipt of social security benefit but was rumoured to be in the process of having a luxury house built for himself on the coast.

What had once been voluntary aid to a paramilitary defence organization from people looking for protection against the IRA terror campaign had, it was clear, been transformed into a full-scale extortion racket, with the East being carved up into individual bastions of control among UDA men reminiscent of Chicago in the 1920s at the time of Prohibition. Tartan gangs toured houses and shops in the area collecting levies. They were known often to demand more than the requisite amount and to collect more than once a week. Most people were aware what failure to pay would mean and did not refuse. But most of the money never reached the UDA headquarters, and Harding Smith and the militants were extremely concerned at this state of affairs, and were determined that it should end.

The Protestant working class was being exploited by the Mafia element in the UDA, and this incensed the UVF. In many ways the counterpart of the Official IRA, the UVF never believed in bleeding the working-class Protestants for funds. They preferred to rob banks and large business concerns. The UVF was smaller the the UDA. It was selective about its membership, and it was composed mainly of men of principle. These men were Ulster patriots as well as being men of action. Like all men guided by principle and not materialism, the UVF could understand and respect like men of principle on the other side. The UVF respected the Official IRA and *vice versa*, though they had different political positions and realized that they were opponents. Both recognized that the other stood for legitimate and honourable ends for their respective communities. Both regarded as distasteful the practices of the Provincials and the Mafia element in the UDA. The history of the Troubles in Northern Ireland contains a number of incidents where the UVF and Official IRA have behaved with chivalry towards each other. Perhaps the most notable was the occasion when two UVF men were captured by the Officials in the Markets area. The local Official IRA commander, Joe McCann, having satisfied himself that the two UVF men had wandered into the area by accident and had not been on a spying mission, released them unharmed, though he knew who they were. It was a gesture that illustrated the mutual respect the two organizations held each other in. It was never forgotten by the UVF leader, Gusty Spence. When McCann was shot dead by troops in 1972, Spence sent a letter of condolence to McCann's widow. He wrote that though he and McCann were on opposing sides, he recognized and respected the dead man as a soldier fighting for a cause in which he believed, just as he himself was.

Such men were therefore disgusted by stories of UDA extortion such as that of an elderly widow in East Belfast who had been told by Tartans that she would have to pay them 50p per week. When she told them that she could not afford to pay this much a brick was thrown through her living-room window, and a number of youths sat in a car outside her house every night. After that she paid up punctually every week. A shopkeeper was asked if he would contribute towards the cost of a colour TV for a local UDA unit. He was not very keen on the idea until he was asked how much his shop window cost. He took the hint and paid up.

When Harding Smith was in Canada everything came to a head. On the morning of Thursday 7 June the *Irish News* carried a story that militants had taken control of the UDA in a bloodless *coup*. The following day it was revealed that the militants had set up a new UDA headquarters on the Shankill Road in West Belfast, and that two important UDA leaders, John Haveron and Tucker Lyttle, were being held there. But in the East, the UDA headquarters in the Newtownards Road denied that any *coup* had taken place. However, Herron appeared to be missing. Later in the day, spokesmen at Newtownards Road said that Herron was being held captive in a bar elsewhere in the road. A TV news camera team was permitted to film Herron in the bar, and interviewed him sitting in a chair flanked by masked men. He was asked whether he was being held voluntarily or against his will, and replied: 'I suppose you could say a bit of both.'

Herron did not appear to be unduly worried, and the wives and families of the three men being held did not seem too upset either. The whole thing was not taken seriously by most observers in Belfast. It was mainly thought that it had all been stage-managed by Herron while Harding Smith was away to consolidate his position. The story given out was that Herron and the other men had been kidnapped by young and more militant officers in the UDA who wanted the organization to adopt a more militant line. Herron and the two others were later released. It was thought that the purpose behind the supposed *coup* had been to rally support behind Herron, in much the same way that the meeting of UDA commanders in January had saved him. But the events of the next week seemed to contradict this, and suggested that there was perhaps more teeth to the '*coup*' than at first seemed possible.

Early on Saturday 9 June a journalist representing the Dublin-based *Sunday World* was summoned to the new headquarters of the UDA in the Shankill Road. At this precise time there were two UDA headquarters, as the upheaval was still in progress. The reporter was shown into a room and given a cup of tea while a press statement was prepared for him. He asked his hosts who they were, and they replied that they were the UDA and that the house was their headquarters. He asked about the Newtownards Road headquarters, and was told emphatically that the headquarters was now in the Shankill Road and that they were the men in charge. The reporter concerned got the clear impression that the events of the previous few days were not a stunt and that the men he dealt with were in deadly earnest. He was given a hand-written press statement. The statement was very long, but it is reproduced in full in the chapter dealing with the Protestants. It is an eloquent and well-thought-out apologia of the militant Protestant position in Ulster, and it argues with some force that this cause has not received a favourable coverage by the press. We give the text in full on pp. 280-83.

June 1973 first UFF claim

It criticized the bias the press had adopted during the Troubles and complained of the misunderstanding it had shown of the Protestant reaction to the events of the previous four years. It explained in some detail the ethnic origins of the Ulster Protestants, and listed a number of grievances that it believed the press had overlooked. The statement referred to the growing opinion in Britain that wanted the troops pulled out of Ulster. It added that the British politicians did not understand the Protestants of Ulster, whom they left defenceless against the attacks of the IRA. It was signed by Andrew Terry and Mrs Jean Moore. Mrs Moore, it will be recalled, was the sister of Ingram 'Jock' Beckitt, the UDA man who had been killed in the Shankill Road in March 1972. She had been head of the women's section of the UDA. Beckitt had been a hard man in the Shankill Road and one of the founder members of the UDA along with Harding Smith. He was killed by Protestants, and Mrs Moore at the time publicly blamed a 'UDA faction' for his death whom she described as 'hoodlums and gangsters'. It was the UDA faction, concentrated around Herron in the East, that she and her colleagues in the West were trying to eliminate. The last line of the statement given to the *Sunday World* reporter – 'we think you should watch the events of the next month with extreme care' – had an ominous ring. Within a few hours of the reporter leaving the new UDA HQ in the Shankill Road, it became apparent what was meant.

At just after 3·00 in the afternoon a car pulled up outside the Avenue Bar in Kent Street, a Roman Catholic pub just off Unity Flats. The bar was crowded when without warning a bomb was thrown inside. A barman picked up the bomb to throw it out of the bar, but it exploded immediately, blowing off his hand and causing him severe injuries. He took the full force of the blast, and probably saved many of the customers from serious injury. Fifteen people were taken to hospital. Fifteen minutes later, a man telephoned the *Belfast Telegraph*, and used the name of Ulster Freedom Fighters for the first time. Calling himself Captain Black, he said that the UFF would bomb Catholic pubs and businesses without warning in future and assassinate

232

known IRA men. This would be in retaliation for the continuing bombing and terror campaign of the Provisional IRA.

Later that night a Roman Catholic was walking drunk along the Crumlin Road when he was picked up by Protestant assassins. Daniel O'Neill, 35, of Arizona Street, off the Glen Road, had been to a social function in Legoniel parochial hall until 11·0 p.m. He left the social with his wife and a Protestant friend who had offered to drive the O'Neills to their home at Glen Road. But Daniel O'Neill was extremely drunk, and asked his friend to stop the car on the Crumlin Road. He then got out and told his wife he would walk home. At 4·00 a.m. the next day, Sunday 10 June, residents of Deerpark Road in the Oldpark area heard a shot and one person, on looking out of his window, saw a man crouching beside the railings of a near-by playing-field. The man was Daniel O'Neill, and he had just been shot in the head. None of the residents in the area had the courage to go to his assistance. Detectives arrived two hours later to find O'Neill dead. They also found marks on the grass where the dying man had been crawling around in agony after being shot. Had assistance been called promptly he might have survived. At least, he could have been relieved of the untold pain of his last moments. But such was the climate of fear that was yet again demonstrated that local people dared not go to the aid of a dying man lest they become involved in the assassination campaign.

The following night, Monday 11 June, Protestant gunmen again took on the Army, and it cost them dearly. Soldiers claimed at least six victims in the battle with no casualties on their own side. But, as happened on other occasions, attention was swiftly drawn away from Protestant militants by another IRA bombing. On Tuesday afternoon, 12 June, the Provisional IRA killed six people and wounded scores of others when they left a car bomb in the centre of a crowded shopping centre in the quiet Londonderry town of Coleraine. As had happened on countless other occasions, an IRA warning had been given but it was too late, and did not specify the correct location of the bomb. To all intents and purposes, there was no warning for the blast. Coleraine had previously escaped unscathed from the Troubles. As a result, security precautions in the town were lax, and it was possible to leave a car unattended in the city's main shopping centre. Prevented from attacking targets in Belfast by the tough security measures, the IRA had turned its attention to 'soft' targets, with deadly effect.

The following night, Tuesday 12 June, a Roman Catholic hall of residence attached to Queen's University was bombed. In a telephone call to the *Irish News* a man claimed to be a spokesman for the UFF said: 'We blew up Aquinas Hall. We meant to kill – and we will kill. We will blow up every Catholic place until the Protestant internees are released from Long Kesh.'

That same evening a Roman Catholic youth was shot in the chest by men in a passing car near his home at Clifton Crescent, off the Cliftonville Road. The incident was witnessed by several other youths who claimed that there had been six men in the car. On Thursday 14 June, a Catholic-owned pub in the city centre, the Duke of York's in Commercial Court, was destroyed by a bomb. No warning was given, and none of the customers was killed. In a telephone call to the *Irish News* the UFF claimed responsibility.

By this time Harding Smith had returned from Canada, and had been fully briefed on the turmoil in the Protestant camp. It is now clear that in his absence the UVF in West Belfast, with whom he had close links, had attempted to take over the UDA and clean the organization up. Whether this was a plan agreed with Harding Smith before he left for Canada, or whether it was a counter-stroke to a move by Herron and his group, is not clear. Herron may have realized that Harding Smith intended to arm the UVF and loyal UDA men and might then move against himself. Herron, according to this theory, decided to make a pre-emptive strike to consolidate his position, and this led to the counter-strike by the West Belfast UVF. What tends to support this line is that the timing of the move, if it was a planned UVF take-over, could hardly have been worse, since Harding Smith was abroad. Again it may be that the truth lies in the story current that the move was caused by young and impatient junior officers in the UDA, who felt the leadership was too soft. What is clear, however, is that when he returned, he found that West Belfast was more firmly than ever under his control and that of the UVF, but that the *coup* had failed to remove Herron in the East.

Early in the morning of Friday 15 June, two armed youths went to Herron's home in the Braniel estate. Herron was not there. The door was answered by his wife who told the men that he was out. The men were unmasked, but then produced guns and put on masks. They pushed past Mrs Herron and forced their way in. The only other adult in the house was Mrs Herron's brother, who was Herron's bodyguard. Michael Wilson, 19, was asleep in an upstairs bedroom. He was recovering from injuries he had received a week earlier when Catholic women in the Seaforde Street area of East Belfast had beat him with hurley sticks. The gunmen burst into the bedroom in which Wilson was sleeping and shot him in the head. He died instantly. Before they left, the killers told Mrs Herron that had her children not been present they would have shot her too.

The gunmen then made their escape on foot through the Protestant estate. Despite the subsequent UDA claim that the IRA were responsible, there was never really any doubt that Wilson was killed by Protestant assassins from the West who came to kill Herron. The car they had used to get to the Braniel had been hijacked earlier in the day on the Shankill Road.

Wilson was given a massive UDA funeral. The top men in the UDA and UVF in West Belfast all attended, led by Harding Smith. Everyone was very upset at Wilson's death, they said. An Army officer had only told Herron a week before that the IRA were out to get him. Alas, they had got poor Wilson instead. Presiding over the interment was the Rev. Ian Paisley, making a return to the militant Protestant camp. However, his flirtation with the UDA was to prove only passing. When it became apparent who had killed Wilson, and why, Paisley wisely withdrew once again. But the pretence had to be maintained. The men in the West took their public show of sorrow to even greater lengths. The night after Wilson was murdered,

Saturday 16 June, Daniel Rouse, 16, a Roman Catholic of River-dale Park South, Andersonstown, was returning home from a night out with friends. He got out of a taxi on Finaghy Road North only several hundred yards from his home. As he made his way home he obviously failed to notice a dark-coloured van at the side of the road. Two men got out of the vehicle and bundled Rouse into it. The van then drove off towards the Lisburn Road. Shortly after midday the next day a caller telephoned the *Belfast Telegraph*. He said he was from the UFF and said that a youth from Riverdale named Daniel Rouse had been kidnapped and shot twice. The caller gave the precise location of the body, and said: 'He is dead. He was killed in retaliation for the IRA's murder of Michael Wilson. There will be plenty more of this happening.'

The information was correct, and the police found the body face downward on a grass verge at Dunmurry Lane. He had been shot twice through the head, and had been dead for some hours. The following day the *News Letter* received a similar call from the UFF. This time the caller said: 'Listen carefully. I represent the Ulster Freedom Fighters. We have just assassinated an IRA man on the way to Larne. We gave him two in the back and one in the head. He is dead. This is in retaliation for Wilson.'

Shortly afterwards James Kelly, 25, a Roman Catholic of Ferris Street, Larne, was found, lying in a ditch by a motorist at Corr's Corner, five miles from Belfast. A police spokesman confirmed that he had been shot in the head. Another motorist reported later that he saw Kelly more than an hour before police found him: 'Apparently the driver thought Mr Kelly was drunk and carried on,' the spokesman said. It was later revealed that Kelly had still been alive when seen by the first motorist. He died only a few minutes before police arrived on the scene. It is thought that Kelly was picked up by his killers as he attempted to hitch a lift home.

The following day, the Protestant-orientated *News Letter* carried a story on its front page headlined 'SPLIT IN UDA RANKS WIDENS–REPORT'. The information contained in the story was remarkable for its accuracy, though the source was not named.

Clearly, however, the writer had been in contact with an element in the UDA. For the first time, the true dimension of the turmoil in the Protestant paramilitary movement was spelt out to the Protestant readership of the *News Letter*. The story ran:

There were firm reports last night that the split in the ranks of the Ulster Defence Association, is widening. Disputes that now beset the once-powerful paramilitary movement have recently been underlined by the emergence of the Ulster Freedom Fighters. This is a breakaway group which, within the first few days of its existence, has claimed responsibility for two murders and two explosions. Anonymous phone callers claiming to represent the UFF say its members have killed to avenge the death of Michael Wilson on Friday. One of the callers threatened many similar 'happenings' in the future.

The UDA is considering strong action against the UFF which, it believes, is 'creating a situation where the UDA could be proscribed as an illegal organization'. *The East Belfast section is under fire from many directions.* Younger members within the section feel the leadership has allowed the movement to deteriorate. *The West Belfast hierarchy also feels the order of priorities on the other side has been lost. They believe East Belfast members are more intent on lining their own pockets than protecting the Protestant population.*

There have been allegations that a 'protection racket' – with Protestant publicans and shop-keepers forced to 'pay up or else' – is in force. Former vice-chairman Tommy Herron has admitted that UDA men were paid for protecting property in East Belfast. But he is adamant that there is no protection racket and claims the people involved were quite happy to pay the money. *This has angered the hard-line Ulster Volunteer Force as well as the militants within the UDA.* The 'freedom fighters' align themselves more closely with the outlawed UVF on the grounds that it is a far more idealistic body than the UDA.

Some security chiefs are now convinced that Michael Wilson, Tommy Herron's brother-in-law, was killed by militant Protestants as a warning to the UDA to get back in line. The Provisional IRA in Dublin has denied that any of its members was involved in Wilson's murder. When the UDA was formed hundreds of men from the Protestant working-class areas flocked to its banner. But as it grew its control weakened until now there are so many splinter-groups within the movement that no one knows quite who supports whom. As one disillusioned man commented last night: 'We got too big for our own good.' Tommy Herron resigned his position so as to stand as a candidate in the Assembly elections. He still acts as spokesman for the organization.*

Just who was the 'disillusioned man' referred to who had spoken to the paper the previous evening is not clear. One reading of the last three sentences would suggest it was Herron. A few days after an unsuccessful attempt on his life, he was no doubt a disillusioned man at this time. Whoever it was who spoke to the *News Letter*, this article shows how important it was felt to be that the Protestant people should know what was going on within the UDA. The UDA still depended to a very large degree on the support of the Protestant working classes to survive as an organization. Just as the IRA used the *Irish News* as a mouthpiece for its press statements and claims, so too the UDA used the Protestant *News Letter*. Someone in the UDA was trying to explain to the people at the grass roots just exactly what was going on.

Wilson received his hero's burial at Roselawn Cemetery. Two days later the Provisional IRA hit back in retaliation for the killings of Kelly and Rouse. On Thursday 21 June, David Walker, 16, a mentally retarded Protestant youth who lived in the predominantly Protestant Belvoir estate in East Belfast, was walking towards Shaw's Bridge. It was 3·35 a.m. when a car stopped by him and two men bundled him into the rear seat. A woman witness immediately contacted the police, while the car disappeared across Shaw's bridge in the direction of the Upper Malone Road.

The youth's father was a prison warder. The family had moved to Belvoir from Suffolk the previous year. Just beyond Andersonstown, Suffolk had once been a mixed and trouble-free area. But the Troubles had spread from Andersonstown and forced many Protestant families to flee to safer areas. David Walker had been to a special school for backward children. When he moved to Belvoir he left school and got a job at the Government Training Centre at Shaws Bridge helping to lay pathways and tend gardens. His only recreation appeared to be walking with his dog, and he had no friends. After the kidnapping police and Army roadblocks were set up around the area, but they were in vain. Just before

*Italics ours – M.D. and D.L.

midnight several people living at O'Neill Street in the heart of the Lower Falls found Walker's body in an alley. He had been shot in the head and chest, but was still alive when he was found. An ambulance took him to hospital, but he died half an hour after admission.

The killing of a mentally retarded boy was widely regarded as a cowardly act. The Provisional IRA issued a denial but nobody believed them. Although Protestant assassins had become more daring and entered IRA strongholds to effect their killings no one seriously believed that they had kidnapped Walker at Shaw's Bridge and taken his body into the Lower Falls. A Roman Catholic youth was later charged with the killing.

A few days later the UFF struck again when they shot dead Joseph Cunningham, 26, at his street door at Nore Street, in the River Streets area of the Oldpark. Cunningham had been born a Roman Catholic, but had been converted to Protestantism when a teenager. The area he lived in was Protestant. After midnight in the early hours of Monday 25 June Cunningham answered a knock at the door. A gunman shot him five times with a revolver and then made off on foot. The UFF later admitted the killing and claimed that Cunningham had been shot because he was an IRA spy. There is no evidence to support this claim, but it may simply have been that Cunningham's Catholic background brought him immediately under suspicion.

The UFF had certainly made their presence felt in the few short weeks they had been in existence, and their most spectacular killing took place two days later. The night of Tuesday 26 June saw the first meeting of the new Belfast City Council which had been elected the previous month. After the meeting at which the councillors filled various committee posts and chairmanships, many of them retired to McGlade's bar behind the *Belfast Telegraph* for a drink. One of these was former Stormont Senator Paddy Wilson. Wilson, 39, an SDLP member and election agent of party leader Gerard Fitt, lived in the Ballysillan area at Liscoole Park. He left the bar at 11·30 p.m., and was accompanied by Miss Irene Andrews, 29, a Protestant, who lived on the Crumlin Road. Wilson was very popular and was well known in

McGlades, as was Andrews, who was a keen ball-room dancer. She had appeared on the TV programme 'Come Dancing' and had worked for five years on the *Belfast Telegraph*. Wilson and Andrews were last seen walking towards his mini car parked on waste ground near by. At 1·30 a.m. the *News Letter* received a call from a 'Captain Black of the UFF'. The caller was reported to have been in a state of excitement. He said: 'We have just killed Senator Paddy Wilson and a lady friend. The bodies are at Hightown Road. After the IRA have murdered a retarded boy, we are not going to stand by for what those animals have done to us in the past four years. There will be more deaths in reprisal.'

The Hightown Road is a lonely deserted place high above the city on the way to Aldergrove Airport. Police treated the call with a certain degree of suspicion, as they were afraid that it might be a trap by the IRA to lure the security forces to a deserted spot for an ambush. They first checked to make sure that Andrews and Wilson were missing, and then a police and Army team searched the Hightown road area. At 4·30 a.m. they discovered the two at a deserted quarry a few yards off the road. Wilson's car was parked facing the road. Both doors were open and a few feet from the passenger door Andrews's body lay. She had been stabbed twenty times in the head and chest. Fifteen yards from the driver's door was Wilson's body. He had been stabbed thirty times in the head and chest, and his throat had been cut from ear to ear. Wilson had apparently put up a struggle with his killers. His body showed the marks of a fierce struggle.

The circumstances of this killing, coming only thirty-six hours before the elections to the first Ulster Assembly, were thought particularly shocking. Gerard Fitt, overwhelmed with personal grief, at first said he was unable to go ahead with his election campaign. He later changed his mind, and topped the poll in North Belfast. During the course of the assassination campaign, only one other politician had been killed.* Wilson was the first SDLP man to be killed. The following month in an interview with journalists from the *Sunday Telegraph* and *Daily Telegraph*,

*An elderly Unionist Senator, John Barnhill, was killed two years ago by the IRA on the border.

the UFF were to claim that the entire SDLP Assembly party would be assassinated.

Twenty-four hours before his death, Wilson had discussed at the Fitt home the possibility of being assassinated. Fitt's daughter, Joan, had asked him if he was afraid to die, and he replied: 'If you've got to go, you've got to go.' He was an extremely popular man on both sides of the sectarian divide in Stormont. He was one of the few politicians who refused to carry a firearm. He explained his reasons for this to a Belfast journalist weeks before his death. 'I couldn't shoot anybody,' he said. 'How could you live with a thing like that afterwards? I couldn't sleep at night knowing I'd shot somebody's son, husband, or father'.

The *Belfast Telegraph* leader on the assassination later in the day the bodies were found said:

> Belfast's reign of terror has reached its lowest point. In the name of common humanity, it must stop. If ever there was an ill-conceived and brutally carried-out murder, this was it. Paddy Wilson was a Roman Catholic politician, but sectarianism was foreign to his nature. He was a working-class representative, nothing more, nothing less, and while others grabbed the headlines with grandiose ideas he grafted away at grass-roots level on workaday problems.

It was ironic that Wilson should be killed, for he was the only SDLP member who refused to secede from public life when internment was introduced. As a result he was never forgiven by some of his colleagues in his own party. He had only been elected to a post on one of the new council committees the night of his death on the votes of the Unionists and Loyalists on the council. Paddy Devlin, his SDLP colleague, had stood against him, and was reported to have been bitterly annoyed at his defeat. Wilson's death, coming so shortly before the Assembly elections, seemed to augur ill for the future. Far from getting better, the situation as Ulster went to the polls seemed to be worse. The Loyalist candidates, led by Craig and Paisley, stood on a platform pledged to wreck the Assembly. Even the pro-White Paper Faulkner Unionist Party could not guarantee that, once elected, its candidates would support the programme on which they were elected. June had seen unprecedented turmoil in the ranks of the Protestant paramilitary groups that had not yet revealed itself. A new and ruthless Protestant group had emerged and claimed for the first time that Protestants were taking part in the killings. Everything seemed gloomy. Politically the future looked bleak. And the assassinations just went on.

[When this book was written in August 1973 Tommy Herron, the former vice-chairman of the UDA, was still alive. Shortly before the book went to press, on Friday 14 September, Herron was kidnapped close to the UDA headquarters in Newtownards Road, East Belfast. His body was found on Sunday 16 September at Drumbo in an isolated spot south of Belfast. He had been shot in the head. Herron's death occurred too late for references to him in this book to be altered.]

Part Four
The Killers

13. The killers (I) – the IRA

As the first assassinations in the current Troubles were the work of the IRA, it is perhaps fitting that the first of our three chapters dealing with the killers should be concerned with this organization. Of the 198 assassination victims that we have tabulated, including the 3 UVF victims in 1966, 42 were victims of the IRA, a ratio of slightly less than one in five. But, as we have seen, in the early days of the Troubles, the only assassins in Ulster were the IRA, and it was not until 1972 that the first Protestant assassins appeared. The IRA, therefore, can lay no claim to innocence, and the large tally of 142 victims of Protestant assassins that we record was due in part, at least, to the early activities of the Catholic organization.

The myth-laden history of the Irish Republican Army is riddled with stories of secret court-martials, kangaroo courts and executions. Their justice, in the form of a bullet in the head, has claimed a considerable number of victims in their tally. But as well as those sentenced by kangaroo courts, there have been also plain sectarian killings in revenge for those committed by Protestants. Like its equivalents on the Protestant side, the Catholic IRA has been composed of men genuinely committed on principle to the movement's ideals, and others less scrupulous, who joined for less lofty motives, some for action, others to make money.

The IRA, or 'RA' as it is known in the Catholic community in Northern Ireland, has always been a very secret organization. Until the arrival of the secessionist Provisionals in January 1970 the recent activities of the movement had remained clouded in secrecy since the failure of the 1956–62 campaign. This had been the latest of a series of campaigns waged by the IRA against the State set up in 1921 against the wishes of the majority of the

Irish people. Ireland had been annexed to the British Crown by conquest. The greater part of the island had become independent after a successful rebellion against the Crown, and it was the consistent belief of the IRA until the 1960s that the only way in which to complete the aim of a united independent Ireland was by military means. The campaign of 1956–62 was in many respects a decisive moment in the history of the IRA. Like its predecessors it had been confined to the countryside. Here the IRA could expect more support than in the province as a whole. Though Catholics are outnumbered by something under two to one in Northern Ireland as a whole, the large Protestant concentration in Greater Belfast, whose population nears half a million, meant that in the country areas the ratio is something closer to even. In counties Fermanagh, Tyrone, and Londonderry, the Catholics are in a majority, and in many parts of Armagh and South Down too. But the significance of the campaign that ended in 1962 was that, despite this advantage, the IRA effort collapsed in a total failure, and was unable to rouse any mass popular support for its campaign. This led the leadership of the IRA to come to the conclusion that military means would not secure their aims, and consequently the IRA made an important policy-shift towards a policitical solution.

The men who led the unsuccessful campaign in 1956–62 were a different breed entirely from those who formed the militant Provisionals in the 1970s. They were men who saw military action only as a means to an end, and not the end itself. They were well-disciplined and dedicated republicans and were not involved in sectarian violence which had continually been a feature of the province since 1921, and even before. These men maintained a strict code of silence about their activities, and respected, as well as feared, the authority of their leaders. The movement at this time embodied the traditional values passed down through the generations of Irish republicanism. As well as being ruthless, determined men, they were also chivalrous and honourable. They were proud of their association with the IRA and were accorded respect for their beliefs, even by those who opposed them. The IRA in this period had a continuous history that stretched back to 1916. It was organized along military lines, and a strict military discipline was enforced upon its members.

At this time a civilian killing could only be sanctioned by the brigade commanders, after a thorough investigation had been carried out, and its findings presented to a specially convened court. Battalion and unit commanders did not have the authority to make on-the-spot decisions or to order an act of retaliation. But, as we shall see, after internment in August 1971 the depleted ranks of what had become the Provisional IRA were filled with men who were not dedicated republicans or military disciplinarians. The men who filled the vacant positions at command level in the Belfast Brigade allowed individual volunteers to carry out assassinations without the authority of either brigade or battalion commanders.

From their formation, the Provisionals created a sectarian image by involving themselves in confrontations with the Protestant community, and later bombing Protestant-owned businesses, and shooting members of the RUC and UDR. They also shot, it is true, Catholic members of these bodies but in the hate-charged atmosphere of Ulster the Protestant population reacted with instinctive fear and, not unreasonably, felt that such attacks were directed at their community alone.

The Provisional IRA had been formed by Catholic militants who believed that the IRA's political involvement after 1962 at the expense of its military policy had been wrong. It had resulted, so these men claimed, in the Catholic community in Belfast being left defenceless when sectarian riots and violence erupted in August 1969.

When Protestant mobs invaded the Falls on 13 and 14 August the only weapons available to the local IRA were one Thompson submachine-gun, one .22 rifle and a shotgun, and these were quite insufficient to prevent the destruction of Bombay Street and numerous shops and houses in the Divis Street area. A similar situation existed in the Ardoyne where the only weapons in IRA hands were a few .45 revolvers, and shotguns with a limited supply of ammunition. The younger element in the Army couldn't understand why the Schmeisers, grease-guns,

Thompsons, .303s, and Mausers which they had seen and used at training camps across the border in Donegal prior to August 1969, had not been available for the defence of the people. They were even more disillusioned when they learned that the Marxist IRA Chief-of-Staff in Dublin, Cathal Goulding, had sold most of the IRA weapons to the Free Welsh Army, a Welsh nationalist body with pretentions in the 1960s to repeating the success of the IRA in 1916. IRA brigade leaders in Belfast, Jim Sullivan and Liam McMillen, had few answers to satisfy the militant men. Men like Joe Cahill, a well-known gunman in the 1956–62 campaign, had left the movement in disgust at its departure from the traditional military policy. By August 1969 Cahill and others like him had come back into the reckoning. They saw their military line justified and the political line of the existing leadership discredited. And they had the support of the young men in the Catholic community – men who had seen Bombay Street razed to the ground while the IRA had stood by powerless.

Sullivan and McMillen were not surprised therefore when they later learned that some of the militants under their command had been plotting to assassinate them because of their alleged lack of militancy, and take over the IRA. It was militant men who a few months later organized the Provisional IRA. Unlike the leaders of the 1956–62 campaign who had suffered a humiliating defeat, these men still believed that political power comes from the barrel of a Thompson machine-gun.

The seeds of their discontent had been sown at the end of the last campaign in 1962 when republicans were encouraged to become involved in housing action groups and, eventually, the Civil Rights movement, which they successfully infiltrated and used as the major vehicle for their aims in the late 1960s. The semblance of a military force had been maintained and volunteers had been regularly sent to training camps in the Donegal hills across the border, but nearly all the weapons used were left in dumps in the Republic or on the border in Ulster. The younger men who found the weapons and explosives training they had in Donegal more attractive than Marxist political thought were among those who later turned away from the existing IRA after August 1969 and formed the backbone of the Provisionals. What they left behind became known as the Official IRA, which continued to pursue its political and non-sectarian policy despite the military offensive begun by the Provisionals.

The Official IRA hardly figures at all in the civilian assassinations. Among the only definite instances we have been able to record was the killing of Meehan and McMillan in the Lower Falls on 9 July 1972. These men were killed when they refused to stop at two successive Official IRA check-points after dark, and were then shot. There are probably two main reasons why the Officials did not engage in the assassinations. First, ideologically they were opposed to and disgusted by such a policy. Anyone in the Catholic community attracted by the idea would not be in the non-sectarian Officials. And secondly, despite the fact that in 1970 the Official IRA was much smaller than the Provisionals, it still maintained its traditional structure of command and enforced a strict military discipline. Such killings would not be tolerated by the Official leadership as they were by the Provisionals. One exception to this rule was the killing on 12 December 1971 of Unionist Senator John Barnhill at his house at Strabane near the border. He was shot dead by Official IRA men. Immediately the Official IRA leadership in Dublin alleged that the killing had been committed by a British Army SAS squad, as, the statement said, the killing could only exacerbate sectarian tensions. But shortly after, the Official IRA in Northern Ireland issued a statement accepting full responsibility. It claimed that the men sent to the senator's home had been instructed only to destroy the property as a reprisal for the destruction of working-class homes in the province by the British Army under the Faulkner administration. But Senator Barnhill had attacked the raiders and been killed in the ensuing struggle, which had only lasted a minute. The senator's house was destroyed by a bomb with the dead man still inside. It was a grisly act, and the Officials came out of it badly. But such acts were not common among the Official IRA, and the Barnhill killing was the exception rather than the rule.

The fundamentally non-sectarian policy of the Officials is

recognized by their opponents across the sectarian divide. Throughout the sectarian conflict the Officials have maintained links with Protestant paramilitary groups like the UDA and UVF. The fact that men in these organizations have felt able to talk to the Officials says much for the success of the latter's efforts to present a non-sectarian image. Fogel, Elliot, and Herron engaged in informal talks with representatives of the Officials, and even a man such as Gusty Spence recognizes, and admires, men whose ultimate goal he has vowed to prevent by force. Spence, as mentioned earlier, sent a letter of condolence to the widow of Official IRA man Joe McCann. McCann was the first, and perhaps the only, charismatic figure to emerge on the republican side in the 1970s campaign. Like the traditional IRA heroes, he combined ruthless determination and commitment to the cause with chivalry and honour – values opponents could share and respect. When McCann was shot dead in 1972 he was unarmed, and it was claimed that a British soldier shot him in the back and then pumped bullets into his prone body in the street. Spence wrote to McCann's widow:

My Dear Mrs McCann,

I would like to tender to you my deepest and profoundest sympathy on the tragic death of your beloved husband, Joe.

There are those who would find it strange to hear from someone such as myself but I can assure you that whilst your husband and I may have been opposed to each other in politics we shared that common bond that is known only to those who fight their own respective corners to the best of their ability. He was a soldier of the Republic and I a Volunteer of Ulster and we made no apology for being what we are or were.

Joe once did me a good turn indirectly and I never forgot him for his humanity and even though I never got the chance to thank him personally I am almost sure that he knew how I felt and that I was grateful to him.

In such circumstances, my inept words are little comfort to you but if you believe that these words are from the bottom of my heart it may go some little way to enabling you to understand them.

I, too, am a family man with a wife and four lovely children and this aspect is the most heart-rending of all because the women suffer in our coming and in our going and it is they who must have the most courage.

May God bless your 'wee' ones and yourself in your hour of extreme grief and may He give you that strength required to face the future as Joe would have wished it.

I salute your husband as an honourable and brave soldier.

Very sincerely and truly,
Gusty Spence

The 'good turn' that McCann once did Spence illustrated the difference in outlook between the Officials and the Provisionals. McCann hated what he termed the 'sectarian tactics of the Provos' and condemned assassination. The two UVF men who wandered into the Markets area by accident one night were released by McCann, the commander in the area. It was an act of chivalry that drew the respect and admiration of Spence and his colleagues, and the scorn and contempt of the Provisionals.

A clear example of the different attitudes of the two wings of the IRA was seen in August 1972. On the 19th two Protestant men were spotted by Provisionals drinking in a Catholic bar near Mayo Street on the Springfield Road. James Neill, 44, of the Limestone Road, and a friend had gone for a drink to the pub unaware of the dangers involved. They were seized by the Provisionals and Neill's friend was handed over to local Officials for questioning. This man was released subsequently as the Officials were satisfied that he had been doing no harm. Neill was found shot dead the next day on the banks of the Flush river. The Provisionals bitterly attacked the Officials for releasing the other man, alleging that both were spies and that both should have been executed immediately. Once again, the Official IRA had insisted on judging a man on his merits and not making an assumption, leading to a life-or-death decision, simply on the basis of a man's religion. People could scoff at and deride them, but the Officials stuck to their ideals and their principles. As such, men of principle on the other side can respect them. There are few Protestants who accorded similar respect to the Provisionals.

Protestant attitudes to the Provisionals were given a violent birth in June 1970, only six months after the movement surfaced. At this stage the Provisional IRA were well equipped and had more members than the Officials – more indeed than the IRA had been able to recruit in any of the earlier campaigns. Among the ranks were numerous men who still vividly remembered the destruction of Bombay Street and similar incidents of Protestant violence, and hoped for the day of revenge. When an opportunity came on the afternoon of 30 June to attack Protestants, heavily armed Provisional units were waiting in the Ardoyne and in the tiny Catholic enclave surrounding St Matthew's Church in East Belfast. They were armed with Thompson submachine-guns, .303 rifles, and numerous other automatic weapons which had reached them from Donegal.

On the Crumlin Road border of the Ardoyne, the IRA claimed an easy victory against the near-by Protestants, with only a few minor casualties against three Protestant dead and scores wounded. In East Belfast, the firing from the Catholic Seaford Street area was so heavy for three hours that all Army units were ordered to remain outside. The battle in East Belfast was considered an even greater victory by the Provisionals because the Catholics there were outnumbered by as much as twenty to one by the surrounding Protestants. Experienced gunmen from the New Lodge Road, Turf Lodge, and Falls Road areas were positioned near St Matthews Church when the gunfire erupted and the Protestants were not prepared for the attack which followed, in which as many as five people may have died and at least twenty were injured. The only IRA fatality was Henry McIlhone, who was shot towards the end of the battle, after he had shot several Protestants with a .303 rifle. He was the man who had started the fighting, when he ran onto the Protestant Newtownards Road with a .45 revolver and wounded at least five unarmed Protestants who were making their way from an Orange demonstration in the Shankill Road across the Albert Bridge. A high-ranking police officer who saw a Protestant sniper shoot McIlhone from the roof of Sirocco Works later commented that McIlhone had shot 'a considerable number of Protestants' before he was killed.

One of the other IRA casualties was Billy McKee, who had been a founder of the Provisionals. He was shot several times in the stomach. He was seen during the battle firing magazine after magazine from a Thompson from the grounds of the church which he had been guarding. He was rushed to a secret hideout in the West of Ireland where he recovered from his wounds; but six months later he received a prison sentence for a firearms charge and he has been in gaol ever since.

These two confrontations on 30 June paved the way for numerous other sectarian clashes, until the Protestants finally reacted to the Provisionals' sectarianism with the full-scale assassination campaign in 1972. The assassinations of 1971, with the exception of the Barnhill killing, were carried out in the traditional IRA style on the orders of kangaroo courts and it was at this time that the technique of hooding a victim was first used. The significance of this still remains something of a mystery, though it certainly added more horror to the gruesome sight which confronted those who found the bodies. The same technique was subsequently adopted by the Protestant assassins. The Kavanagh shooting in January 1971, which was regarded by the State Pathologist's department as the first assassination, was in many ways a typical IRA execution. Kavanagh had been sentenced by a kangaroo court in his absence after he had ignored repeated warnings from the IRA to avoid contact with the police, to whom they believed he was giving information. A squad of two or three men was sent to carry out the sentence of the court. They picked him up in a car as he walked to work one morning, took him to the banks of the polluted river Blackstaff half a mile away at Roden Street and shot him. The manner in which the fatal shots were delivered is significant. Kavanagh was shot first through the left nostril while he knelt on the ground, and when he fell the final bullet was fired from close range through the back of the head. The efficient manner in which the killing was carried out was, in fact, the traditional IRA execution, and was rarely departed from in the killings that followed. The men who carried out such a killing were almost certainly very experienced men, probably officers in the IRA. They were well trained in such executions and always followed the same procedure, permitting the condemned man a few minutes to make his peace with his maker before killing him. It was therefore not always too difficult to distinguish the professional I R A executions from the amateur and freelance ones, once the assassinations began in earnest.

Such a freelance killing was almost certainly that of the three Scots soldiers who were killed in March 1971. This killing was not a typical I R A killing. It was carried out by Provisional I R A men. The triple killing shocked the whole of the United Kingdom, and contributed in no small way to the downfall of James Chichester Clark as Ulster's Prime Minister later in the month. The killing also helped harden the image of the Provisional I R A as ruthless sectarian killers without any scrap of humanity. Protestants in Ulster were particularly angered because the three young off-duty soldiers were Scots Protestants, all members of the First Batallion, the Royal Highland Fusiliers.

I R A history and folklore is full of stories about condemned men being allowed to have a few minutes to themselves before they are killed in which to prepare for death. But the three Scots soldiers were never given the opportunity to do this. They were shot down at close range as they urinated into a ditch by the side of a quiet country road high above Belfast by two men who had befriended them in a city pub earlier in the evening. The soldiers: Joseph McCaig, 18; his younger brother, John, 17; and Douglas McCaughy, 23, had been drinking in Mooney's Bar in Cornmarket hours earlier. At this time, it was still considered proper for unarmed soldiers in civilian clothing to frequent Belfast in their off-duty hours. After all, the troops had been sent in the previous August to protect the Roman Catholics of the city from their Protestant neighbours. No one had yet seriously suggested that the Protestants might attack the Army, and it seemed inconceivable that Catholics would turn upon their protectors. Yet this is precisely what was to happen.

In Mooney's bar the three unfortunate soldiers were befriended by some local men. One of them was quite a comic, and regaled the assembly with tales of his days in the British Army. The company drank for a time and then moved on to Kelly's Cellar bar, several hundred yards away. Then the Provisionals invited the three soldiers to a party on the outskirts of the city, where there would be women. On this promise they all left Kelly's for the party, still holding their half-filled beer glasses. The group got into a blue mini car provided by the IRA men and headed out towards Ligoniel, high above the city on the way to the airport. Several hundred yards from Squire's Hill Tavern on the Ligoniel Road, the mini stopped, and the three soldiers got out of the car, beer glasses still in their hands, to relieve themselves in the ditch at the side of the road. As they did so their companions produced revolvers and calmly shot each of them in the back of the head. Joseph McCaig was extremely drunk, and was shot three times. His brother John was only slightly drunk. He had been shot twice, and damage to his skull indicated that he had also received a severe blow from the butt of the gun that killed him. The bullets had been fired only inches from his head, as was the case with the single bullet fired into the brain of Douglas McCaughy. All three were killed instantly. The bodies of the two brothers were found one on top of the other. McCaughy was propped up beside the embankment, his beer glass still clasped in his hand.

A group of Scotland Yard detectives headed by Chief Superintendent Payton arrived in Ulster a few days after the killing to track down those responsible. They left seven months later without any success. On their arrival police investigations centred on the Ardoyne area which was only half a mile from the murder scene. Three well-known Provisionals came under suspicion: Martin Meehan, the Provisionals' Ardoyne commander, Anthony 'Dutch' Doherty, and the Provisionals' quartermaster in the area, Paddy McAdorey. These men were known to be among the most dedicated and most experienced men the Provisionals had in their ranks in the city. But attempts to apprehend them were unsuccessful, and any chance of questioning McAdorey about the killing vanished when internment was introduced on 9 August. McAdorey was shot dead in a gun-battle with British troops at Jamaica Street, on the fringe of the Ardoyne. Meehan and Doherty were later captured by troops who raided a club in the Ardoyne on 9 November, but neither was charged with the killings of the three soldiers. Meehan refused to talk to the police about anything, but Doherty talked a great deal, and was grilled for several days on the killings. Both men were removed to Crumlin Road prison, and it was believed that charges were imminent when both escaped and sought refuge in the Irish Republic. Doherty, who has since been expelled from the IRA for recognizing a court in Eire, was believed to have been the man who had told humorous stories about his life in the Army. He had been in the Parachute Regiment when a teenager.

Sources close to the Provisional IRA at the time of the killings believe that they never received the sanction of the movement's leadership at brigade level. It was believed that the Provisionals at battalion level in the Ardoyne decided on the action because they felt the movement's overall leadership was not militant enough. Echoes of this killing were heard in March 1973, two years later, when four NCOs from the Army's head-quarters at Lisburn were lured to a flat in the Antrim Road with promises of a party and girls. It is possible that the same people were involved in both killings, although Doherty and Meehan could not have been involved in the latter. There were sugges-tions after the 1971 killings that more people had been involved and that some might have been girls. Certainly, the one vehicle known to have been used in 1971, a blue mini, would hardly have been large enough to carry six grown men, at least three of whom were carrying full glasses of beer. It is probably that two cars were used, and therefore at least possible, that others were involved.

These killings represent a more ruthless and callous attitude than that adopted by the IRA in previous campaigns. This atti-tude has, of course, more commonly been displayed in the wanton and indiscriminate bombing of civilian targets carried out by the Provisional IRA. The proclamation of an independent Irish Republic on Easter Sunday 1916, drawn up by Patrick Pearce, and revised by James Connolly, enjoined all who served the Republic not to dishonour its name with cowardly acts of needless violence. It also proclaimed complete civil and religious liberty for all the inhabitants of Ireland. It is to be wondered how many Provisionals in the 1970s, particularly the teenage youths who plant bombs in crowded city centres, have ever read this document. Certainly the Officials have, for they loathe the Provisionals and their acts of useless violence. But one wonders how men like David O'Connell or Rory O'Brady, the Provisional IRA's leaders, could justify the actions of these men and still claim to be the legitimate heirs of the men who fought and died in 1916 under the banner of that proclamation. For according to the men of 1916, every Protestant in Belfast was an Irishman, no matter what his political views. Every shop or factory that the Provisionals bomb is an Irish shop. Every person their bombs maimed or killed was Irish. The Provisionals claim they are 'liberating' Northern Ireland from the yoke of British Imperialism, yet most of the oppressed people want to remain under that yoke, and the people who suffer most from the Provisional IRA's tactics are the population in the North – the people who live and work amid the ruins of cities destroyed by Provisional bombs. To give both the history of Irish republicanism and the Official IRA their due, nothing like the campaign of terror undertaken by the Provisionals in 1970 has ever been seen before in Ireland, and there are many traditional republicans who regard what the Provisional IRA has been doing with nothing less than disgust, and consider it a disgrace to what they see as the honourable tradition of Irish republicanism.

Internment in August 1971 effectively removed many of the restraining influences over the excesses of the Provisional IRA, when many of the older and more experienced officers were picked up in the dawn swoops of Catholic areas. Their places were filled by younger and less experienced men, who had not seen active service in the previous campaign and who did not care for, nor appreciate the need for, tight military discipline. These people were attracted by the huge quantities of modern weapons now reaching the Provisionals from abroad, purchased with American money, and they looked for action. One result was that it became easier for individual IRA men and units on the ground to carry out assassinations on their own initiative the following year.

These occurred mostly in the north of Belfast because it was here that sectarian warfare was on a greater scale due to the close proximity of both Catholic and Protestant ghettos. The Ardoyne had seen the violence that had erupted in 1969, but the near-by area of the Oldpark had remained free of disturbance in that year. But at the beginning of February 1971, one year after the Provisional IRA had been established, large-scale riots broke out between rival Catholic and Protestant mobs in the area. During the confrontation between the Catholics coming from the Bone area and Protestants in Louisa Street, the gunmen on both sides came out and several people were killed. One of the dead was James Saunders, a young Provisional volunteer. His death was never forgotten by the Provisionals, and, in turn, the Protestants never forgot their dead. This was the way, on both sides, in Ulster.

Saunders had been shot 'on active service' by British troops who had moved into Louisa Street to engage the Provisionals who were fighting the Protestants. When the Army moved out, the Protestant gunmen took over, and fired into the Catholic Bone area wounding a number of people just before midnight. Many other Catholics might have been killed or injured had not a Sterling submachine-gun jammed in the hands of a Protestant gunman as he aimed it at a crowd. The IRA blamed the Protestants for Saunders's death and, in the months that followed, the Oldpark saw further sectarian violence which turned the area into one of the most dangerous in the city.

It was in this hate-filled atmosphere that the assassins were to operate the following year. Throughout the killings in 1972 and 1973 the IRA have not had specific assassination squads, as have the Protestants, because their units were already in existence and can be used for this purpose without trouble. As well as this, it has to be remembered also that the prime activity of the

IRA, except for the brief period of the June–July truce in 1972, is not sectarian assassinations. The Provisionals' main activity has been the campaign of bombings and attacks on members of the security forces. Had they devoted more of their resources to a concerted campaign of sectarian killings, the total number of assassinations would have been far higher, and would almost certainly have precipitated the massive rioting and gun-battles that have long been feared in the province. This event, with its accompanying result of wholesale slaughter of besieged communities on either side, has become known in the province as 'civil war' to distinguish it from the happenings of the previous four years which are known simply as 'the Troubles'. That Ulster is in a state of civil war, as it is usually known, with rival armies on both sides, can surely not seriously be doubted. But it may be that the fear of the possible eventuality of the most extreme definition used in the province prevents the Provisional I R A from engaging more completely in a campaign of sectarian assassination. However, one of the ironies of the Ulster situation is that the Provisional IRA have never appreciated that to the average Protestant in the province the killing of soldiers, UDR and RUC men, has always been a sectarian act, as too have been the bombings of civilian targets.

There are almost certainly other reasons for the low proportion of the killings that we have recorded being done by the Provisional I RA. The leadership do not approve the killing of Protestants as a general rule. Many in the leadership believe that they themselves are not sectarian, and they oppose such killings on the grounds that they are sectarian acts, though they do not regard bombings in this light. It is interesting that when the Official IRA killed Senator John Barnhill in December 1971, the Provisionals issued a statement in which they said the killing was to be deplored as a sectarian act that would only inflame relations between the communities. The Officials replied bitterly and accused the Provisionals of hypocrisy. As well as this, the Provisionals always insist that their enemy is the British Army, and tend to ignore the Protestant population. They believe that having achieved their united Ireland by force, those

Protestants who do not want to live in it will go quietly to Scotland. It is a strange belief, but it tends to mean that the Provisionals, while they ignore the genuine and deeply held Ulster patriotism of many Protestants, also discount their political importance in deciding the fate of the province and, as a general rule, leave them alone when it comes to overt military action. One has again to apply the caveat that the Provisionals do not regard their bombings or shootings of security forces as being directed at Ulster's Protestant population. If one accepts that in these activities the Provisionals believe they are attacking 'British Imperialism' then one can begin to understand their approach to the Protestant population in the context of the assassinations.

But this applies only to the leadership, many of whom have been across the border in the Republic for much of the campaign. On the ground things are slightly different, and there individual men or units do have personal grievances and grudges against neighbouring Protestants. This was the case of those in the Lower Falls who had seen Bombay Street burned to the ground by rampaging Protestant mobs in 1969, and of the men in the Ardoyne and the Bone areas who had similar grudges about similar incidents. Protestants, too, have their reasons to hate Catholics, and these grudges and feuds on the local level are the basic fuel of the assassination campaign. It became easier on the Catholic side after internment for men with hatred in their hearts for their Protestant neighbours for some personal wrong, either real or imagined, to take their own revenge without recourse to brigade or even battalion HQ for permission. Unlike the situation of the previous IRA campaign, officers commanding individual units are now not required to seek permission to carry out a bombing or a shooting. The result is that the decision on whether or not a man should live or die is taken at ground level with reports of the incident frequently not being relayed through the command structure. Provisional IRA leaders in Belfast and Dublin often do not know that their men were responsible for specific assassinations.

One example of this was the killing in January 1972 of the

Protestant bus-driver, Sidney Agnew. A teenage boy and girl, both Provisional IRA volunteers, were ordered to kill Agnew, who was the principal prosecution witness against several IRA men charged with hijacking his corporation bus. The teenagers shot Agnew in front of his wife and children at his home in the Mount, in East Belfast. The decision to kill him had been taken at a meeting of the Ballymacarret Provisional IRA earlier in the evening. It was believed that if Agnew were killed and could not testify in court the following day, the accused would be able to leave court free. The Provisional brigade staff in Belfast, and the battalion staff covering the area, could not have been warned in advance that this decision had been taken. They would probably have been sufficiently aware of the law to know that as Agnew had already made depositions in court on oath about the incident these could be used at the trial if he was killed. Thus killing him was a futile act.

When the summer of 1972 neared and the killing increased, IRA involvement reached its height – particularly during the truce with the Army. This was in part due to the fact that military activities were suspended and many Provisionals found a vent for their frustration at enforced inactivity in participation in the killings. It was in part also a response to the killing of Catholics by the Protestant assassins. Once again, however, this involvement was not ordered by the high command, but was allowed to happen spontaneously, unchecked at unit level in certain areas of the city, often unknown to, and not approved by, many of the movement's titular leaders.

When men like Clawson and Fisher are found in the Oldpark area those responsible probably justify their actions to their superiors with the allegation that both men must have been spies to have been in a Catholic area at midnight. Such an allegation, difficult to refute once the men are dead, is nonetheless easy to make if a Protestant wanders into a Catholic area. Ultimately the leadership of the IRA is responsible for they have taken no steps to stop the assassinations or attempt to discover those responsible, and whether the allegations made about the victims are true. Such indiscipline in the ranks is unprecedented, but it is really only a sign of the times, and the calibre of the membership of the movement at all levels.

Many of the Provisional IRA victims in the summer of 1972 were people who found themselves, under the influence of drink, wandering by accident into dangerous districts. It was only on a very few occasions that IRA men went out searching for victims. Men such as Turkington, Johnston, Clawson and Fisher were killed after being picked up by IRA squads after they had lost their way going home. They were interrogated by the same people who picked them up, and then executed by them. No quarter was given, whether or not the victims were members of the UDA or UVF, or just ordinary Protestant working men.

Geoffrey Walter Hamilton, who was shot in the Grosvenor Road in October 1972 walked, like the four other victims mentioned, into the clutches of IRA men, and the fact that he was carrying a camera and no press card immediately sealed his fate. Nothing he could tell his captors would convince them that he was not working for the Army. But Hamilton was an exception. As a rule, the Provisionals have seemed to assume that all Protestants they find in their areas are UDA or UVF men, in much the same way that the Protestant paramilitary bodies tend to believe that all Catholics are in the IRA. But most of the Protestants who have died at the hands of IRA squads– like most of the Catholics who have been killed by Protestant assassins – were in fact only ordinary people who found themselves in the wrong place at the wrong time. Usually the fate of the victims has been decided at local level, although in some cases the traditional kangaroo court is used. Martin Paul Owens, 22, a Roman Catholic from Andersonstown who was killed in April 1972, met his fate this way. Another IRA kangaroo court was held on Samuel Boyde, 20, in September, and in January 1973 a court sat in judgment on the UDA man Francis Smith, 20, who lived in the village, and whose car was believed used in the killing of 14-year-old Peter Watterson.

The shooting of the Roman Catholic magistrate, William Staunton, in October was almost certainly sanctioned at brigade level before being carried out. This killing had more of a political motive than most of the others, and it is doubtful if local unit commanders would have dared act against Staunton without the go-ahead from above. Throughout the Troubles the IRA have compiled an assassination list of prominent people, who will be killed if and when the opportunity arises. Chief among the names on this list are Brigadier Frank Kitson, who was Army commander in Belfast during the introduction of internment, and the two former GOCs, Generals Tuzo and Freeland. Also prominent on the list are the names of RUC Special Branch men such as Detective Inspector Harry Taylor, who played a major role in the interrogation of IRA men at the Palace Barracks, Holywood, and later at the Police Holding Centre, Castlereagh. If men such as Tommy Herron are to be believed, the IRA lists contain the names of prominent Protestant extremists also.

The fact that few of the important people on the IRA's death lists have been killed should not lead one to believe that these lists are kept merely for the amusement of the leadership. The memory of the IRA is traditionally very long. Many years after previous campaigns they have settled old scores. Men who had thought they could sleep soundly in their beds because a campaign has been formally ended have discovered to their cost that the IRA neither forgives nor forgets. During the past four years more than enough old scores have been created to fill Ulster's future with deepest gloom and foreboding. The assassinations began with a trickle in 1970 and 1971. They grew to a torrent in 1972, and have continued in 1973. Who can today say with confidence when they will end?

14. The Killers (II) – The Protestants

The six counties of Northern Ireland have a large Protestant majority. In round terms there are one million Protestants compared to half as many Catholics. The state was created in 1921 on the sole basis that it ensured a permanent Protestant majority. Historically Ulster also contains the three Catholic counties of Donegal, Monaghan and Cavan, but at the time of partition these counties were left in the then Irish Free State, later the Republic, for the simple reason that such a nine-county Ulster could not guarantee a permanent Protestant majority. The Protestants in the Northern Ireland state have always been an embattled community, fearing absorption by the Republic on the outside, and wary of the birth-rate of the Catholics on the inside.

Such a society created on this fundamentally sectarian basis could expect poor community relations at best, and at worst was a powder keg waiting for the spark that would ignite the whole charge. As we have seen that spark was produced in the years leading up to 1972; and there can be no doubt that the majority of assassinations carried out in Ulster were committed by Protestant groups. As recently as August 1973 the Vanguard Unionist Party of William Craig could issue a statement claiming that there was no evidence to connect Protestants with the killings and demanding that the press should not make such assumptions – but in fact evidence abounds of the activities of the Protestant involvement in the killings. There are now recorded a number of court cases where Protestants have been convicted of assassinations, and where the overt involvement of one or other of the Protestant paramilitary groups is admitted. In the trial of Welshman, Swain and McAllister for the murder of Bernard Moane, for example, it was not challenged in court that the men were members of the Ulster Defence Association. After their conviction they all shouted loyalist slogans to the public gallery, where supporters responded with cheers. In 1966 the Government of Terence O'Neill banned the UVF, after the killing of Peter Ward but before any court case had legally proved the connection of that body with illegal acts. Curiously, despite the wealth of evidence from numerous court cases of the complicity of the UDA in killings, attempted killings, robberies and kidnappings, Mr Whitelaw has taken no steps to ban it.

There is no doubt that the UDA has been the main vehicle through which Ulster's working-class Protestants have channelled their grievances against the Roman Catholic population during the past few years. The most dramatic action taken by Protestants has been the assassinations. This is not to say, however, that the killings have been the result of an overall strategic plan drawn up at command level in the UDA. Rather like the IRA, the UDA has tended to evolve during the Troubles into a body where the most important decisions are taken by local commanders on the ground without recourse to the leadership. This has led to the absurd picture of the UDA's spokesman, Tommy Herron, announcing that the Association had 'declared war' on the British Army on a number of occasions. Herron was merely legitimizing the actions of local men on the spot over whom he had no control. So too with the killings. There are, and have been, far more splinter groups and groupings on the Protestant side than the Catholic. As well as the UDA and UVF, there are the various Tartan gangs, the Red Hand, Tara, the Loyalist Defence Force, the Shankill Defence Association, and the Orange Volunteers, to name but a few. The membership of these groups has always tended to overlap, and the UDA has tended to embrace them all in a sort of loyalist umbrella. But each group has always retained its own peculiar structure and operated independently of the rest, and acknowledge no overall control. In January 1973 the UDA leadership under Herron was able to call off these various groups of assassins for almost four weeks. It was a remarkable feat, and showed the degree of physical force Herron had at his disposal to compel the pause. But his power was limited. With nothing in return from the other side for the concession, Herron was unable to restrain the killers, and he was forced to let them continue.

The composition of these Protestant assassination squads is of some interest. They are not usually the rank-and-file members of the UDA, though, again, it has to be stressed that like virtually all the Protestant militants they do belong to the Association. They are also members of the other groups. These groups tend to be small, secretive, and tightly knit organizations and contain the men of action within the Protestant community who are not content to sit back in a posture of defence, but who want to go out and hit back hard at the 'enemy' Catholic community. The sort of people they are is well illustrated in the letter to the *Loyalist News* of July 1971 that was quoted earlier (see pp. 50–51).

In the two years that followed the publication of that letter, a number of organizations grew up to fill the vacuum left by the UVF. One of these was Red Hand, a group formed in East Belfast by a leading Protestant militant. It had been founded well before the Troubles began, and is credited with a number of acts of violence – notably the blowing-up of the Belfast water-mains – before the autumn of 1968. But the onset of the Troubles and the accompanying violence provided a boost for the men of action, and it is reliably reported that Red Hand grew from having a membership of only a couple of dedicated men to a considerable size in this period.

The troubles had this effect on the other organizations too. The UDA which grew to prominence in 1972 was not geared to offensive action against the Catholics and this displeased many Protestants. These people were angry at the collapse in law and order in the province because of the Catholic–IRA campaign of violence and civil disobedience. They were frightened lest their accustomed way of life might be destroyed through lack of a stout defence on their part. As the letter-writer in the *Loyalist News* wrote, they were 'willing to give their lives to hold on to what others gave their lives for'. More importantly, they saw the best way of hitting back as not so much giving their own lives, but taking those of their opponents. Such people existed in significant numbers in the Protestant community. They only needed the opportunity to strike back. In this context, it is, perhaps worth looking at another quotation used earlier on. This is the letter written to the *Ulster Militants* from a group of men who described themselves as disillusioned UDA and UVF men, who had discovered that there was in existence an organization on the Protestant side that was hitting back hard at the Catholics (see pp. 52).

The letter gives a fairly detailed account of how in the summer of 1972 militant Protestants were organized into commando groups to attack the 'IRA Provisionals and their "passive" sympathizers'. It is interesting that it is the Provisionals who are singled out for attack, which could suggest that a different attitude was taken towards the Officials. The most sinister phrase is that referring to the Provisionals' 'passive' sympathizers. As these men were defining their own terms, it is not immediately apparent just what action, or degree of inaction, would qualify one as a passive sympathizer of the Provisional IRA. To some Protestants at least, the mere fact that one was a Catholic would be sufficient to damn one as a passive sympathizer of the Provisionals and make one guilty of all their excesses. This was certainly the attitude of the woman who wrote to the *UDA Bulletin* in February 1972, also quoted earlier on pp. 56–7. She said she had reached the stage 'where I no longer have any compassion for any nationalist, man, woman, or child. After years of destruction, murder, intimidation, I have been driven against my better feelings to the decision – it's them or us.' To her, at least, and almost certainly to countless thousands of other working-class Protestants, Ulster was engaged in a bitter struggle for survival. If the state were destroyed as seemed likely the Protestant people with their own peculiar culture and heritage would be wiped out and their Ulster would be replaced by a Romish priest-dominated republic. This woman called for the men in the Protestant community to form themselves into 'commando groups', to hit back at the Catholics before it was too late. 'Why have they not started to hit back in the only way these nationalist bastards understand?' she asked. '*That is, ruthless, indiscriminate killing*

... If I had a flame-thrower I would roast the slimy excreta that pass for human beings.'* Quite clearly there were men in the Protestant community prepared to take precisely the action the woman asked for. What sort of people were they?

Before the Troubles, Ulster had one of the lowest murder and crime rates in the western world. How is it that overnight, as it were, this could change, and something in the region of 1,000 people could be killed here, mostly in a space of two years, and over 200 the civilian victims of assassinations? Had a large number of dangerous psychopaths on both sides suddenly emerged? This is an explanation that many would subscribe to; but opinion is divided, even among the experts. Some medical and psychiatric authorities believe that the Troubles have acted as a catalyst for the psychopathic element in Ulster society. They point out that in all societies there are those who deviate from normality. The term 'psychopath' in the sense that it is generally understood by laymen – that of a violent and sadistic madman – is only one aspect of the mental illness it denotes. There are two other non-violent types of psychopath, the loner or outcast who finds himself unable to mix with the other members of society, and the person who believes he is being persecuted by that society. All three types of people are present in society, but, the experts say, in a normal society the harm that the violent, sadistic or aggressive psychopath is capable of doing is severely circumscribed. But Ulster is not a normal but a sick society. Such people here, in the climate of fear and hatred on both sides of the sectarian fence, found that for the first time they had a role to play in the society that had always shunned them. They discovered that the violent acts that earlier caused them to be reviled and imprisoned were later greeted as acts of patriotism and lauded by the same people who had once despised them. Their illness had become respectable. One has only to look at the details of killings such as that of Thomas Madden, Francis Arthurs, Patrick Benstead, or Henry Russell, to begin to understand this argument.

Such mentally ill people are, of course, not confined to one side in the conflict. At least one psychiatrist has expressed the

*Italics ours – M.D. and D.L.

belief that many of the leaders of the paramilitary groups on both sides are probably suffering from mental illnesses that would, in other times, have seen them confirmed to mental institutions. Since the Troubles began, there has been a marked drop in the incidence of mental illness treated in the province, and this could be explained by the fact that those who in normal times would have sought treatment from doctors and psychiatrists now no longer feel the need to so so. The abnormal situation of the sectarian conflict has made their abnormality 'normal'. Killing and torturing is no longer a crime, but an accepted and honoured social activity on both sides. Consequently there is no need for those who feel personal tendencies towards such practices to go and seek therapy for it. On the contrary, such men are much valued within their communities, and instead of seeking to eliminate their tendencies they may have felt obliged to exaggerate them for the public good.

Most of the leaders on both sides of the fence have, during the course of the Troubles, come to prominence from complete obscurity in a few short years. But to say that all the killings have been the work of aggressive psychopaths, for the first time allowed to let their feelings run unchecked, is perhaps too simple an explanation. It is not a view that is held by everyone in the medical and psychiatric professions. An alternative view that has been advanced is that the killers are in no way abnormal. Our society is founded on the acceptance of the principle of taking life: we recognise the right, indeed the duty, to take human life when necessary. Hundreds of thousands, probably millions of men in the United Kingdom from the Prime Minister downwards have almost certainly been involved in taking human life. Mr Heath was an officer in an artillary regiment during the Second World War, and along with millions of other British soldiers he took part in active service in which the prime aim was to kill as many of the enemy as was necessary to win a military objective. No one, the argument goes, would seriously describe Mr Heath and those who served in the British Army during that war as 'aggressive psychopaths'. And so it is with the members of the paramilitary groups on either side of the Ulster conflict.

In all modern, and indeed earlier, societies, the right to kill other human beings is admitted as something that can, in certain circumstances, transcend the usual sacrosanct nature of human life – indeed, refusal to fight and kill has often been deemed immoral. So it was that in 1946 those French men and women who had refused to accept the orders of the Vichy French Government to cease fighting the Germans in 1940 were lauded as heroes while those who accepted the order were condemned as traitors. The men and women who fought in the French Resistance from 1940 to 1944 would not be regarded as mentally ill. But they were no more popular among their fellow countrymen and women at the time than, say, the Provisional I R A were in Ulster in 1970–73. Like the Provisionals, the terrorists activities of the French Resistance were regarded as futile and brought down the wrath of the security forces, whether German or Vichy French, on the innocent local people. Odette Churchill was made a heroine because she lured German soldiers to their deaths by the promise of sex. Today in Northern Ireland when Provisionsl I R A girls lure British soldiers to their deaths in a similar way they are unanimously condemned as sub-human.

Where is the normality in these situations? The cynic may be forgiven if he concludes that 'normality' and 'morality' are relative terms and depend more on the final consequences of any given action or series of actions than on their intrinsic merits at the time. So the French Resistance was just and honourable in its activities, but the Provisional I R A is not, because the one ultimately succeeded whereas the other has not. Should the Provisionals by some quirk of history actually succeed, would history be rewritten to justify their actions after all? One can only recall that in 1921, only a few short months after the British government had decried and vilified the I R A leader Michael Collins as a 'gunman' and 'murderer', they were treating with him on equal terms and describing him as a great patriot. In 1916 the British wanted to hang Eamonn DeValera: in 1940 when he was the Irish Prime Minister Churchill was begging him to enter the war and offering Ulster as an inducement.

Thus history would tend to suggest that the instant judgements made on insurgents at the time are not always borne out in the long-term view. A higher duty is on occasion accepted as justification for acts that would normally be regarded as barbaric and abnormal. In Ulster at the moment, on both sides, the argument of a higher duty is used to cause otherwise normal people to commit acts of complete abnormality that they would in other circumstances never personally consider and would condemn in others. In the opinion of one leading medical man, what happens to such people is that a mental shutter comes down inside their minds when they commit one of these acts. It is this mental shutter that enables hundreds of thousands of ordinary men to go to war and then come back without serious mental disturbances. In Ulster those on both sides responsible for the killings have regarded themselves as soldiers engaged in a war. This had enabled them mentally to 'dehumanize' their victims. The victims cease to be individual human beings to their killers, but merely part of the 'enemy', not 'one of us', but 'one of them'. As the woman writing to the *U D A Bulletin* wrote, she no longer had 'any compassion for any nationalist man, woman, or child'. The actions of certain sections of the Roman Catholic community were for her so serious that she attached the blame to the whole community, including those personally innocent. They would have to suffer in revenge along with the guilty. It is basically the same philosophy that could accept the pattern-bombing of German cities in 1944 and 1945, and the atom-bomb attacks on Hiroshima and Nagasaki in Japan in 1945, when countless thousands of innocent women and children, old people and the sick, were destroyed. Those who would justify such actions in the Second World War would seem to have no right to criticize, on moral grounds, the woman who wrote to the *U D A Bulletin* or the tactics of either side to the Ulster conflict.

One is faced with two explanations for the killings in Ulster. Either they are the work of psychopaths who naturally gravitate towards leading positions of activist movements in a violent situation; or they are committed by ordinary people, who feel no moral guilt because they are moved by a higher duty than that which requires them not to take life. There are, no doubt, some aggressive psychopaths on both sides, but this would not account for many of the killings. Very many of the people involved do appear to be perfectly normal – perhaps the great majority of them. On the Protestant side, three young men from the Shankill area who were sentenced to ten years each for attempted murder in 1972, afford us an insight into the sort of people who are involved in the assassinations.

In the early hours of 28 July 1973 a young Roman Catholic student, Joseph Henry Hall, 23, was making his way home to the Oldpark area of the city. Hall was a young man with a bright future ahead of him. At the age of 15 he had left school in Ulster without any qualifications and gone to work in England. There he regretted his lack of qualifications and worked hard at evening classes and won a scholarship to Rupert Stanley College of Further Education in Belfast. There he gained more qualifications and had been accepted by both Queen's University Belfast and Trinity College Dublin for degree courses. He was due to begin a history degree at Queen's in the autumn of 1972.

As Hall walked on 28 July along Upper Library Street, not far from Unity Flats and the foot of the Shankill Road, a blue van containing three young Protestants of about the same age as himself pulled up alongside him. A few words were exchanged before one of the men in the van emptied the contents of a revolver into Hall and left him for dead. He had been hit by at least ten bullets from virtually point-blank range. The killers sped off towards the safety of the Shankill Road, and there the matter might have ended as, to quote the usual police statement, 'another apparently motiveless murder', but for two things. First, despite his terrible injuries Hall survived the attack; and second, the killers did not make good their escape. In the few seconds they needed to reach the Shankill Road from the scene of the shooting, they came across an Army–RUC patrol, and in their panic crashed the van and were apprehended.

The three men in the car were: Thomas Reid, 23, of Carnan Street; Ronald McCullough, 20, of Silvio Street; and William Smith, 18, of High Pass. All lived in the Shankill–Woodvale area, and all came from respectable working-class homes.

Reid had been injured in the crash and spent some time in hospital before he appeared at a remand hearing at Belfast Magistrate's Court on 19 August. At this hearing his solicitor, Trevor Smyth, requested bail for his client. The charge was attempted murder, and bail on such a charge would have been most unusual, but Smyth told the court that Reid would resist the charge strenuously. He said that the accused, a labourer, came from a respectable working-class background. He had never before been in trouble with the police, and there would be no difficulty obtaining satisfactory surities. Bail was denied.

Reid's two accomplices came from similarly impeccable working-class backgrounds. McCullough was an apprentice electrician and Smith an apprentice printer. These were young men learning a trade, preparing for the future, young men who at other times and in other cities in the United Kingdom could be expected to form the backbone of the skilled working class. But these men did not live in Birmingham or Manchester, where, in the course of time, they would have married, had families, and settled down to be solid citizens with their own homes, cars, and possessions. They came from the Shankill and Woodvale in Belfast – areas, as Gusty Spence said, that had known poverty and hardship, and where they had grown up on a diet of sectarian hatred and bitterness.

Over the previous three or four years these men had seen everything they had been brought up to and revere and respect crumble away. Old-fashioned Unionism had disappeared, followed by the B-Specials and then Stormont itself. All the indications were that the long-feared republican take-over had arrived. What were young men such as these to do? What, from their backgrounds, could they be expected to do?

At their trial all three men pleaded guilty to the charge of attempted murder. They had little option. They had been caught virtually red-handed. The Crown Prosecuter, Mr Michael Lavery Q.C., told the court that as far as he knew the three men had never met or known of their victim before the night they shot him. Defending the men, Mr Desmond Boal said that they all came from the same part of Belfast, and they each shared the

273

same religious and political affiliations. 'They are subjected to the same social pressures and are swayed by the same prejudices and mindlessness and thoughtlessness that permeates that section of the community from time to time,' he said. The men, in a mindless and thoughtless way, were doing something they thought was an expression of the needs of their community.

It was an eloquent defence, and contained a strong element of truth. Glimpses of the background in which such attitudes have been cultivated were seen at earlier pre-trial hearings. At the first hearing on 31 July, three days after the attack, Smith and McCullough appeared at Belfast Magistrates Court wearing UDA and UVF badges. (Reid was still in hospital at the time.) When the three men first appeared together in the dock on 29 August to be remanded again, one shouted to the court 'No surrender!' and another 'Keep up the fight!'

When they appeared again for remand on 14 September there were about twenty young men in the public gallery of the court all dressed uniformly in blue anoraks. As the three left the court, the youths got up smartly and saluted. They applauded their three accused colleagues and shouted UVF slogans. A week earlier, the court had been cleared by a magistrate when a similar demonstration had taken place: a number of women had clapped, cheered, and shouted slogans, while Reid, Smith, and McCullough replied with shouts once again of 'No surrender!' and 'Keep up the fight!'

The picture that emerges from scenes such as these is one of three young men totally without remorse for the act they had committed. Quite the contrary, in fact; they seemed to be proud of themselves. Within their own community they are regarded not as criminals, but as heroes, soldiers fighting for the cause. 'No surrender!' and 'Keep up the fight!' are fighting slogans, the war-cries of an embattled community. In the eyes of this community Reid, McCullough and Smith are prisoners of war, soldiers caught by the enemy on active service. Their comrades-in-arms lend them moral support by attending the court hearings in uniform and according them military salutes. These three young men did not know Joseph Henry Hall personally. They did not need to. For them his shooting was a military operation. Hall was a Roman Catholic and therefore an enemy. Personalities did not come into it. They sought to eliminate him and gained only partial success – he is now paralyzed from the chest down. They were captured, but the war goes on: 'No surrender!', 'Keep up the fight!' The three men did not doubt that their action was just. Nor did they doubt the ultimate success of their cause, which they knew to be just. Lord Randolph Churchill said during the Home Rule debates in the English House of Commons in the 1880s: 'Ulster will fight, and Ulster will be right!' These words are carved on the hearts of countless thousands of Protestants in the province from birth.

An interesting footnote to the Hall case came in January 1973. On 12 January at Belfast Recorder's Court, the injured man was awarded £56,000 criminal injuries damages. At the court Joseph Hall declined to be photographed by press photographers, and his counsel asked the press not to publish his address. It was feared that the colleagues of the three UVF men – now serving ten years for the attack – who had cheered them so loyally at the court hearings, might seek to finish the job. Such fears were not totally unjustified. On the night of 14 January just two days after the award, 'unknown men' set fire to the Counsellor Bar in Everton Street, off the Crumlin Road. The fire completely destroyed the bar which was owned by Mr Robert Hall, Joseph Hall's father.

The previous day, 13 January, on the steps of Belfast City Hall, Joseph Hall's mother, Mrs Imelda Hall, had made an impassioned plea for peace in the province at a rally organized by Women Together, a non-sectarian group of women. 'I want the women to please, once and for all, stop the assassins knocking on our doors,' she said. 'Please forget who started it all. Let's help finish it.' Her words have a special poignancy: Joseph Hall, the Catholic victim of Protestant gunmen, was the product of a mixed marriage. His father is a Protestant and his mother a Catholic. The Halls mirror the tragedy of Ulster.

The Hall case is interesting because it allows us to see the organization of the various assassination squads operating at this time, for Reid, McCullough and Smith are a fairly typical group. Such a group usually consists of three or four men, only one of whom will carry a gun. A revolver is the most common weapon. The killers are usually well briefed before they go out, they will know the quickest escape routes from the scene of their shooting, and in almost every case this planning is good enough to get the squads back into friendly territory before the killing has been discovered. In an area such as North Belfast where the rival communities are so close together, escape can be made in a matter of seconds.

In the Hall case, for example, the shooting took place no more than 300 yards from the Shankill Road. It was the misfortune of the would-be killers to come across a passing RUC–Army patrol. Even then, such a contingency had been catered for. Each squad that is sent out receives a piece of paper with a solicitor's telephone number. The name of one of two well-known Belfast solicitors will be on the piece of paper. The members of the squad are instructed to make no comments to the police until the solicitor has been summoned. The man who possesses the gun is then to admit this, but to claim that the other members of the car did not know he had it. They will each protest that they did not know of its existence. Thus it is that on many occasions patrols stop squads in suspicious circumstances late at night in cars, but can only in the end convict one man for possession of a firearm. Sometimes the gun is legally held, and then the police can make no charges stick, even though they have a pretty shrewd idea that the men they have stopped were looking for an assassination victim.

Another important feature of the Protestant militants has been the growth of interrogations in depth. It would be wrong to see these interrogations solely in the context of the assassinations. They are an integral part of UDA and UVF rule in the Protestant areas, and as such have become a common practice in assassinations where the victims are picked up and detained beforehand. Here again, one cannot but help notice the parallel with what has been happening on the other side of the fence. The IRA too have conducted in-depth interrogation of victims before executing them. However, the scale on which the Protestants have operated has exceeded that of the IRA. A new term entered the Ulster vocabulary with the frequency of such Protestant interrogations. 'Romper Room' is the title of a popular children's TV programme where an adult tells young children stories. For some reason, the Protestants have chosen to call their interrogation rooms 'romper rooms' and the activities that take place inside them, 'romperings'. It is clear that the Protestant organizations have read well the Compton report – the judicial investigation of the interrogation techniques used by the British Army during and after internment – for one finds that many of the techniques used by the British Army have been adopted by the Protestant militants. In addition, electric shock treatment has been used by them. A number of people have been admitted to Belfast hospitals with curious marks that only later were revealed to be caused by the electrodes of simple but effective electric-shock machines used in romper rooms.

By far the largest number of people subjected to romperings have been Protestants, for, as mentioned earlier, in the vacuum created by the absence of the RUC the effective control of law and order in the Protestant working-class areas passed to the paramilitary bodies. Here again there is a parallel with the Catholic areas. The hard men on both sides of the sectarian divide are usually punctilious in their enforcement of the law when it comes to non-political offences. For example, on both sides, it has been insisted that taxi-drivers possess both Public Service Vehicle licences, and the corresponding insurance before they are allowed to operate. This is to guarantee the safety of the people in the area. As far as Motor Taxation is concerned, they could not care less, but insurance and PSV licences are crucial. And so it is in all other spheres. In the absence of the traditional law-enforcement agency, the paramilitary bodies have taken over. In Protestant areas petty crime has, if anything, been punished more harshly than before the Troubles. Harding Smith, for example, is well known for dragging petty criminals down to RUC stations to be dealt with. Significantly, the men concerned have usually had the benefit of a UDA rompering beforehand, and are only too pleased to see the inside of a gaol after that.

One element of the romperings that has tended to develop during the assassination campaign is the increasing participation of young people. The young people who have tended to gravitate to the ranks of the militant bodies are often the most likely to engage in gratuitous violence for its own sake. In a number of the assassinations it is clear that many hands were at work. The Madden killing is an obvious example. There would seem very little explanation for the treatment that Madden received – 150 stab-wounds before he was strangled – unless a number of people participated in a kind of ritual killing. The element of ritual in the killings has been of interest to the authors. If one assumes that many of the killers have been normal people, then one has to look on occasion for an additional stimulant to their actions over and above their traditional hatred of Catholics. One such stimulant that immediately presents itself is alcohol. The 1966 killings were committed by men who had had an enormous amount of drink in them. The killing of Bernard Moane in August 1972 took place after the killers had drunk all the samples of drink he carried as a salesman. Most of the assassinations have taken place late at night when the killers have had the opportunity to have a drink. In addition, those where the victim has been taken to a club for interrogation have also presented the killers with the opportunity to drink, probably during the interrogation. But as well as this, or perhaps side by side with it, there is also the suggestion that in at least some of the killings a number of people have taken part in a ritualistic manner. Possibly, new additions to the group have beeen ceremonially 'blooded' in this way. We know from the trial of a juvenile who admitted that he 'took a dig' at Felix John Hughes at a club inside the UDA No-go area of Portadown in July 1972, that there were at least a dozen people involved. Hughes was badly beaten, and it would appear that most of the company 'took a dig' at him, one managing to break his skull. The killing of Patrick Benstead in East Belfast in December 1972 also seems like a killing where a number of people could have inflicted injury on the dead man before he died. He was branded with a figure 4, a cross, and 'IRA' on his back. This would not appear the sort of thing a single killer would concern himself with. Rather a group of people, wrapped up in the excitement of their action and wishing to boast of it, would seem a more likely answer. So too with the killing of Henry Russell, the UDR man who was found in Larkfield Drive, Sydenham, in July 1972. Russell received very similar treatment to Benstead. In these two killings there is strong evidence to connect very young people, the local Tartan gangs. This was also the case with one of the earliest killings, that of Patrick McCrory, in March 1972. In all these killings, there seems to be some element of ritual involved, possibly not conscious, but nonetheless there. The killings of Francis Arthurs in West Belfast in July 1972 would also seem to come into this category. Arthurs's body bore the marks of a number of stab-wounds remarkably similar to those inflicted on Thomas Madden the following month in the same area. Yet in neither killing were these wounds the cause of death. Arthurs was shot and Madden was strangled. It would seem that where the knife is used as a weapon of torture, or where branding or severe beating prior to death take place, a form of ritualism can be suspected. In July 1973, in an interview with journalists about the killing of Paddy Wilson and Irene Andrews the previous month, a spokesman for the UFF admitted that such ritualistic killings might have taken place, when he referred to this killing with the words; 'That was a ritual killing.' So at least some of the assassins have been conscious of this element in the killings, and possibly it has been more prevalent than one has suspected.

The arrival of the Ulster Freedom Fighters on the scene brought a new dimension to the assassination campaign. They were born as a result of the turmoil in the ranks of the UDA. Once again, as in January, a compromise had been agreed between Herron in the East and the hard men in the West led by Harding Smith and the UVF. Herron's position was slipping badly, and he was forced to concede virtually everything demanded. He had seen his brother-in-law killed in his place, and was deeply shocked and frightened. But he was still strong enough to

279

keep some power in his own area, though his prominence as a spokesman for the UDA as a whole diminished. One point he was able to carry with Harding Smith was that the assassins should not be allowed to get the UDA banned. As a result the new Ulster Freedom Fighters emerged. In reality they were only the hard men in the West, mainly the UVF men and militant UDA men, who had tried to take over the UDA and turn it towards a more militant political role. By taking on the form and title of a new and distinct group, it was hoped that the UDA would not be blamed for the assassinations. The decision was logical. While they did not have a separate identity, the Protestant assassins had always maintained strict secrecy and had created a group within the UDA. Herron was not interested in the assassinations, and did not want to see the UDA banned because of them. Harding Smith for his part did not want to see the Association banned, and thus the arrangement suited both sides.

The people who emerged in June 1973 consist of dedicated Protestant Ulster patriots motivated by a high idealism. They are the first militant Protestant group to formulate and articulate a cogent and compelling justification of their actions. Parts of the statement handed to a representative of the Dublin *Sunday World* on Saturday 9 June have been quoted in an earlier chapter, but to understand the feelings of the people involved, one has to read the statement full. It runs:

We accept that the press of the world is sick of the sound and sight of Ulster, sick of our orgy of destruction, sick of our rancour and sick of our brutalities. Why, therefore, you ask, should you be interested in the self-delusive ravings of a band of extreme Protestants? A band of men cast in the role of wicked 'heavies', the 'bad guys' of the story, the narrow-minded bigots of Ulster, the cause of all the present troubles?

Mountains of words have been written about us in the past four years and our role in the affair is cast by the press in a certain way and all comments about us are based upon these assumptions:

That we are narrow minded. That we are fanatical. That we are similar to the I R A. That we hate all Catholics. That we are repressive, 'right wing' Fascists. That we cannot be reasoned with.

With all that has been written about the Scots-Irish of Northern Ireland, you would have thought that someone would have eventually grasped the essential truth of it all. The real cause of the bloodshed, the real cause of the hatred. We think you, the press, have done nothing of the sort, and it is high time that you did; for, if nothing else, we do feel you owe our people a little latitude. Just this once.

It seems a lifetime ago that our competent, if partisan, government came under fire from a Civil Rights movement which, it has to be admitted, did have a justification for many of its grievances. Cast inevitably in the role of St Bernadette came a pint-sized lady of fiery oratory and poverty-striken background. How the press loved this little lady, pictured her swinging prettily in a garden as her victories over the repressing, misruling Unionists were announced.

You, the press, made a heroine of this girl and you bear a heavy responsibility for what followed. The blundering, incompetent and seemingly repressive antics of our leaders confirmed your attitude that she and her associates were right and that we were wrong. The B-Specials, the reactions of our police forces, and the so-called ambush of Burntollet, hardened your views which, in turn, hardened ours, and the die was cast.

It is such a pity that you do not consult your history books, for the real truth lies there, repeated over and over again, like a gramophone record. We are a hybrid race decended from men who colonized Scotland from Ireland in the fifth century, and who then colonized Northern Ireland from Scotland in the seventeenth century. Our existence was not placid in Scotland, but that was heavenly compared to our life in Ireland. For four hundred years we have known nothing but uprising, murder, destruction, and repression. We ourselves have repeatedly come to the support of the British Crown, only to be betrayed within another twenty years or so by a fresh government of that Crown. What is happening now mirrors similar events in the seventeenth, eighteenth, and nineteenth centuries.

We are not good at propaganda and not good at extolling our virtues or admitting our faults. We just stick to our points of view, bow our heads and pray for it all to die down again for another fifty years or so.

Gradually, however, we have come to realize that this time other factors have come into the age-old conflict of the Scots-Irish versus the Irish-Irish, or if you prefer it that way, the Protestants versus the Catholics in Ireland.

Traditionally the English politicians let us down – betrayal we call it. The Catholics try to overwhelm us so we are caught in between two lines of fire. Second-class Englishmen, half-caste Irishmen, this we can live with and even defeat, but how can we be expected to beat the world revolutionary movement which supplies arms and training, not to mention most sophisticated advice on publicity, promotion and expertise to the I R A?

We do not have large funds from over-indulgent sentimentally sick Irishmen in America who send the funds of capitalism to sow the seeds of communism here. We do not have the tacit support of the government of Southern Ireland and we do not have the support or interest of the British people.

We are betrayed, maligned and our families live in constant fear and misery. We are a nuisance to our so-called allies and have no friends anywhere. Once more in the history of our people we have our backs to the wall, facing extinction by one way or another. This is the moment to beware, for Ulstermen in this position fight mercilessly till they or their enemies are dead.

We would like to remind you of a few salient facts: The Russians who condemn our people have millions in slave labour camps and their government is the biggest mass murderer since Adolf Hitler. Edward Kennedy, the heroic night-swimmer of Martha's Vineyard, is hardly in a moral condition to criticise his pet rabbit let alone us. The ruler of Libya is a raving fanatic. If the Unionist Government of Northern Ireland was corrupt, it was as pure as the driven snow compared to the Government of John Mary Lynch. If the press likes scandals then let them examine the private fortunes of government ministers in the Lynch republic. Fortunes made out of a divine intuition about future planning permissions. If the Protestants in the south of Ireland are so content, why do their numbers dwindle and why do they never complain?

If the Southern Irish government wants us then it will have to win our hearts, rather than have us as bitterly hostile losers in a bombing war of attrition tacitly backed by them. Their own history should tell them this will never work. Our troubles destroyed their tourist industry, and a few well-planted disease-ridden animals could very rapidly destroy their economic growth. They too are not immune from trouble, and they should not support evil men of violence lest it rebound heavily upon them.

The British Army in Ulster has good soldiers who are being set up like dummy targets. The orders of the politicians are tying both hands behind their backs. The British public says: 'Send the soldiers home.' We say: 'Send the politicians and the officers home and leave us the men and the weapons – or, why not send the soldiers home and leave us the weapons and we will send you the I R A wrapped up in little boxes and little tins like cans of baked beans.'

The politicians who rule our lives from England do not understand us. They stop the Army from defending us properly and stop us from defending ourselves. We do not like these flabby-faced men with pop eyes and fancy accents. We do not like Heath and we do not like his 'side-kicks'. We had to stomach Reggie until Poulson saw him off, and Lambton and Jellicoe went in a more interesting way. We should really like to see wee Willie waddle off to cut the throats of his colleagues in Westminster and leave us to sensible ideas and policies which *will* work.

We ourselves are not perfect. We ourselves do not always see eye to eye, but the time is fast coming when the Scots-Irish of Ulster will have to reconsider their future actions. The bloodbath could very soon be a reality, and you who condemned us for it could have precipitated it unjustly on decent people because they jerrymandered a few constituencies to avoid giving power to people who were educated and dedicated to destroying a way of life.

You turned an adulterous little slut into a revolutionary saint; a soft-voiced failed priest fanatic was called a moderate, and you gave a terror organisation all the publicity it desired. It was not an *Irish* leader of the I R A who said we were all fit to be bombed but a sick little pop-eyed Englishman with a false name and with no Irish connections whatsoever. We the Scots-Irish are fighting for survival. We think we have been greatly wronged, and we think you should watch the events of the next month with extreme *care*.

This document contains certainly the most eloquent statement of the case of Ulster's Protestant militants given throughout the course of the Troubles. It was directed at the press, and there is much truth in the claim that the press have been unsympathetic to their cause, while at the same time putting a favourable gloss on the activities of many of the Catholic side. Significantly, this book is the first publication in which the statement has appeared in full. The *Sunday World* transmitted a copy to the *Belfast Telegraph*, but only a few short snippets were printed. This was clearly not the coverage the statement's authors had sought.

It has to be made perfectly clear that the statement was not issued in the name of the Ulster Freedom Fighters. Those who entertained the Dublin newspaper's journalist to tea at a house in the Shankill Road were emphatic that they represented the new leadership of the UDA and that the house was the Association's new headquarters. The UFF was not heard of until later in the day when, after the bombing of the Avenue Bar in Kent Street, a man telephoned the *Belfast Telegraph* and claimed the attack for the new body. But it is clear that those who wrote the statement were extreme Protestant patriots who had become bitterly disillusioned at the policies adopted by successive Stormont and Westminster governments over the preceeding four years.

The document is a lucid and frank exposition of the position of working-class Protestants in Ulster at the present. The historical background is substantially correct, and it is interesting that, as Spence had done the previous year on TV, the legitimacy of some of the claims of the Roman Catholic Civil Rights Movement were accepted. Also of interest is that the writers accept that under the old Stormont system Catholics had been gerrymandered in elections. But this is justified on the grounds that it was necessary to preserve the State. Unionist politicians until the time of the Troubles continually rejected charges of gerrymandering, although it was an integral part of the Unionist system, and for the reasons given in the 9 June statement. There is little doubt that had Catholic and republican politicians been given power at local government level in any degree corresponding to their popular support from 1921 onwards the result would have been virtual secession by the Catholic majority in large areas of Ulster. As the statement asserts, gerrymandering was necessary to preserve the Ulster State.

The language and the structure of the statement would suggest a highly intelligent hand behind it. Words like 'rancour', 'self-delusive', 'latitude', 'partisan', 'hybrid', 'placid', 'over-indulgent', 'maligned', 'intuition', 'tacitly', and 'precipitated' are not as a rule found in working-class vocabularies in the United Kingdom. And despite the political sophistication of the Ulster working class, few men or women living in the Shanhill or Sandy Row could have written the document. It is a clear and concise statement aguing its case point by point in a logical and cogent manner, as a good press statement should. There had obviously been a lot of work put into it drafting out the points to put forward, and they come across simply but powerfully. For the first time it was apparent that the Protestant militants have begun to formulate their own coherent ideology, quite separate from, and in many ways opposed to, the traditional Unionism they blandly supported for fifty years until it was found to be wanting.

One month later, two English journalists, Gerard Kemp of the *Daily Telegraph* and Peter Birkett of the *Sunday Telegraph*, were given an exclusive interview with the UFF. They were taken to a house in Belfast where they were shown into a small room and given tea. Two UFF men told them that all the nineteen newly elected SDLP members of the new Ulster Assembly would be killed. One of the men explained why he was so hostile to the Roman Catholics and the IRA.

The day I started turning bitter was 'Bloody Friday' in Belfast last year.* I saw it all in colour on the BBC news. Clifford Luton was the reporter. Very few people here had colour TVs at the time. But they should have seen what I saw: people putting pieces of bodies into plastic bags. I will never forget it.

When questioned about the killing of Paddy Wilson and Irene Andrews, one of the men said: 'Wilson and Andrews was a ritual killing. It was a godsend to get rid of vermin like that.' When asked why Andrews, a Protestant, had been killed, the man said: 'She was carrying information to the Officials. Wilson belonged to the Officials. We were after both of them. They had been together numerous times.'

The journalists were given a written statement to read, which ran as follows:

The world is condemning us as murders – we call ourselves patriots. We are fighting for Ulster's freedom. During the past four years we have waited for the authorities to take positive action against the gangsters who have ravaged and raped our country. We have, alas, waited in vain.

Even our own Protestant defence forces have seemed unwilling to walk that extra mile and stamp out themselves the cancer which has been eating away at the very bowels of Ulster. Unfortunately, the

*A reference to the bomb attacks on 21 July 1972, when the Provisional IRA killed nine people and injured scores of others with nineteen bombs.

Ulster Protestant, knowing his cause is right, has been foolish enough to sit back, believing that right will prevail.

The events that have taken place over the years have clearly shown that unless positive action is taken now, our Ulster will fall. We are now fighting for our very survival. Our backs are to the wall. We have more in common with the State of Israel, the Star of David on our flag. Those brave people fought and won their battle for survival. We intended to win ours. And like the Jewish people, each time an act of aggression is committed against our people, we shall retaliate in a way that only the animals in the I R A can understand.

We would appeal to the R C populace: throw these gangsters out of your midst. Until you do this, you must bear the agony. Our fight is not with you, but the animals you shelter. We trust that when our fight is won – as win we will – Ulster will be filled with people working for a common purpose:

The fight to live in freedom and worship God in whatever way we choose; the right of our senior citizens to live out the balance of their well-earned retirement in peace; above all, we fight to keep Ulster for the Ulster people.

In closing, we would make it clear to our people, and indeed to the world, that our methods, although extreme, are necessary. When the cancer within the human body lies deep, the surgeon must cut accordingly. If we must forfeit our lives, we will do so gladly, knowing that our cause is just.

Taken with the statement given to the *Sunday World* reporter this leaves one in little doubt as to the basic ideology of those in the Protestant camp ready to take offensive action against the Catholics. 'The world is condemning us as murderers – we call ourselves patriots' – this shows clearly that these men believe they are acting in the pursuit of a higher duty, an ideal. 'We are fighting for Ulster's freedom,' they say. The woman who had written to the *Loyalist News* had called upon men such as these to come forward prepared to fight 'for the cause . . . willing to give their lives to hold onto what others gave their lives for'.

The U F F make it plain in their statement that they have only been forced to act themselves because they have been let down by the normal authorities, who have stood by while 'gangsters' 'ravaged and raped our country'. Even the Protestant para-military defence forces have been guilty of inaction, and so

Ulster's Protestants have been forced to protect themselves, to go on the offensive, and the UFF have taken the inspiration of the Jewish State of Israel, a State preserved from destruction only by the military might of her people. The UFF will adopt the Israeli policy – tough reprisals against the Arab population for acts of terrorists – in their reaction to the actions of the IRA. Just as the Arabs suffer in Israel because they harbour and shelter the guerrillas, so, too, the Roman Catholics in Ulster will suffer the same fate. It is perhaps a good analogy. The State of Israel, with a Jewish majority, contains a large minority of Arabs opposed to its very existence, who are a natural fifth column for the terrorists. As the Catholics were for many years in Northern Ireland, the Israeli Arabs are denied equal rights with the Jews, although they comprise about a quarter of the population. The Israeli Arabs would prefer to be absorbed within a predominantly Arab state and see Israel and the Jews disappear from the map. The Provisional IRA would like to see a 32-county all-Ireland republic in which the Protestants would have ceased to exist, having all gone back to Scotland where they came from. In Israel, when Arab guerrillas attack Israeli troops or property, the Jews hit back by blowing up houses in the nearest Arab settlements to discourage the inhabitants from giving aid and shelter to the guerrillas.

This is the policy the UFF will pursue, it would appear. 'And like the Jewish people, each time an act of aggression is committed against our people, we shall retaliate in a way that only the animals in the IRA can understand.' They make it perfectly plain that the Catholic population as a whole will suffer at their hands because of the acts of the IRA. They refuse to make any distinction between the two until the Catholics turn their backs on the IRA and close their doors to them. It is insufficient for average Roman Catholics not to participate in the IRA's campaign. They must take positive steps to rid themselves of the gunmen and bombers, or else their failure to do so will be construed as tacit support.

If this statement is to be taken at face value – and there is no reason not to do so – the UFF would appear to be a fundamentally non-sectarian body. They offer the Roman Catholics a partnership in the Ulster state in which 'Ulster will be filled with people working for a common purpose'. Freedom of religion is to be guaranteed in this new Ulster, whose fate will be decided by Ulster people alone – surely an attack on the British link in its existing form. The men behind the statement appear to have felt the need to explain, though not to apologise for, the extreme nature of the actions they take. Dire circumstances require drastic, if unpleasant, measures. 'Our methods, although extreme, are necessary. When the cancer within the human body lies deep, the surgeon must cut accordingly.'

The precise form the new Ulster would take is left vague, probably deliberately so. It would seem that it would be autonomous, and could either exist within the United Kingdom, but with Westminster only holding jurisdiction over foreign policy, or else it could be independent. Such an independent Ulster would be feasible, especially within the EEC where payments from the community's social fund could maintain the province's standard of living. The statement seems to suggest that Ulster's Catholics would be given a fair deal in the new system, though it does not go into detail except to guarantee religious liberty. No formula for resolving the province's social problems is put forward, and this can be only guessed at. But the document is an extremely bitter statement, from a group of people who, one presumes, are basically working-class Protestants, about the betrayal they have received at the hands of the Unionist and British governments. Like the people who wrote the statement given to the *Sunday World* journalist in June, the UFF would appear to be opposed almost as much to the Unionist Party and the British government as to the IRA. They feel let down by the two former and attacked by the last.

It is highly likely that both statements came from the same source. A close textual analysis of each shows that the language and the phraseology used, as well as the political views expounded, are identical. It is also beyond reasonable doubt that the UVF is a big factor in both. It is known from impeccable sources, such as Tommy Herron and David Fogel, that the UVF are closely allied to Harding Smith in West Belfast. The 9 June statement was issued in West Belfast at a time when elements in the UVF were trying to take over the UDA. If this is the case – and if the UVF are *not* involved, one must assume the existence of another Protestant paramilitary body with identical political and military policies – the attitude of the UFF towards the Official IRA needs explanation, if earlier passages in the book are to be justified.

The men who spoke to Kemp and Birkett described themselves as 'brigade staff of the UFF'. They said that Wilson had been a member of the Official IRA, and that Andrews had been a spy for the Officials, and described the couple as 'vermin'. In addition, in June the UFF had left a car bomb outside a Republican Club (a branch of the Official IRA) in the Lower Falls area. Such an attitude towards the Official IRA would tend to conflict with the known views of UVF men such as the leader Gusty Spence. But the crucial point is to be found in the theory of guilt by association put forward in the UFF statement. Certainly, the Official IRA, with its well-known non-sectarian attitude, have made the right noises for extreme elements in the UVF and UFF; but they have not taken the right actions. There is a basis for discussions between them and the Protestant working-class leaders, but these cannot take place while the Provisional IRA campaign is still underway. In an earlier chapter it was explained how the failure of the Official IRA to respond to the overture made by the Protestant militants by calling off the assassins led to even more killings. Those men in the Protestant community who had some respect for the Official IRA despaired of them. The Provisionals were known to be weak on manpower and to be losing popular support in the Catholic community. The Officials were gaining manpower and popular support. They were known to be well-equipped with weapons from Eastern Europe, and to be well-trained and disciplined. Yet they sat back and did nothing while the Provisionals continued their campaign – a campaign that aroused the contempt and disgust of average working-class Protestants. This was why there is no sympathy for the Official IRA in the UFF. If the Officials were to move against the

Provisionals and stop the violence, then there would certainly be support for negotiations with the UFF. But not before then.

Until that time, the UFF made it clear to Kemp and Birkett, they would pursue their campaign with the utmost vigour. Kemp asked one of the men if he was the Captain Black who issued press statements, and if he had killed anyone. He replied: 'You can say that Captain Black and Captain Jones [another issuer of statements] have both killed. They have killed the enemies of the country. The IRA put bombs into Protestant places and blow things up. This is our answer.' The two men stressed that the UFF was not in any way connected with the UDA.

When questioned about the assassinations, and the repeated use by the police of the phrase 'motiveless murders', one of the men said: 'There are no sectarian assassinations without cause. You don't just bloody well kill people for the sake of killing them. If you dig into their backgrounds you find they are associated with the republicans.' One can appreciate from this last statement the frustration the Protestant militants have felt at the treatment they have received at the hands of the press. They claim that the assassinations are not indiscriminate acts of murder, but calculated military actions taken against known enemies. 'If you dig into their backgrounds you find they are associated with the republicans,' they said. But how often has such digging taken place before the police issue their stock phrase 'another apparently motiveless murder'? Precious little, if the truth were known. The police have been overworked and prevented by the virtual state of civil war from pursuing the most routine of inquiries. In the majority of killings, all their statements really boil down to is that they have no information whatsoever on the killings. Every crime is 'apparently motiveless' until one acquires information.

The emergence of the UFF was the logical result of the development of Protestant militancy during the Troubles. During the years of violence caused by the Provisional IRA countless thousands of ordinary Protestants have been angered at the Catholic population and dismayed at the reaction of their own elected leaders to what they see as armed insurrection against the state. The events of 1972 when Stormont was virtually abolished and the British government treated with the IRA convinced the militants that they must take action themselves if all they hold dear was to be preserved. Ulster's fate was in the hands of her own people. One way of striking back was through the assassinations. Most of them were not random, but based on information, not always accurate, that the victims were in some way connected with the other side. Catholics could be killed simply because they were Catholics, even though they may have no connection at all with the IRA. But these killings were still seen as political by the killers. They did not kill for the sake of killing, but because of what they saw as military necessity. The Protestant militants regarded themselves just as much at war as the IRA. They were fighting for their very existence, and they were not going to give in without a fight, no matter how ruthless and extreme their methods. They have a cause which they believe to be just, and they are prepared to die, as well as to kill, for it: 'No surrender! Keep up the fight!' are their slogans, as they have been in the past.

15. The Killers (III) – The British Army

A great proportion of Ulster's Roman Catholic population believes that many of the Catholics killed by assassins have been killed by plain-clothes British troops. So pronounced is this belief that an issue of *Civil Rights*, the fortnightly journal of the Northern Ireland Civil Rights Association, contained the following advice on its front page. Under the heading 'WHAT TO DO IF THE SAS SHOOT YOU', it said:

> From the files of gems of advice to citizens from members of the British Government a Civil Rights team has devised some advice for citizens shot by SAS/MRF squads. Provided you are alive when the shooting stops, pretend to be dead until the squad moves away, otherwise they might try to finish the job. If there is an army post near by do not worry. It will not be manned, or if it is the occupants will be busy writing a press statement to say that no military personnel were involved in the shooting. Shout for help and get yourself carted to hospital; the police will take a statement and investigate. Revealed evidence suggests that they may find within a few hours that you were shot by the SAS/MRF. However, you may not have proof of this fact until months later and only then if you can get someone into court. This may happen when your claim for damages finally reaches a hearing.

This passage was published in June 1973 and accurately reflects opinions held among widely differing sections of the Catholic community. Many Catholics believe not just that the British Army has been involved in the assassination campaign, but that it has been responsible for the bulk of the killings on either side. Our investigations contradict this. Only two deaths out of over 200 examined can categorically be laid at the door of the Army. Of the handful of eight killings which we have been unable to attribute, none seems likely to have been committed by the Army. Nor are there statistically very many cases of attempted assassinations where Army involvement is conclusive. Nonetheless, the belief in large-scale Army activity remains.

The Civil Rights Association referred to the Army's 'SAS/ MRF' squads. The context in which the term was used, and in which it is usually understood in the Catholic community, is such that it is assumed that the two are synonymous. This is not the case – a point which will be expanded later. For the time being, it is necessary to know that the SAS is the Special Air Services, a crack British Army regiment of relatively recent origin. Many people assume that its prime occupation is assassination, but this is untrue. In fact the Special Air Services Regiment is a uniformed unit of the British Army just like the Parachute Regiment, though, as we shall see, its duties are somewhat specialized. MRF has been the subject of some discussion in Ulster. The Catholics claim that it stands for Military Reaction Force, while the Army usually maintains that it means Military Reconaissance Force. The difference in the second word may or may not be crucial. What is certain is that the MRF squads are regular troops out of uniform who travel into and out of civilian areas in unmarked civilian cars. What they do once they get there is the moot point.

The two instances where there is incontrovertible evidence that the Army's plain-clothes troops killed civilians are those of Patrick Joseph McVeigh on 12 May 1972, and Daniel Rooney on 27 September 1972. There is no controversy as to who killed both these men – the Army have accepted full responsibility for the deaths, and the injuries to five others in the same incidents – but there are sharp differences in the versions of the Army and other witnesses concerning the circumstances of the shootings.

The first man to die was McVeigh, a 44-year-old married Roman Catholic of Ladybrook Park, Andersonstown. He was a member of the Catholic Ex-Serviceman's Association, and on the night in question CESA were mounting a number of vigilante patrols in the Andersonstown area. Andersonstown is very susceptible to incursions from outside because of the M1 motorway, and a number of strange cars had been seen cruising through the area after dark. McVeigh, an electric welder and father of six, was standing talking to four CESA vigilantes on Finaghy Road North late on the night of Friday 12 May when just before midnight a car drove up Riverdale Park South. None of the five men was armed, and after the attack CESA issued a statement in which they stated that the dead man was not on duty that evening, but was merely talking to the four other men.

As the car passed the five men, one of those inside opened up with a submachine-gun, spraying the men with bullets. McVeigh was killed and the four others were seriously injured. The car is reported to have continued for 100 yards down Riverdale Park South and then made a three-point turn and passed the scene of the shooting before escaping in the direction of the Lisburn Road. One version of the incident claims that on their way from the scene of the killing, the killers were stopped by an Army patrol. It is claimed that they were allowed to pass on after they had shown documents to the troops.

A uniformed Army patrol was at the scene of the shooting within minutes. They found four of the men lying in pools of their own blood, and, significantly, there were no weapons there, nor did the patrol at any time suggest that the men were terrorists. An Army spokesman the next day said: 'When troops reached the street they found one man, who they believed was dead, had already been taken away in an ambulance. Another four men who were wounded were taken by personnel-carrier to Musgrave Park Hospital.' An earlier statement issued by the Army had said that the five men had been shot after a one-hour gun-battle between troops and the IRA. Soon after a third statement was put out which said the killing and woundings were committed by unknown persons.

The immediate reaction of local people in Andersonstown was to assume that the culprits were Protestant assassins. In the *Belfast Telegraph* on 27 May it was said: 'Local people maintained that McVeigh had been shot by Protestant extremists but no evidence has been found to substantiate this.' However, on 1 July the *Irish News* carried a story headlined 'NEW LIGHT ON FINAGHY MAN'S KILLING'. It told how each of the four survivors of the attack had been called separately on their recovery to Springfield Road police station. A high-ranking police officer is alleged to have said to each of them: 'You realize that a plain-clothes Army patrol was responsible for that shooting.' This was not known to the men until told by the police officer, and the Army had not issued any statement altering the one issued the day following the killing which attributed the incident to unknown persons. The chairman of the Andersonstown branch of CESA, Liam Devlin, immediately put a number of questions to the Army as a result of the disclosure. 'Why has it only come out now that soldiers were responsible?' Devlin asked. 'Are the soldiers involved going to be brought to justice? Will compensation be paid to the deceased man's family and to the four men who were wounded?'

No charges were ever brought against the troops involved, and the question of compensation is still pending court hearings at the time of writing. At the inquest on McVeigh in Belfast on Thursday 21 December the Army accepted responsibility for the incident. Statements made by the soldiers in the car were read to the court in their absence. They claimed that they were fired upon by the men, a number of whom carried weapons. They returned the fire. They said they had been fired upon earlier that evening in Andersonstown. As they drove down Riverdale Park South they saw two groups of men. Two armed men were in one group and the second group contained four men armed with rifles. They were fired upon, and returned the fire.

This version of events was strongly contradicted by the four men who had been wounded with McVeigh. All the men said they were members of the Catholic Ex-Servicemen's Association, although none had been in the services. They all claimed there had been no shooting from their group on the evening in question at the junction of Finaghy Road North and Riverdale Park South. They claimed that none of them was armed, and that the dead man had not been on patrol with them, but had merely stopped for a talk. One of the wounded, Patrick Donnelly, 41, of Riverdale Gardens, said: 'This was a completely unprovoked attack by the Army on unarmed men.'

Detective Chief Inspector Drew of the RUC attached to Springfield Road police station told the court that forensic tests carried out on the clothing of McVeigh and the four wounded men to ascertain whether any of them had fired a gun that night had proved negative. He said he had been informed at noon the following day – within twelve hours of the shooting – that the Army was responsible. However, the Army officer in charge of the troops who arrived on the scene after the shooting, claimed he was not informed that the Army were responsible. Under cross-examination from Mr Charles Hill representing the next of kin of the dead man, the officer said he had not known until the day of the inquest that a plain-clothes Army patrol was responsible. He had thought it had been a sectarian assassination.

The soldiers responsible for the killing did not appear in the coroner's court, and were not available for cross-examination. This is a perfectly legal course of action to take. Coroner's courts are held to determine the cause of death and not to determine guilt. If a party to a case is likely to be charged with a crime in connection with a death, or if there is reasonable ground for supposing such charges might be laid at a later date, they may decline to attend to answer questions. Chief Inspector Drew told the coroner that no proceedings had been brought against any Army personnel arising from the shooting. An open verdict was returned, and the coroner, Mr James Elliot, said there was a possibility that two other men, not in the group shot by the Army, had opened fire on the plain-clothes Army patrol.

The second known fatal victim of the Army plain-clothes patrols, Daniel Rooney, 19, of Rodney Parade, Andersonstown, died in September 1972. In the early hours of Wednesday 27 September, Rooney and a friend, Brendan Brennan, 18, were shot from a passing car at St James's Crescent near the entrance to the M1 motorway, close to the Protestant Village area, but in the Falls. An Army statement issued the following morning admitted that the youths had been shot by an Army 'surveillance patrol' but claimed that the two were gunmen.

'At 12·15 this morning five shots were fired at a "surveillance patrol" in the St James's Park [Falls Road] area,' the statement said. 'Fire was returned and two hits are claimed. There are no casualties suffered by the security forces.'

A member of the Robert Emmet Sinn Fein Cumann (a 'political', though illegal, wing of the Provisional IRA) telephoned the morning *News Letter* a few hours after the attack and gave the following statement on the incident:

Two cars came into St James's Crescent, and the occupants of the second one opened fire with two machine-guns at two young men who were standing at the corner of St James's Crescent and St Katherine's Road. Both of the young men were struck by bullets. One of them, Daniel Rooney, died later in hospital. The second, Brendan Brennan, was seriously injured. There had been no shooting in the area before the cars appeared, and the two young men were merely standing on the footpath when they were fired at.

When told that the Army had issued a statement admitting that one of its plain-clothes patrols had shot the youths, when fired at, the Provisionals' spokesman said: 'I am glad that the Army is now confirming that their plain-clothes patrols are operating in the area. The Robert Emmet Sinn Fein Cumann is calling all the women in the area out at 11·00 a.m. today to protest and to ask that the Army should evacuate the district and hand the duty of protection of the people back to the Provisional IRA.'

In a television interview later in the day of the shooting, the commanding officer of the Third Battalion, the Royal Green Jackets, Lieutenant-Colonel Robin Evelegh, whose troops were stationed in the area of the incident, claimed that Rooney was a known IRA gunman. He said that Brennan, the youth who was injured with Rooney, was also in the IRA and that he had 'got his just deserts'. Colonel Evelegh told the BBC interviewer that plain-clothes patrols did operate in the area, but that their job was reconaissance. They were to 'see what the IRA are doing'. He said that Brennan had been seen carrying a gun by a soldier in the Green Jackets on a previous occasion, and during the ceasefire period in June and July, he had boasted to the officers of another regiment, who had been stationed in the district, that he had shot soldiers. The Army produced a car for the television interview which contained a number of bullet-holes. Colonel Evelegh said that this had been the car used by the Army patrol and the bullet-holes had been caused by the shots the two youths had fired.

A decidedly different version of the shooting was given by the sister of the dead youth, Miss Mary Rooney, 22, who was one of the first people at the scene. She said she had just crossed the junction of St James's Road and St James's Place when she saw a car drive slowly out of St James's Crescent and turn down St James's Road.

Suddenly I heard bursts of gunfire coming from both sides of the car and saw the flashes. I heard screaming and thought to myself, 'My God! Someone has been hit.'

She ran down to the Crescent. As she ran she saw a further burst from the car as it turned into Rodney Parade, where she and her brother lived with their parents.

When I got to the Crescent I saw my brother Daniel lying flat on the footpath and bleeding. I also saw another boy bleeding whom I now know was Brendan Brennan. I heard no other shooting in the district before, during, or after the time I heard and saw the gunfire from the car. My brother was not a gunman and had been screened more times than I can remember by the security forces in the area. They knew him by name, and I just cannot understand why they shot him down so callously. They have been satisfied with gunning him down in cold blood. They have reached the depths of cruelty and said that he was a gunman and that he got his deserts. May God forgive them.

Other witnesses to the shooting made statements to the Civil Rights Association. Two girls made a joint statement of what they saw. They were standing at a corner talking before parting to go to their homes. Two young boys came over and told them that some strange cars which had entered the area the previous week were back again. They told the boys that if they saw any-body else on the streets to tell them to go into their homes. Just as the boys had moved to go down the street a car turned off Rodney Parade and drove up St James's Road.

We ran up St James's Crescent and into a house and the car had passed on up St James's Road. We came back out again and it was only a matter of seconds when another car came off the Donegal Road and up St James's Crescent, and a young boy from one of the houses shouted: 'Get off the street. Those cars are back.'

We ran into a hall and got down and the car passed. We thought it was safe. We just came out and a car was just turning the bend. When it was turning they opened fire out of the back window. They went on down St James's Road. They were still firing. We heard moaning from the corner. We ran over, and two young men were lying and moaned and we realized who they were.

In a separate statement one of the girls said she saw a weapon coming out the back window of the car and anything up to twenty rounds were fired: 'The sparking and flashing of the weapon lit up their faces,' she said. 'We could see the profiles of four faces in the car. We ran over and heard moaning at the corner of St Catherine's Road.'

Another witness who also made a written statement was a widow of St James's Gardens, Mrs Maria Canning. She and a friend were talking at the St James's Road end of St James's Place at about five minutes past midnight. Their attention was attracted by the glaring headlights of two cars which they could see driving up the lower part of St James's Road.

Knowing of the frequent car attacks in the area we immediately stood close into the hedge. We saw the first car turn into St James's Crescent, the other car passed us, and went up St James's Road. Seconds later the same car re-appeared coming out of St James's Drive – the next street up from where we were standing. It then passed us again going down St James's Road where we saw it meet up with another car which was coming out of St James's Crescent.

The car leaving St James's Crescent turned out in front of the other car and as they left the junction [St James's Drive/St James's Road] shots were fired from the second car. I want to make it clear that the street was completely peaceful and still at the time. No shooting occurred except from the car.

Mrs Canning went on to stress that the headlights of the cars were more powerful than the lights on ordinary cars, and she suggested that there might have been an arrangement for one of the cars to light up the area where the young men were standing at the corner as the other car approached it. She said that the glare from the headlights was so powerful that it was frightening.

The collected statements of various witnesses to the shooting were compiled into a dossier by the Civil Rights Association and sent to the Attorney-General of the Irish Republic in Dublin as additional evidence for the case that government presented to the Commission of Human Rights at Strasbourg later that week. In a statement the Civil Rights Association alleged that Rooney and Brennan were shot by any Army 'murder squad':

The incident clearly reveals the hand of a British Army plain-clothes murder squad which has been operating in the Lower Falls, Broadway and St James's area over the last few weeks. It also bears out earlier evidence gathered by NICRA about SAS-type activity in the Bawnmore area of Belfast. When we warned the people of Northern Ireland about this possibility, the British Army scoffed at the idea. Who is scoffing now?

The anger in all sections of the Catholic community at Rooney's killing by the Army was great. As the statements of witnesses indicate, the Army plain-clothes patrols in the area were far from unobtrusive. Residents had known of their existence for a number of weeks, and would retire to their homes when the cars appeared. It was generally believed that the purpose of the patrols was not reconnaissance, but assassination. The statements made by Colonel Evelegh on television aroused deep controversy. On the day after the shooting, 30 September, the following letter was printed in the *Irish News*, signed by a resident of the area:

Sir,

I would be most grateful if you would publish this letter, as it concerns a statement made on television by Lt.-Col. Evelegh against a young man shot by a 'plain-clothes military patrol'.

In his statement the Colonel stressed that this young man was a well-known gunman and was on their wanted list, having been observed just two weeks ago carrying a gun.

I now challenge Col. Evelegh to prove this, as Daniel Rooney, the young man in question, was a visitor in my home and when he decided to leave in the early hours of Saturday morning [23-9-72] I insisted on accompanying him to his home. As we approached the street where he lived, a foot-patrol of the Green Jackets apprehended us and, when I protested, they said they were just taking him to Broadway military post for a routine screening. He was released a few hours later. Had this man been the well-known gunman as stated by Col. Evelegh, why was he released? I await an answer.

Yours, etc.,

A RESIDENT OF THE AREA

The following day, Sunday 1 October, from the pulpits of all the Roman Catholic churches in the area where Rooney lived, the following statement was read by the priests:

Three weeks ago we had to express the revulsion of the people of this parish to a brutal murder committed at that time. Today we have to refer to the killing that took place during the past week, the violent slaying of Daniel Rooney, aged 19 years, and the serious wounding of Brendan Brennan.

No one in the area has any doubt that Daniel Rooney was an innocent victim. He was talking peaceably with his companion when the fatal shots came from a passing car. The fact that the Army has since then admitted that these shots were fired by military in plain clothes only increases the indignation felt by everyone about the brutal attack that led to his death.

You have heard us frequently denounce and condemn in the strongest possible terms other murders committed in this parish. We would be quite inconsistent today if we did not take the point clearly that this kind of killing is totally indefensible, no matter who its perpetrators are. It is in direct contravention of the law of God. It is an assault on the most basic of all rights, the right of life itself. It calls in question the discipline and control of the forces supposedly devoted to the security of the community. And it undermines any possibility of creating the understanding and trust that will be necessary if there is ever to be a solution to our problems.

To the parents and family of Daniel Rooney we want to offer our deepest sympathy and the promise of our prayers for the happy repose of his soul. We will pray to for the recovery of Brendan Brennan, and for his parents and family also, to give them support in their ordeal.

Rooney and McVeigh are the only fatal shootings where the British Army's responsibility has been proved conclusively and, indeed, admitted by the high command. But there are a number of other incidents where local people believe the Army was involved. In February 1973, for example, two civilians, Brendan Maguire and John James Loughran, were shot outside a café on the Antrim Road from a passing car. Immediately afterwards the Provisional IRA on the New Lodge Road came out and engaged the Army. Four IRA men were shot dead by the Army, who claimed that the other two men had also been shot by them. The Army insisted that the two men were terrorists who had been shot by uniformed soldiers during the gun-battle. Despite the evidence of witnesses in a Chinese restaurant in the Antrim Road, who had been forced to dive for cover as the machine-gun fire that cut down the two men outside raked their building too, the Army said they had been shot in the New Lodge Road. Local people believed that the two men had been shot by an Army plain-clothes patrol, so as to bring the IRA onto the streets for a confrontation. Indeed, soldiers operating with the new infra-red sights on their rifles were too good for the youthful and inexperienced volunteers they faced, and they easily picked off four Provisionals. But there is no other evidence to support this except the Army's staunch insistence that it did indeed shoot the men, but with uniformed troops during the battle on the New Lodge Road. It would be difficult to understand why the Army should have chosen that particular night to provoke a confrontation with the IRA. Elsewhere in the city, troops were under fire from Protestant extremists, and unless it was believed that the Protestants might think twice about shooting at the Army when the IRA were doing the same, this was possibly the worst time to have a full-scale gun-battle in the New Lodge Road. A more likely explanation that fits the known facts is that Maguire and Loughran were killed on the Antrim Road by Protestant assassins, and that this led almost immediately to the IRA coming onto the streets to attack the Protestant Duncairn Gardens, into which the killers' car was seen to disappear. As a result, the Army was obliged to take on the IRA gunmen, and killed four, but believed that it had hit more. When two further bodies were produced, the Army just refused to believe the claim that they were not gunmen, and did not consider the later evidence either impartial or trustworthy.

In addition to these three incidents, there have been two shootings where Army involvement has been clear, but which did not result in any deaths. On the morning of 15 April 1972 two Roman Catholic brothers, Gerry and John Conway, were walking along the Whiterock Road in the Upper Falls area. The Conways ran a fruit and vegetable stall in the city, and were a familiar sight on the Belfast streets selling their produce, obtained directly from the countryside, usually well below the price in the shops. They lived on the Ballymurphy housing estate and were heading for a bus on the Falls Road. When they reached the gates of St Thomas's School near the junction of the Whiterock Road and Ballymurphy Road, a civilian car drew up in front of them. Three armed men jumped out of the car and opened fire at the brothers. The two brothers ran off and managed to escape down a narrow alley. They both received gunshot wounds, however, and local people called ambulances which took the wounded men to the Royal Victoria Hospital.

The incident happened in broad daylight, and in a residential area. There were a number of witnesses, therefore, to the shooting. According to their reports, one of the men had pursued the Conways as they escaped, and shot them both. He was described as being fair-haired and wearing grey trousers and a brown pullover. After the shooting witnesses alleged that he returned to the car and spoke into the microphone of a car radio. Almost immediately after, two Saracen armoured cars arrived on the scene and spoke to the civilians. A uniformed officer is alleged to have said to the fair-haired civilian: 'You stupid bastards, you've got the wrong bloody men.' After this short exchange, the two armoured cars left accompanied by the civilian car. Later the Army press office issued a statement in which it said an Army 'mobile patrol' had come across two men on the Whiterock Road. One of the men was wanted by the Army; the patrol came under fire from one of them. It returned the fire, wounding one man, who dropped his pistol and escaped.

Despite this statement which claimed that the Conways had

opened fire on the Army, neither brother was ever charged with an offence. Indeed, neither was ever questioned by the Army about the incident. The pistol which one of the brothers is alleged to have used to shoot at the Army was never produced, though presumably it might carry the fingerprints of whichever brother used it. Nor was any attempt made to test either brother for forensic evidence to prove that he had fired a weapon recently. Both brothers made statements about the incident to the Civil Rights Association and to the Association for Legal Justice, and have initiated proceedings for damages against the Army.

It is reliably reported that the Conways were mistaken by an Army plain-clothes patrol for two top Provisional IRA men. James Bryson and Patrick Toland were two of 'The Magnificent Seven' detainees on the prison-ship Maidstone who had escaped, while the ship was anchored in Belfast harbour, by swimming to the shore. It is known that the two men were in the area of the Whiterock Road on the morning of the incident, and one of the Conway brothers did bear a passing resemblance to Bryson. It is also known that the Army has a list of wanted men whose photographs were at one time on a wall in the Maidstone, under the heading: 'Shoot on sight'. Presumably both Bryson and Toland would have been on this list, and presumably the instruction would have applied to both uniformed and plain-clothes troops. The existence of such a list and this instruction could more than account for the Roman Catholic population's fear of the Army's plain-clothes patrols.

The second incident in which the Army's plain-clothes troops were involved in a non-fatal shooting took place on 22 June 1972. That afternoon three Roman Catholic taxi-drivers – Hugh Kenny, Joseph Smith, and James Patrick Murry – were standing by their cars on the Glen Road in Andersonstown. Their taxis were parked a short distance from the junction with Shaw's Road when a blue Ford Cortina civilian car came down the Glen Road heading towards the city centre. A burst of machine-gun fire from a rear window of the car cut down the men, and also wounded a man in a near-by house. A statement issued by the

Army press office in Lisburn shortly after said: 'About eighteen shots have been fired in an incident in which security forces were not involved. When a patrol of the Second Field Regiment, the Royal Artillery arrived at the scene they found nothing.' The statement ended by reaffirming that the Army was in no way involved in the shooting: 'Our men were not involved in this shooting at all,' it said.

But a few hours later the Army issued a second statement which accepted responsibility for the shooting, but which claimed that the car, which contained plain-clothes troops, had only fired when it had itself come under fire from the three men:

'Shortly after mid-day a mobile patrol wearing plain clothes and on surveillance duty was travelling eastwards on the Glen Road. A group of men standing at a bus turn-about opened fire on the patrol and a number of bullets passed through the rear window, narrowly missing a soldier. The patrol immediately fired back, and the men were seen to fall.'

But as in the case of the Conway brothers when similar charges were made, no attempt was ever made to bring any of the three men before the courts. Presumably the part of the first press statement which said that the patrol that arrived on the scene soon after the shooting and found nothing, still stood. At no time was the weapon that the three men were alleged to have used against the 'mobile patrol' produced. Nor was the car with gunshot holes at which they were supposed to have directed their fire ever produced and shown to the press as it had in the Rooney and Brennan shootings.

However, the most interesting aspect of this shooting was that, unlike the other cases where the soldiers who were responsible were never produced, two British soldiers were charged with offences connected with the incident. Seven months later, on Tuesday 27 February 1973, Captain James Allister McGregor, 29, and Sergeant Clive Graham Williams, 25, appeared in Belfast Magistrate's Court. McGregor was charged with the unlawful possession of a Thompson submachine-gun and ammunition. Williams was charged with the same offence but, in addition, he was charged with attempting to murder the three taxi-drivers, causing them grievous bodily harm and with maliciously wounding the fourth man, Thomas Gerard Shaw.

When charged with his offence, McGregor was alleged by a detective to have said: 'That ammunition had nothing to do with me. It belongs to the police at Castlereagh and was issued by the Special Branch.' Neither man denied being in possession of the weapon and ammunition; but they maintained that they held them legally. It is interesting to note that the weapon involved was a Thompson submachine-gun. It is not a standard Army weapon – the Army uses Sterlings – but it is the standard weapon of the IRA. Why the Army should have issued its 'mobile patrols' with a weapon it considers obsolete, is a matter for conjecture.

McGregor was said to be a member of the Parachute Regiment, but he was also said to be attached to Thiepval Barracks, Lisburn, the Army HQ, and was, therefore, working away from his unit. None of the Parachute battalions was stationed there. Williams's unit was not given in court. At a later hearing on Wednesday 2 May in Belfast Magistrate's Court, the Crown announced that it had withdrawn the charges against both men relating to the firearm and ammunition. McGregor was thus allowed to go free, although Williams had still to face the other charges. Both men had been on bail.

Williams appeared on trial in Belfast in June 1973. He told the court that he was a former Royal Military Policeman and that in June 1972 he was the commander of a unit of the Army's Military Reconnaissance Force attached to the Thirty-Ninth Infantry Brigade. He explained that the force was set up to carry out surveillance duties in areas where it was difficult for uniformed troops to travel freely. At the time of the shooting there were forty men in the force and they were supplied with civilian powers to move about areas and had their own armoury. He said there were fifteen men in his unit and that a squad consisted of between two and four men in one civilian vehicle.

He told the judge that on 22 June his group were inoperative because they knew the truce with the IRA was about to take place. There was a fresh intake of NCOs into the unit. The morning of the shooting he gave the new recruits a briefing, and then took them to Kinnegar firing-range to familiarize them with general weapons and those used by terrorist organizations – particularly the Thompson submachine-gun. His unit had two Thompsons in its armoury, and he had that morning demonstrated its use to the new recruits.

Later he went to Lisburn to have a radio fixed in his car and sent two squads of men in civilian vehicles to patrol the city centre and South Belfast – Andersonstown is south of the city. On his return from Lisburn he said he had two new recruits in his car with him, and the Thompson he had been using earlier on the firing-range was underneath the back seat in a hold-all. He took the new men through the Andersonstown area, and had made two passes through the area to familiarize them with the work they would have to do. Williams explained to the court that a Thompson was not generally carried by a squad, and that a Sterling was the usual weapon. When a squad of three men was on duty in a civilian car, one man generally carried the Sterling while his two companions were armed with automatic pistols. When asked by counsel why the Thompson was concealed that morning, Williams replied: 'Soldiers were our biggest enemy because if a gun was seen in the vehicle they would open fire and we would be shot dead.'

He told the court that he had come under fire on several occasions on armed MRF duties. The morning of the Glen Road shooting, after making two passes through the Catholic Andersonstown and Suffolk areas, he ordered another squad to move down the Glen Road. The squad radioed back after their pass that they had spotted a man armed with a revolver at the Bunbeg bus terminus – close to where the three taxi-drivers were standing. Williams said he ordered the squad to make a second pass down the road, and the squad confirmed their previous observation. When Williams's own squad made a pass, he claimed they came under fire and returned the fire and believed they had hit three gunmen. On this defence Williams was acquitted by the jury of all the charges laid against him.

These four cases, of McVeigh, Rooney, the Conways, and the

Glen Road shooting, constitute the sum total to date of the really solid evidence that would suggest that the British Army has played a role in the assassination campaign. Many Catholics would claim that this evidence provides the proof of a massive Army involvement in the killings; but one could with equal consistency conclude from this evidence that the Army is not involved in any coordinated way in the killings. The British Army is by far the largest, best-trained, and best-equipped fighting force in the Ulster conflict. If it intended a massive campaign of sectarian assassination – for whatever reason – it could surely manage more than the handful we see here. Indeed, if it chose so to act then the total of over 200 dead to date would probably pale into insignificance beside the hundreds or thousands the Army could kill. And it has to be asked, what possible motive would the Army have for such a campaign? No individual or group has yet produced a satisfactory answer to that question. It has been suggested that the motive is rather esoteric. That the Army believes that the quickest way to solve the conflict is to let the Northern Irish indulge in a bout of ritual blood-letting far surpassing what has already taken place. According to this theory, the Army has therefore tried to provoke sectarian conflict. It has sought to bring about the long-feared civil war, in the belief that a few thousand dead on either side after a few weeks' bloody rioting and killing would soon bring the Irish to their senses, and that afterwards they would all settle down and live together happily ever after. It is a nice theory, but there is not a shred of evidence to support it. There is also a theory that the Army is killing Catholics to cause sectarian trouble, not for overall strategic reasons, but for short-term tactical ones. This argument holds that at certain times the Army finds such troubles useful to take the heat off a more dangerous situation. Thus, it is claimed, an Army MRF squad shot Maguire and Loughran on the Antrim Road in February 1973 to bring the IRA on the streets in the New Lodge Road, and take the heat off its confrontations with Protestants elsewhere in the city. Apart from the dubious logic behind this argument, there is again no hard evidence to support it.

A more down-to-earth interpretation of the known facts of Army involvement in shootings is to be found basically in the explanations the Army themselves gave for every one. One ought to bear in mind in the four cases mentioned where Army involvement is accepted, that there was no need for the Army to accept their role if they had chosen not to. For six weeks the four men injured in the incident when McVeigh was killed were under the impression that they had been shot by Protestants, and would presumably still think so to this day but for the fact that the security forces told them that the Army was involved. So too with Rooney, and the other two cases. If the Army were engaged in a campaign of assassination it would seem illogical for them to admit any involvement whatever, unless forced to do so by the amount of evidence proving their connection. And the fact is that the bulk of evidence conclusively proving the Army connection in these four cases has come from the Army. Suspicion of collusion between the killers of McVeigh and a uniformed Army patrol there was, but no proof. So too with the shootings of the Conways. But had the Army been in the midst of an illegal undercover campaign of sectarian assassination, it is most unlikely that it would have thought twice about denying any connection with the incidents. It at first denied responsibility in all four incidents, but later reversed the denials with statements accepting not only that its troops were involved, but also that they were in civilian clothes.

So we are left with four cases of Army involvement in killings or attempted killings. In all four the Army accept the fact that armed plain-clothes patrols opened fire on civilians in Catholic areas. In each case, too, they claim that their patrols were fired on first. Thus the main difference of opinion between the Army and those who chose to regard these admissions as *prima facie* evidence of a massive campaign of assassination, is simply the nature of the role the plain-clothes patrols were assigned to perform in the areas where the incidents took place. The Army says they were reconaissance units, used because uniformed patrols would in certain areas of Belfast be both ineffective and likely to be attacked. The Army's opponents claim that the sole purpose of such squads was to cruise round the Catholic areas to assassinate the residents. To discover where the truth lies, it is useful to turn our attention to one of the British Army's top experts on counter-terrorism, Brigadier Frank Kitson.

Brigadier Kitson is widely regarded as one of the foremost authorities in the world on counter-insurgency operations. He served with distinction with the British Army in Kenya, Malaya, and Muscat and Oman, and with the UN peace-keeping force in Cyprus. He was the Belfast Army commander from the spring of 1970 to April 1972. He was, therefore, in charge of the city when internment was introduced in August 1971, and is generally believed to have been the man responsible for the interrogations that took place after the big swoops on IRA men in that operation. It is also generally accepted that he brought in SAS units for the internment operations. The IRA have cause to dislike Brigadier Kitson, for he masterminded the policy that led to the virtual destruction of the Provisionals' command structure, and it is reported that, as a consequence, he heads their 'death list' as the number one target.

Brigadier Kitson's views on counter-insurgency are extremely interesting. Before he took up his present post in Northern Ireland, he had briefly served there before, although not during the Troubles. In the year prior to taking up his command he was at the University of Oxford writing a book in which he set out his views on counter-insurgency operations. Entitled *Low Intensity Operations – Subversion, Insurgency, and Peacekeeping,** Brigadier Kitson's book appeared in 1971, when the situation in Ulster had developed into a major crisis; but at the time of his writing it, Ulster was relatively quiet, and it might have been thought that the worst had been seen off.

Kitson's book is an argument for the creation of a special force within the British Army to combat insurgency. He states that he believed that the Army was not at that time capable of meeting the threat of internal disorder, and argues that in the future such insurgency would tend to be a more common situation for the modern Army than conventional national wars. The

*Faber & Faber 1971.

book, though it mentions the future possibility of internal disorders within the United Kingdom, is an argument for the creation of a special force within the British Army ready to serve in any part of the world where there is a need for a trained counter-insurgency force.

The work received acclaim from military circles when it was published, and is now a standard military textbook on counter-insurgency. It is of especial interest for us, as the author was given command of the biggest trouble-spot in Northern Ireland immediately he had finished the book. It is surely no coincidence that Brigadier Kitson should have at this time been put in charge of Belfast, especially as he was only a brigadier and not a full general, and was therefore the youngest man in the British Army to hold a command position. The most junior officer in a command position in the Army and given the toughest assignment. There is therefore a strong probability that Kitson was given his command for the purpose of putting into practice the policies he had advocated in his book. He had stated that there was a need for a special counter-insurgency force within the British Army. Was he told to go to Northern Ireland and create the force he required there?

In the introduction to his book, Kitson discusses the role of an Army on a peace-keeping mission:

One . . . term which merits a definition is peace-keeping, which will be used in this study to mean preventing, by non-warlike methods, one group of people from fighting another group of people. Peace-keeping does not involve the activities of an Army which *formally* attacks one or both parties to a dispute in order to halt it, because although this might be done with a view to re-establishing peace, the activity itself would be a warlike one and would be of a totally different nature to a peace-keeping operation.* [p.3]

Taken completely out of context, as this quote is, one might be tempted to place some stress on the word 'formally'. Could not an Army 'informally' attack one or both parties to a dispute, that is, with plain-clothes troops masquerading as one of the warring factions – if it was thought this might bring peace nearer?

*Italics ours – LD and DL.

This would be to agree with the Army's critics in Ulster, but it is by no means clear that this is what is meant in the passage quoted. What Kitson seems to have meant is that the traditional role of an Army, dating back to the Romans – to produce peace by successful military action – was not relevent to an internal insurgency situation. In other words, there can be no military solution in the usual sense of the term, and therefore, it followed that if the Army is to succeed, it would have to adopt tactics not usually associated with a military campaign. He said elsewhere:

> ... It is worth pointing out that as the enemy is likely to be employing a combination of political, economic, psychological and military measures, so the government will have to do likewise to defeat him, and although an army officer may regard the non-military action required as being the business of the civilian authorities, they will regard it as being his business, because it is being used for operational reasons. At every level the civilian authorities will rightly expect the soldier to know how to use non-military forms of action as part of the operational plan, although once it has been decided to use a particular measure they will know how to put it into effect. [p.7]

Again, one can read many things into this. If one wanted to, one could claim that in this passage Kitson implicitly sanctioned assassinations when he said that the government would have to take the same measures to defeat the enemy as the enemy used towards the government. There is scope for this view. Kitson argued for a revolutionary reappraisal of the British Army's traditional attitude towards its role. He believed it would be faced in the future with not so much the conventional forces – to all intents and purposes structured and motivated like itself – but with opponents much more flexible, both in their approach and in their ends. It would be rather naïve to assume that faced with a ruthless and dedicated enemy prepared to use immoral means to achieve its end, the force Kitson envisaged would not use similar means if it thought they would be successful. The question of the morality of war, which was raised in the previous chapter, is virtually impossible to answer satisfactorily. Every individual has his or her own subjective view, and governments too have their views which they make binding on their citizens. Kitson's book was a thoughtful attempt at a definition of a future military campaign strategy, and he did not overlook the moral issue:

One final matter which requires mentioning in this introduction concerns the moral issues involved in preparing to suppress subversion. Many regard subversion as being principally a form of redress used by the down-trodden peoples of the world against their oppressors, and feel, therefore, that there is something immoral about preparing to suppress it. Undoubtedly subversion is sometimes used in this way, and on these occasions those supporting the government find themselves fighting for a bad cause. On the other hand subversion can also be used by evil men to advance their own interests, in which case those fighting it have right on their side. More often, as in other forms of conflict, there is some right and some wrong on both sides, and there are high-minded and base people among the supporters of both parties. Fighting subversion may therefore be right on some occasions, in the same way that fostering it might be right on others, and the army of any country should be capable of carrying out either of these functions if necessary, in the same way as it should be capable of operating in other forms of war. In a democratic country it is the duty of the soldiers to know how to wage war in any of its forms, and it is the duty of the people to elect representatives who will only make war when it is right to do so. When conflicts occur, soldiers, like other people, have to have faith in the moral rectitude of their government to some extent, because it is not usually possible to know enough of the facts to make an absolute judgement as to the rights and wrongs of the case. But if any man, soldier or civilian, is convinced that his country is wrong he should cease to support it and take the consequences. The fact that subversion may be used to fight oppression, or even that it may be the only means for doing so, does not alter the fact that soldiers should know how to suppress it if necessary. Moral issues can only be related to the circumstances of a particular case, and then they must be faced by soldiers and civilians alike on moral grounds. [p.8]

Kitson, therefore, argues that an individual is just as morally accountable for his actions in uniform as out of it. The Army is in no way distinct from the State, but an arm of it. As such, moral responsibility for its actions is spread throughout that State over civilians and soldiers alike. Many commentators on this passage have tended to argue that Kitson was putting the Army beyond the realms of morality, but Kitson would seem to be saying the opposite. The Army is the creation, and is governed by the prevelant morality, of the State to which it is accountable. Ultimately it is the State – in our democratic society the elected government – which controls the actions of the Army, and therefore is responsible for the moral implications of those actions. If an individual soldier cannot stomach these actions, he can refuse to support it, but, Kitson says, he must 'take the consequences'.

From this a natural conclusion can be drawn with reference to Northern Ireland. The spirit of Kitson's book would seem to countenance under certain circumstances a campaign of assassination by the British Army undertaken by plain-clothes troops. There are few, if any, courses of action that Kitson would not have his special force take if they seemed likely to achieve the ultimate aim. But the crucial point is that these actions would have to be sanctioned at government level, not at a military level. One has to ask oneself whether or not the British government would be prepared to sanction this course of action.

In another passage of his book Kitson discusses the possible roles of a British Army in the future, and says:

But one commitment will inevitably remain, which is the obligation for maintaining law and order within the United Kingdom. Recent events in Northern Ireland serve as a timely reminder that this cannot be taken for granted and in the historical context it may be of interest to recall that when the regular army was first raised in the seventeenth century, 'Suppression of the Irish' was coupled with 'Defence of the Protestant Religion' as one of the two main reasons for its existence. [p.24]

It is doubtful that Kitson intended that he should be taken literally when he recalled that the primary aim of Cromwell's New Model Army was the 'suppression of the Irish'. In the historical context – and no people know their history better than the Irish – it was perhaps an unfortunate analogy to make, though, indeed, the Provisional IRA in Belfast have for Kitson the same degree of hatred as their predecessors had for Cromwell. A better view of Kitson's attitude to situations such as that in Ulster is given elsewhere in the book:

Translated into normal terms, the aim of the government is to regain if necessary and then retain the allegiance of the population, and for this purpose it must eliminate those involved in subversion. But in order to eliminate the subversive party and its unarmed and armed supporters, it must gain control of the population. Thus, in the same way that the first aim of those involved in subversion is to gain control of the people so that the purpose of the uprising can be achieved, so also the first aim of those involved in counter-subversion is to gain control of the people because, in most cases, this is a necessary prelude to destroying the enemy's forces, and in any case, it is the ultimate reason for doing so. [p.49]

Those who would see in Northern Ireland a concerted campaign of assassination by the British Army against the Roman Catholics must justify their belief in the context of this statement by the man who, for two crucial years, commanded the British forces in Belfast. Kitson makes it quite clear that the main aim of a force such as he advocated was to gain the allegiance of the population on behalf of whom the insurgents claim to be acting. An assassination campaign would not in this context seem logical. Quite clearly, Kitson's main concern in his book – and therefore, one may assume, in his later command in Belfast – was not with the rights and wrongs of individual tactics such as assassination, but with the effectiveness of a number of approaches to the problem of combating insurgency. He was concerned that the British Army should be adequately equipped to deal with a situation in which it had not been accustomed to operate. Towards the end of the book he set out in some detail the sort of forces he believed should be created as counter-insurgency units. A prime concern is political indoctrination of the population:

One form of specialist activity, provision for which requires discussion in more detail, concerns the ability of a government to disseminate its views and policies in an advantageous way in a situation of subversion and insurgency ... [p.187]. In practice the Psychological Operations resources controlled by the Services at the time of writing are very limited ... [p.188]

Although the British seem to persist in thinking of Psychological Operations as being something from the realms of science fiction, it has for many years been regarded as a necessary and respectable form of war by most of our allies as well as virtually all of our potential enemies. Some evidence of this can be adduced by comparing the two instructors, four staff officers and twelve team members employed by the British with the numbers maintained by some of our allies. For example the West Germans maintain Psychological Operations units totalling 3,000 men in their regular army to say nothing of reserve army units. [p.189]

Thus was the British Army equipped when it embarked on its duties in Northern Ireland, with just eighteen men trained for psychological warfare. Nor, when Kitson was writing, were there any plans to improve this. He argues that in the early stages of a campaign insurgents would be most vulnerable to infiltration by intelligence units, and it would be then that there is the greatest need for action on the part of the Army.

He later discusses '. . . the sort of situation in which troops are deployed rapidly and unexpectedly into an area where no intelligence organization exists . . .' [p.191]. Such was the situation when in August 1969 British troops were sent to Northern Ireland. Kitson goes on to give his formula for success in this situation:

An effective way of dealing with this problem would be to establish a unit which could carry out the two separate functions of setting up or reinforcing the intelligence organization and of providing men trained in operations designed to develop information by special means. If a unit of this kind were formed the element designed to set up or reinforce the intelligence organization would consist of a number of officers available to move at short notice when needed. These men would be majors or captains and they would be backed by a number of other ranks to act as drivers and clerks. The unit could be a relatively large one in which case there might be three or four groups each consisting of a major and several captains, the major being intended for deployment to a provincial or county intelligence headquarters, and the captains to districts; a unit of this size would be commanded by a lieutenant-colonel or senior major who could deploy to the intelligence headquarters of the country concerned. [p.191]

Kitson then goes on to talk about the teams that would be built by the men he has described. The teams would contain mainly younger men, and they would be divided into cells: 'The actual organization of this cadre must be geared to the fact that, once deployed, the men in it will be used to direct indigenous teams rather than to operate themselves. On this assumption, it should be in a position to provide a number of cells each consisting of an officer and one or two training sergeants' [p.192].

What is to be made of this in the context of Northern Ireland? If it is assumed – and the authors do – that it was primarily to enable him to put his theories into operation that the Army sent Brigadier Kitson to Belfast in 1970, a number of suggestions can be made. To come back to the difference between the SAS and the MRF, the preceeding passage gives a clue. The SAS, as said before, is a regular although specialized unit in the British Army. Its operations entail much of the counter-insurgency duties that Kitson outlined. During the past few years the SAS has been heavily committed fighting Arab insurgents in Oman and Muscat where, coincidentally, Brigadier Kitson also served.

The officers of the SAS would have formed the nucleus of a counter-insurgency psychological unit as outlined by Kitson above on his taking up the Belfast command in 1970. Indeed, as the British Army, on his own admission, had so few such men, Kitson could hardly have got such specialists from any other source within the British Army. The smaller units, or cells, that he said should be set up by these men, with one officer and two sergeants, bear a remarkable resemblance to the MRF or 'mobile patrols' that the Army in Northern Ireland admits to using, though it has consistently denied SAS involvement. Kitson reproduced in his book a diagram of a command structure of a Special Unit. Such a unit would operate independently of the main-force Army on the spot. Kitson argued that such a unit should preserve its independence. The purpose of such units would be determined in the context of the situation, but certainly the small cells of a single junior officer, two sergeants and a driver could be used for undercover intelligence work. In the context of the Ulster situation, the diagram can be interpreted quite easily to see the cells under the responsibility of the Special Methods Group as the MRF squads, composed of various members of different regiments, brought together for that specific purpose in Ulster. The other group, headed Organization, and composed of more senior officers and various drivers and clerks, would seem to be the SAS, which is not operational, but supervisory.

Thus it would seem that at the time of the assassinations there did exist a structure within the Army that would fit the apparent description of assassination squads, and which did have at least some justification for such a policy in military terms behind them. But Kitson does not in his book refer to political assassination as a specific policy, and this is perfectly consistent. The primary concern of Kitson is with military intelligence and the Army's preparedness to fight a psychological as well as a military campaign. It is clear that assassination for political purposes does come within the terms of reference given by Kitson to his Special Units, but the question one has to answer in Northern Ireland is whether this did indeed occur. On the basis of the evidence produced in this chapter the case against the Army must be declared unproven. On the four clear cases where the Army was involved in killing or attempted killing of Catholics by its plainclothes troops, it is by no means certain that the soldiers' claim to have been fired upon first was not correct, even if the victims were not those responsible for the shootings.

On its own, the paucity of evidence against the Army would be sufficient to rule the troops out of major consideration in the assassination campaign. The Army may or may not be responsible for many abuses in Northern Ireland since it was posted there in 1969. It has not come within the scope of this book to examine any of the allegations laid against it except in the context of the assassinations. In this field, considering the number of assassinations and attempted assassinations, the Army's involvement has been statistically insignificant. As with the Troubles generally, one has to look to the Catholic and Protestant people of Ulster for the causes, and the solutions, of the assassinations.